Paradoxes of the Public School

Paradoxes of the Public School

*Historical and Contemporary Foundations
of American Public Education*

James E. Schul

Winona State University

INFORMATION AGE PUBLISHING, INC.
Charlotte, NC • www.infoagepub.com

Library of Congress Cataloging-in-Publication Data

A CIP record for this book is available from the Library of Congress
http://www.loc.gov

ISBN: 978-1-64113-650-1 (Paperback)
       978-1-64113-651-8 (Hardcover)
       978-1-64113-652-5 (ebook)

Printed in the United States of America

To my mom, Joy Schul, who set me on the path of truth.

Contents

Preface

The American public school seems primal to us. It has always been a familiar part of our lives. However, it is important for us to be reflective of the fact that the public school is a project that emerged in the early to mid-19th century as a means to sustain and support the new nation. Since then, the school became the central force in American society that it remains to this day. John Dewey (1897), the renowned American philosopher, crowned the school as "the fundamental method of progress and reform." He was right. The school has been at the forefront of many of the most pivotal reforms we've experienced as a society, from desegregation to equal rights for women; from inclusion of individuals identified with disabilities to the claim of civil rights for individuals who are transgendered. Yet, while the school has taken a lead on these reforms, it has often done so reluctantly and, often times, while kicking and screaming in resistance. The reason? School, plain and simple, is a byproduct of our society. We seldom like change and are reluctant to do so, despite overwhelming evidence that reform needs to take place. The school reflects this disposition. However, laws are ascribed to the school that force it to change and, often times, we are forced to change because of the compulsion placed on school. This is what Dewey meant when he crowned the school as the fundamental method of progress and reform.

Seldom do we praise the public school—doing so is unnatural for us. It is a beleaguered institution often chastised by politicians and policy makers for being inept at performing its role. After all, we are likely more familiar

Paradoxes of the Public School, pages xi–xv
Copyright © 2019 by Information Age Publishing

with the public school than any other American institution. Like any old familiar place or instrument, we fail to recognize its success. How many times do we complain about the things that are not working in our home despite the overwhelming amount of things that are? The school falls in this rut of the familiar. It is the only institution we have meant to intentionally improve us as both individuals and as a society. Yet, in our contemporary times, the public school is under assault. A plethora of evidence collectively denounces the effectiveness of high-stakes testing and challenges the claimed success of alternative routes to schooling, such as charter schools, to improve students' academic achievement, yet these reforms remain, for the time being, firmly entrenched on the public school, weakening it each day, week, month, and year. It should come as no surprise to scholars of education that a growing faction of the public is ideologically opposed to public education and would like to invoke throngs of privatization within it. The rising tide of libertarianism, the belief that individuals should be free from government power of nearly any kind, targets the public school as an unnecessary social program. This might explain the consistent assault on public education that runs contrary to evidence.

Yet, the general public does not seem to share this hostility toward the public school. A 2014 report from the National Center for Education Statistics projected public school enrollment to increase in the foreseeable future. I have been a member of a local parent–teacher association that vibrantly supported our community's public school in a myriad of ways, including fundraising and after-school programs. Yet, if you were to ask people on the street—"What is the purpose of the public school?"—you might get a variety of answers. Is it a purely academic institution? Is it primarily a social institution? Is it a vocational institution? These competing purposes for the purpose of public school make the school vulnerable to those who seek to threaten its very existence. After all, why should we support an institution that seemingly no one can agree on why we have it? With that said, it is important for us to be reflective of why we have public schooling if we clamor for more of it. The lone blueprint we have for school is its past. There, you will find that these competing factions have always been around. The aim of this book is to study the complexity of the American public school, to shed light on both its achievements and its blemishes. But, mostly, this book aims to move us toward a better understanding of school and its place among the central issues in our society.

I position the reader of this book to look at the public school through a paradoxical lens. As you will see, the American public school is deluged with paradoxes. According to Merriam-Webster's dictionary, a paradox is "a statement that seems to say two opposite things but that may be true." However, this is not meant, by any means, to be an attack on the public school. To the contrary, the public school is not unique in its paradoxical nature as most of our social and cultural institutions possess a plethora of paradoxes. Politicians, for instance, may keep one proverbial eye on the good of their constituency and yet another on their own personal good. Financial credit institutions may tout sound financial decision-making through their educational programs, but prosper most when individuals, to some extent, overuse their credit capacity. Intercollegiate athletics may emphasize student success in the classroom, but have been known to turn the other way when a high profile athlete may have a less than stellar academic performance. In fact, the very foundation of the United States of America is founded on a paradox between democracy and capitalism. The historian H. W. Brands (2010) explained this paradox that is at the epicenter of our political infighting:

> Democracy depends on equality, capitalism on inequality. Citizens in a democracy come to the public square with one vote each; participants in a capitalist economy arrive at the marketplace with unequal talents and resources and leave the marketplace with unequal rewards. (p. 5)

I recently visited New York City and, as I strolled the short distance from the New York harbor to Wall Street, I had an epiphany. The two symbols that define our country's paradox between democracy and capitalism, namely the Statue of Liberty and the New York Stock Exchange, were merely a few blocks away from one another! Awareness of this paradox between the two symbols led me to become increasingly interested in how it causes such infighting among us—especially in the wake of our current political climate! I found myself wanting to read more about our country's history and about the sources of our current angst. Therefore, it is my hope that a paradoxical lens will help you, the reader, to increase your own interest and curiosity on the important topics addressed in this book. In sum, I tried to write a book for you to enjoy and learn from.

I wrote this book, first and foremost, for the person who wants to understand the American public school in all of its complexities. I arranged this book in the spirit of John Dewey's experimentalist conception of teaching and learning of history. Historically speaking, the chapters are arranged in chronological order beginning with the conception of school in the seventeenth century and ending with contemporary times. What I looked for are significant moments in the evolution of the American public school and lined them up chronologically. For instance, racial desegregation was a significant moment that began with the Supreme Court's 1954 ruling in *Brown vs. Board of Education*. Hence, I explore desegregation in Chapter 9 which I placed chronologically in the 1950s. Table P.1 illustrates the chronological

TABLE P.1 Chronological Makeup of *Paradoxes of the Public School*							
17th & 18th Century	19th Century	1880– 1920	1930s & 1940s	1950s	1960s	1970s	1980s– Current Era
Chapter 1 Chapter 2	Chapter 3 Chapter 4	Chapter 5 Chapter 6 Chapter 7	Chapter 8	Chapter 9	Chapter 10	Chapter 11 Chapter 12	Chapter 13 Chapter 14

make-up of the book. The book, however, is not a typical chronological history of the public school. Instead, I organized the book thematically so each chapter emphasizes contemporary issues. In fact, each chapter begins with a fictionalized tale of school meant to place the reader in the real world of school as it relates to the theme of that particular chapter. For instance, the first chapter explores the issue of religion in school. I do so by first providing a contemporary tale on a dilemma that reflects the situation public school teachers may face when it comes to religion. I then proceed by providing historical context of the conception of school in the United States under Puritan New England's theocratic agenda (which is why religion is Chapter 1). I then segue toward the role of religion in the contemporary school that takes us back to the fictional tale provided at the onset. This is the pattern throughout the book: to provide a fictional tale that focuses on the larger contemporary theme, then explore the historical context from which the theme emerges, and then follow it with an exploration of that theme in today's school environment. The topics that I chose are ones that arguably are the most noteworthy and relevant ones in the development of the American public school.

It is my intent that this comprehensive study of the American public school will benefit a wide array of individuals. This will benefit the teacher candidate or experienced teacher who seeks to learn more about the larger issues surrounding their profession; it will benefit the policy maker who seeks to be informed about the nature of the school as he/she seeks to improve upon it; it will benefit the general public who simply seeks to be more informed about the most prominent public institution in American society: the public school. While it is my intent that this book is a resource for anyone interested in a comprehensive study of school, I did add italic lettering to any names or terms that may be of significance. This will help any instructor or student who uses the book in a course. Likewise, I provided a set of questions at the end of each chapter for you, the reader, to reflect upon and enrich your own understanding of the content explored within the chapter.

I hope that you find this book useful as you seek to better understand school. I hope that you enjoy reading it and that it leads to fruitful conversations about school. Most of all, I hope this book is able to, in some respect, play a role in fostering a more thoughtful dialogue on the complexity of school and how best to improve it for the future.

References

Brands, H. W. (2011). *American colossus: The triumph of capitalism, 1865–1900*. New York, NY: Anchor.

Dewey, J. (1897). My pedagogic creed. *The School Journal*. 54(3), 77–80.

Acknowledgments

I wrote this book while on sabbatical provided to me by Winona State University (WSU). I would like to thank WSU's President Scott Olson, Vice-President Patricia Rogers, College of Education Dean Tarrell Portman, and the WSU Education Studies department for their unwavering support for me. I'm also grateful for the many WSU students who were the first to encounter the ideas I've written about in this book—they provided me new insights and the necessary confidence to share it with a wider audience.

This book is the culmination of a myriad of individuals who have invested in me in one way or another. I probably never would have had a career in education without the support, guidance, and encouragement from Michael Fuller, my advisor at Miami University in Oxford, Ohio. I got my start as a high school social studies teacher at Franklin Monroe High School in the tiny village of Pitsburg, Ohio. I'm forever grateful for the opportunity to serve there during a formative decade of my life. My time as a doctoral student at the University of Iowa equipped me with the necessary background and skill set to study the school experience. I am fortunate to be able to call myself a protégé of first-rate scholars from Iowa's Lindquist Center, namely Bruce Fehn, Kathy Schuh, Greg Hamot, and Christine Ogren. However, perhaps no one has been more influential in my writing of this book than Peter Hlebowitsh. The seeds of this book were planted in the countless hours I spent with Peter as his student, graduate assistant, and later as fellow scholar in the field of educational foundations. I'm blessed by not only the good example he set for me as a professor but also by his friendship. The

Paradoxes of the Public School, pages xvii–xviii
Copyright © 2019 by Information Age Publishing
All rights of reproduction in any form reserved.

Society for the Study of Curriculum History has been a valuable resource for me to try out the ideas embedded in this book and conversations with fellow members helped shape my understanding of the American school experience. Prior to my time at Winona State University, I was fortunate to work at Ohio Northern University where I started my career in academia. I had a wonderful time at Ohio Northern and am grateful for all the support my colleagues there provided me.

I'm forever grateful for my parents, Joy and James R. Schul, who always supported me and ensured that I received the best education they could possibly provide. My wife, Christa, remains the most important person in my life whose love and support for me is a priceless treasure. Our four wonderful children, Lani, Wilt, Swin, and Myrene, are constant reminders to me of the wonder of childhood and the need to provide the best possible educational experience for our nation's children.

1

Religion and School

It was early in the morning at Fairlawn public high school. As was typical, the school's social studies teacher, Dan Billups, was among the first to arrive at the school. Dan was beloved by students and admired by colleagues because of his diligence, enthusiasm, and integrity. Always dressed in a dress shirt, tie, and slacks, Dan was the epitome of a professional educator. He liked to arrive early to prepare for the school day long before others pillaged him with requests and a general desire to share some time with him. On this warm spring morning, Dan was spending time writing assignments on the board and searching for an inspiring "Quote of the Day" to share with his classes. Nearly 30 minutes before the start of the school day, Amanda, one of Dan's students, knocked on his wooden classroom door and Dan signaled for her to come in. Amanda was a good student and an active member of her church's youth group. "Mr. Billups," Amanda inquired, "we are having an open prayer vigil around the school's flagpole this morning. Could you please join us?" Amanda, like so many other students, knew Dan was an active member at his church who even taught Sunday school classes. However, Dan did not explicitly proselytize his religious views in the public school because he believed

Paradoxes of the Public School, pages 1–10
Copyright © 2019 by Information Age Publishing
All rights of reproduction in any form reserved.

doing so was not only generally ineffective but also illegal. "Amanda," Dan kindly replied, "while I'm glad you're having the vigil, I cannot join you because I'm a public school teacher." Amanda thanked her teacher for his time and left the classroom. Thoughts began to race in Dan's mind at that moment: "I wish I could do more to support them, but it could create a big problem"; "I'm glad that the kids are taking a moral stance amidst such self-indulgence and immorality in our student culture"; "I never talked to Amanda about my religious views, it is amazing how they know this about me—maybe I am making a big difference by just being who I am." He never saw the flag pole vigil in the schoolyard, but trusted and hoped it went well as he finished his morning preparation. At that moment, the first morning bell blared from the school's intercom system. The parking lot began to fill and students trickled into the building. The school day was about to begin and Dan Billups was ready for them. He walked to the door of his class to greet his first batch of students. "Good morning, it's good to see you," Dan loudly bellowed with a smile for each student. "Good morning, Mr. Billups," could be heard amidst the rustling and chattering of the teens as they filed in his classroom.

The American public school, in its creation, served a much different purpose than its modern conceptualization. Dan Billups probably would not have wavered in his decision to Amanda's request if he was a public school teacher at a much earlier time in American history. The first public school in our history emerged in 1647 in the state of Massachusetts as a means to counter the evil plans of "The Old Deluder," or Satan. This initial rendition of school sought to ensure children could read the Bible and be made aware of the path to eternal salvation. The school in Puritan New England served a theocratic agenda for a homogenous population. However, today's American public school serves a democratic agenda for a pluralistic, heterogeneous culture. What led to this change in agendas will be discussed in Chapter 2. Here in Chapter 1, we will explore the nature of religion in the American public school's past and present. The crux of this exploration will be an unraveling of the following paradox:

The American public school must not establish a religion but yet must also ensure students' exercise of religion.

The New England Puritans

In the early to mid-seventeenth century, a group of people from England flocked to what is now Massachusetts in search of religious freedom. What they desired most, however, was to purify the Christian church through strict obedience to the Bible and Christian doctrine (Morgan, 1966). Historians aptly call this group *Puritans* for their quest to cleanse Christendom. The Puritans governed the Massachusetts Bay Colony as a *theocracy*, or a society where religion and its government were intertwined. These Puritans took seriously the rearing of children and believed that education should run parallel with the aims of the Christian church. For instance, in 1642 they founded Harvard college as our country's first institution of higher education with the admission requirement that all of its students should consider Jesus Christ as the primary purpose of their life and studies (Brubacher, 2017). In the same year, 1642, the colonial government of Massachusetts passed a law requiring that all families should teach their young children to read and write. This *Massachusetts Law of 1642* proved to be a failure as government officials routinely discovered that the families were negligent of this requirement. As a result, 5 years later the *Massachusetts Law of 1647* was passed which required that each township reaching the size of fifty households must hire a schoolmaster and erect a school within the township. This 1647 law, "The Old Deluder Act," was the country's first commitment to formal schooling and subsequently the beginning of the American public school experience.

The Puritan schools adopted a systematic approach to education. Unlike the Native Americans surrounding them who had an informal approach to education that sprouted from within tribal culture, the Puritans sought a formal approach to education that sought to institutionalize the culture's efforts to educate the youth. These institutions, called schools after the Latin derivation *schola* which means "place of instruction," required rules and curriculum that aptly aligned with the religious concerns of the culture. For instance, the first reading ledger called a *horn book* included the letters of the alphabet as well as the Lord's Prayer as the primary text for the children to learn from. This ledger would eventually be replaced by a paper textbook named "The New England Primer" that weaved religious instruction in the midst of literary rhymes (i.e., "In Adam's fall, we sinned all").

The pulpits in Puritan New England were occupied by ministers who were the most revered individuals within the culture. Perhaps none of these ministers was more influential upon Puritan culture than *Cotton Mather* (1663–1728). Cotton Mather was a product of the Puritan culture, having graduated from Harvard college and the son of the very well-known minister and president of Harvard college, Increase Mather. Cotton Mather's influence reached far and wide within Puritan New England as evidenced by his leadership in the infamous Salem Witch Trials and his promotion of inoculation for disease prevention. Cotton Mather's support and endorsement for any venture usually ensured that the public would follow his prompting. In one of Mather's most noteworthy sermons he commanded that children obey their parents and when in school, should "regard their tutors (teachers) as their parents" (Mather, 1699). Mather's matching of the teacher as a parent still holds true in a contemporary court of law under the principle *in loco parentis*, which means "in place of parents." Still today, it is *in loco parentis* that legally empowers school officials to compel children to act against their will such as the case with the child who must do his or her homework despite not wanting to do so.

Toward Pluralism

In the waning years after the Puritans settled in New England, droves of immigrants from reaches of Europe outside of England claimed portions of the American colonies as their new home. Amongst these new Americans were Roman Catholics. The colony of Pennsylvania, known as Penn's colony after the Quaker real estate entrepreneur and philosopher William Penn (1644–1718), was regarded as the most tolerant of all the colonies. This tolerance led to more cultural pluralism within the colony and also laid seeds for what would become a significant cultural conflict within Philadelphia's public school system.

Philadelphia, where the Declaration of Independence and U.S. Constitution was later created in the American Revolutionary era, derived its name from the Greek *philia*, or "brotherly love." Ironically, this city known for its openness and tolerance became the site for a series of bloody and deadly riots in the summer of 1844 that were rooted in religious intolerance. The riots emerged in the midst of a broader nativist movement in the country where American citizens were concerned with the changing population brought forth from an influx of immigrants from Central Europe, particularly Roman Catholics. These Philadelphia riots primarily sprouted from a controversy that emerged between urban Protestants and Catholics over the issue of Bible reading in the class curriculum. Roman Catholics, who do not use the same King James Version of the Bible as Protestants, felt they were becoming increasingly marginalized and began to protest the compulsory Bible reading placed upon their children. Protestants, as a result, reacted against the Catholics in protection of their own stake in the cultural landscape of the city. The result was a series of bloody and deadly confrontations that included the burning down of a Catholic church and necessitated the use of thousands of militiamen. These riots gained national attention and eventually led to the creation of the private Catholic school system that still remains to this day as the primary, legitimate competitor to the American public school system.

TABLE 1.1 Religious Preferences, 1948–2008				
Year	% Protestant/Non-Catholic Christian	% Catholic	% None	% Other
1948	69	22	4	2
1978	58	29	7	5
1998	58	27	7	6
2008	56	22	13	9

Source: Gallup.com

The lesson learned from the *Philadelphia Bible riots* is that a theological agenda for a public school system is not viable within a pluralistic society like the United States. While in Chapter 2 we will explore how the nation came to exist devoid of a theological political structure, unlike that of Puritan New England, it is pertinent that we currently examine how our nation protects the religious liberties of its citizens. This is especially important to know in light of the recent decline in conventional religious preferences within the United States. As you can see in Table 1.1, fewer Americans report to be Protestant Christian with an increase in Americans stating they are neither Protestant nor Catholic.

Despite the increase in religious diversity, remnants of our country's theocratic past remain in place. There are, however, legal parameters in place within our nation's public sphere, in our case the public schools, that serve us well in understanding the relationship between religion and government.

The First Amendment

The most important legal parameter in place pertaining to the role of religion in public spaces is embedded in the First Amendment of the U.S. Constitution. In fact, the topic of religion is featured in the very first statement of freedom given to the people in this opening amendment—before speech, press, and assembly. The First Amendment, like the remaining Bill of Rights, are what political scientists term as "negative rights" in that they are rights in which the government will not impede upon. There are two clauses at the onset of the First Amendment, both pertaining to how the government will not impede upon certain areas of religion in the lives of citizens. The first clause is known as the *establishment clause.* It states as follows:

Congress shall make no law respecting an establishment of religion.

The framers of the U.S. Constitution were well aware of the bloody conflicts that arose from within societies that adopted a national religion, as was the case with England. The framers wanted to avoid this and sought to create a nation without an adopted religion. At first glance this clause may appear to be simple in that the U.S. government is prohibited from creating a national religion, however by the mid-twentieth century an understanding of the establishment clause became murky. At the center of the evolvement of our understanding of the establishment clause was the public school.

Arguably, the most significant Supreme Court case regarding the relationship between the establishment clause and the public school is *Engle v. Vitale* (1962). It is a case that originated with a concern that some families shared with a New York middle school over the following sanctioned prayer: "Almighty God, we acknowledge our dependence upon Thee, and we beg Thy blessings upon us, our parents, our teachers and our country. Amen" (DelFattore, 2004, p. 69). The school district, believing it was meeting the needs of the community's interests as well as complying with constitutional limitations placed upon them, arranged for students who objected to the prayer to "opt-out" of the prayer by momentarily leaving the classroom. The concerned families, who claimed to be atheists, continued their protest of the sanctioned prayer asserting that it still violated the establishment clause. The U.S. Supreme Court heard the case and in a landmark decision ruled, in an 8–1 decision, on behalf of the concerned families stating that the sanctioned prayer as well as the opt-out clause were in violation of the establishment clause. This ruling was controversial at the time, especially in the midst of the Cold War where a fear of a communist (which prohibits religion) takeover of the United States was a serious significant concern by some of the American public at the time. It was also controversial because now it was unclear exactly what was considered a violation of the establishment clause in the public school. Can religion be a topic studied by schools? Can schools partner with religious organizations? The public was put more at ease with this second controversy as a result of the Supreme Court's decision in another important case *Lemon v. Kurtzman* (1971).

The significance of the Lemon case is that with it the court provides a guideline to help us better decipher the parameters of the establishment clause using three pointed questions about a statute or action of a government body (see Figure 1.1). These three questions, popularly known together as the Lemon Test, can be applied to school settings and provide some clarity to school officials in what could be a very difficult matter. For instance, a public school providing a world's religions course in its curriculum clearly passes the Lemon Test because such a course has a clear

- Does the statute or action have a secular purpose?

- Does the principal or primary effect of the statute or action advance or inhibit religious practice?

- Does the statute or action result in an "excessive government entanglement" with religious affairs?

Figure 1.1   Questions of the Lemon test.

secular purpose. Students live in a globally interdependent world where they encounter individuals and cultures with a diversity of religious tenets and practices and it is important that they are educated on these various religions as a means to foster cooperation and tolerance. However, this situation could become more difficult depending upon the execution of the course. As a case in point, let's say that the teacher of the course focuses upon one particular denomination of Protestant Christianity for 95% of the course and glances over all other major religions of the world. This would likely violate the effect prong of the Lemon Test because the action has the effect of promoting a particular religious viewpoint. In another hypothetical scenario, let's say that course is taught in a Roman Catholic cathedral with the help of a Catholic priest. While the explicit course curriculum may pass the first two prongs of the Lemon Test, it can be argued that it would fail the last prong because of an excessive entanglement that the course has fostered with the Roman Catholic church. At times in this latter situation it may seem confusing to public school students and their parents as to whether they are in fact in a public school with a normative mandate or a Catholic school with a parochial mandate. Of course, the courts at all levels consist of people who make judgements. The norms of society have proven to affect court decisions and so it is difficult to know exactly what the court may rule all of the time. However, the Lemon Test provides clarity to the establishment clause after the *Engle v. Vitale* (1962) ruling. What, however, about students' free exercise of religion?

The second clause of the First Amendment, known as the *free exercise clause*, states the following:

> Congress shall make no law respecting an establishment
> of religion, or *prohibiting the free exercise thereof.*

While the establishment clause focuses on the actions of the state, with the school and its officials serving as the agents of the state, the free exercise clause pertains mostly to students within American public schools. This

- Is the student's religious views sincerely held?

- Is an important state interest served while impeding students' religious freedom?

- Is it pedagogically or financially feasible to allow for students' religious freedom?

- Does the religious practice cause a disruption in school?

Figure 1.2 Key questions in free exercise cases.

clause emphasizes the point that individuals must be permitted to practice any form of religion—mostly without any restrictions whatsoever. However, there are general legal guidelines from courts that may lead to a school rightfully restricting a students' religious freedom (see Figure 1.2). For one, a student's religious exercise of religion may be restricted if it is proven to not be sincerely held. For instance, a student who claims to a teacher that they do not have to do any math homework because their religious practices at home are interrupted because of the homework assignment likely are maneuvering their way to avoid the homework assignment rather than out of a true religious motive. However, if somehow this situation is proven to be sincere, the school still may be able to impede on this students' religious practice because doing homework serves the states' important interest to ensure that students are proficient at math, thus schools should be free to assign math homework if they deem it necessary for student math proficiency. While a student's claims of religious freedom may be limited if the beliefs are not sincerely held and/or if the requirement by the school serves an important state interest, a student's religious freedom may also be impeded if their requests are deemed by the school to be administratively, pedagogically, or financially infeasible. For instance, if a request is made by students that requires the school to adopt a specific textbook just for that student or to attend a separate classroom apart from their classmates, then the school may reject the students' request without fear of violating the free exercise clause.

Perhaps the most commonly used condition where the school may impede students' exercise of religion is if the practice causes a disruption. As a case in point, if a student wears a shirt displaying the slogan "God Hates Gays" then the school has the right to either punish or force the student to change their shirt. The reason for this is that the shirt literally uses hate language and that language is directed toward a specific student population that is intended to marginalize those students. If a student, however, chose to wear a "God Loves You" shirt, then the matter is clearly protected under the free exercise clause. It should be noted that most instances of student practice of religion in school is protected by the free exercise clause and courts have historically upheld the students' rights. This has been especially true with regard to the idea of religious-based student groups meeting on school grounds during non-school hours. For example, in the case *Good News Club v. Milford Central Schools* (2001) the Supreme Court upheld a student groups' claim that their school district should allow them to meet during nonschool hours. The school district claimed that since the group was religious based, and spent their meeting time toward what amounted to religious instruction, they should not be permitted to meet within the school. The Supreme Court ruled in a majority opinion that the actions of the school constituted viewpoint discrimination and that the student group that focuses on religion deserved the same treatment as other groups, such as the Boy Scouts, that met on school grounds during nonschool hours (Merriman, 2007). While the Good News Club case focused primarily upon students' free speech rights, it also demonstrated that the Court, to a certain degree, views student religious liberties as something to be protected despite a school's claim that allowing such liberties would be a violation of the establishment clause.

Summary

The American public school was first conceptualized in New England during the seventeenth century. New England at this time was a theocracy and the school served that society's theocratic agenda. However, as new colonies formed, an influx of European immigrants created more diverse, pluralistic societies across the North American continent. This pluralism was particularly evident with the burgeoning diverse religious backgrounds of the American people. As the United States of America was formed, the framers of the federal constitution installed a Bill of Rights to secure its citizens fundamental freedoms. The First Amendment of the Bill of Rights first emphasized religion stating that the federal government will not establish a religion and will not inhibit citizens' free exercise of religion. As the American public school evolved over the course of time to better serve the pluralism present within the nation, the establishment clause became broadly interpreted by courts that schools cannot sanction or promote religion. However, courts also have upheld students' free exercise of religion in many instances. The paradox of the school not being able to establish a religion yet also being required to ensure students' free exercise of religion still exists as a tension that the American public school must pay careful attention to so as to persistently protect the religious liberties within the American democracy.

Reflective Exercises

1. Why do you think religion is the first issue mentioned in the First Amendment?
2. Are there any remnants of the Puritan's religious agenda still at play in the American public school today? Explain your answer.
3. Apply the Lemon Test to the following questions:
   - Can a teacher wear religious jewelry or have a religious tattoo?
   - Can a school observe a religious holiday, like Christmas?
   - Can teachers tell students they believe in God?
4. How should schools interpret the free exercise clause in a case where a student requests exemption from a certain class because of religious reasons?

References

Brubacher, J. (2017). *Higher education in transition: History of American colleges and universities.* New York, NY: Routledge.

DelFattore, J. (2004). *The fourth R: Conflicts over religion in America's public schools.* New Haven, CT: Yale University Press.

Engel v. Vitale (1962). 370 U.S. 421.

Good News Club v. Milford Central School (2001). 533 U.S. 98.

Lemon v. Kurtzman (1971). 403 U.S. 602.

Mather, C. (1699). *A family well ordered.* Retrieved from http://ota.ox.ac.uk/tcp/headers/N00/N00727.html

Merriman, S. A. (2007). *Religion and the law in America: An encyclopedia of personal belief and public policy* (Vol.1). Santa Barbara, CA: Abc-Clio.

Morgan, E. S. (1966). *The puritan family: Religion and domestic relations in seventeenth-century New England.* New York, NY: Harper & Row.

2

Democracy and School

"B-39."

"O 7."

"I-22."

"BINGO!" exclaimed nine-year-old Clara who sat amidst the nearly two hundred people congregated in Belleview's century old gymnasium.

Arnie Derschewitz, the tenderhearted and wildly entertaining second grade teacher, was in his twenty-fourth year at Belleview and was accustomed to hosting this bingo event each year at the time the leaves fell off the town's trees and onto the lawns and streets. It was a festive time for the school community. It was here where girls like Clara sat, side by side, with her classmates, their families, and oftentimes their teachers. Many parents were still donning their work clothes as they sat with their children, often alongside fellow community members who were meeting for the very first time. It was here where community members ate popcorn and sang songs together—led by Mr. Derschewitz—that were familiar to the children and

Paradoxes of the Public School, pages 11–22

Copyright © 2019 by Information Age Publishing

new to the parents. One of the songs was even written by Mr. Derschewitz himself: "Belleview, Belleview, we're glad to be part of you." All of this while everyone patiently anticipated the call of the next letter and number combination.

However, bingo was actually a small part of the night. It was the getting together that mattered most to the school. Belleview was the only place where many of these people would ever be together. Outside the school that night, little connected the people outside. Those at the local McDonalds® eat that evening's dinner amidst their own partition, wolfing down their double cheeseburgers and fries. The nearby Walmart® was experiencing its recurring ritual of cars parking on its large field of pavement, with customers hurriedly doing their shopping errands or just deciding to walk around to see if there might be anything in the large brick building that might interest them. Seldom do the people speak to one another as they peruse the aisles during this rite of the modern era. The masses, in no way, connect with one another. This is what made the bingo night so special—it diverted from community members' conventional practice of going their separate ways and dwelling in their own singular silos of life.

Belleview's bingo night is indicative of the unique purpose of the public school to fulfill our country's democratic agenda. The American public school, conceived by the New England Puritans of the seventeenth century, initially had a theocratic agenda. However, the aims and scope of the public school evolved with the emergence of the nation. As we saw in Chapter 1, American society became more demographically pluralistic once immigrants from a myriad of countries arrived on the nation's shores during the seventeenth and eighteenth centuries. The rise of multiple sects of Christianity dwelling in the same region, often times in the same community, made it increasingly difficult for a theocracy to survive harmoniously with the emergent revolutionary spirit that arose in America at the tail end of the eighteenth century. This revolutionary spirit climaxed into the American Revolution of the 1770s and spilled out into the formation of the American socio-political regime still in place today. This chapter focuses on the nature of this new socio-political regime, including its values and aims, and how the mission of the American public school took shape to reflect this new democratic-minded regime. However, as the new democratic heartbeat emerged in the school's mission, competing aims emerged simultaneously. These competing aims remain to this day. Therefore, at the center of this chapter will be an exploration of the following paradox:

The American public school has a specific mission to foster democratic citizenship but is often expected by the public to have a different purpose, namely vocational and college preparation.

The American Revolution

John Locke (1632–1704), an English philosopher from the late seventeenth century, created a paradigm shift in how people saw the role of government and its relation to the people under its control. The conventional belief of government in Locke's era and earlier was encapsulated in a theory called *absolutism.* Absolutism asserted that God created government, endowed this government with rulers, who in effect benevolently rule over its people. The names of history's most well-known monarchs, such as Elizabeth I, King James of England, Louis XIV, or Louis XVI of France, exemplified the nature of absolutism. These monarchs ruled with prestige and great power over their countries. Locke put a crack in the armor of absolutism with his writings, most notably his *Two Treatises of Government* (1690), that challenged absolutism and sought to replace it with a social contract between the government and its people. According to Locke, this social contract consisted of a guarantee of natural rights (life, liberty, and property) to the people who had the authority to usurp the government that infringed upon these rights. Locke influenced numerous other philosophers throughout Europe in the eighteenth century in what historians call the *era of enlightenment.* The enlightenment was a period when much of European society challenged conventional wisdom in place of a reliance on human reason and an overarching support of human rights. The influence of the enlightenment spread toward the American colonists, among whom many boldly based their own revolution against their ruling country of England.

The seeds of the American Revolution were first sewn in a trans-Atlantic conflict often referred to as the French and Indian War (1754–1763). This war pitted England and the American colonists against France and Native Americans in a bloody fight for who would control the North American land west of the Appalachian mountains. England and the American colonists proved victorious in this war but it proved costly to England. As a result, the English government issued a series of taxes and restrictions upon the American colonists to help pay for the war as well as to prevent further conflicts related to the contested land west of the Appalachians. Many of the colonists were enraged by these actions by England and called these actions "Intolerable Acts" and rallied themselves under the anti-English slogan of "No Taxation without Representation." The protests by the colonists against the English government led to a conflict that ensued for nearly six years (1775–1781) between England and the American colonists famously called "The American Revolution."

One of the pivotal moments of the American Revolution was the creation and signing of the *Declaration of Independence.* This document, today regarded as the cornerstone document of American democracy, contains what is collectively viewed by Americans as the mission statement of the United States:

> We hold these truths to be self-evident, that all men are created equal, that they are endowed by their Creator with certain unalienable Rights, that among these are Life, Liberty and the pursuit of Happiness.—That to secure these rights, Governments are instituted among Men, deriving their just powers from the consent of the governed,—That whenever any Form of Government becomes destructive of these ends, it is the Right of the People to alter or to abolish it, and to institute new Government, laying its foundation on such principles and organizing its powers in such form, as to them shall seem most likely to effect their Safety and Happiness.

Locke's philosophy of a social contract that protects individuals' natural rights ebbed and flowed from this statement. Of course, the American Revolution ended with a victory for the American colonists. With that victory came the need for a reshaping of a nation to befit its fresh, yet challenging, mission statement. This reshaping involved financial, military, and, of course, political reform to assure a workable structure emerged to jumpstart the new nation. However, the struggle for a new type of public education during this time of nation building should not be overlooked for it laid the groundwork for the purpose and vision of the American public school system that exists to this day.

The Struggle for a Public School System

As we saw in Chapter 1, Massachusetts had a public school system in place by the mid-seventeenth century. Although it predominantly served a colonial theocracy and was poorly funded, it nonetheless was more than what existed in other areas of the new nation. To put it bluntly, public education largely did not exist at the inception of United States of America. For many, like the primary author of the Declaration of Independence, Thomas Jefferson, this was a significant problem that needed to be solved if the new democratic experiment was to be successful.

The Declaration of Independence stated that the government derives its power "from the consent of the governed." This simple and romantic idea would have powerful consequences in how the American people would need to view education—for it would now need to be tied to the perpetuation and security of the nation. After all, the people were now in charge of the government rather than visa versa. The Constitution of the United States, conceived nearly a decade after the Revolution itself, stipulated in its *Tenth Amendment* that: "The powers not delegated to the United States by the Constitution, nor prohibited by it to the States, are reserved to the States respectively, or to the people." Public education did not surface anywhere as a power within the scope of the federal government. Thus, the power of public education rests within the realm of the individual states. The post-revolutionary years saw reformers in several states, led by *Thomas Jefferson* (1743–1826) of Virginia and *Benjamin Rush* (1746–1813) of Pennsylvania, embark on a prolonged and unsuccessful fight for public education in their respective states. In his *Notes on the State of Virginia*, published in 1781, Jefferson (1853) proposed a bill to the Virginia legislature that would create a public education system out of a need to "diffuse knowledge more generally through the mass of the people" (p. 157). He asserted that the new nation necessitates public education that is "adapted to the years, to the capacity, and the condition of every one, and directed to their freedom and happiness" as a means of "rendering the people safe, as they are the ultimate guardians of their own liberty" (p. 159). A few years later, Benjamin Rush (1786) wrote to the people of his respective state of Pennsylvania in his *Thoughts Upon the Mode of Education Proper in a Republic* that "the business of education has acquired a new complexion by the independence of our country" (p. 13). This new "complexion" of education, according to Rush, needed to focus on instilling knowledge, skills, and dispositions within the citizenry that reflected the needs of a republican government. Neither Jefferson nor Rush were successful with creating public school systems in their respective states. However, the rhetoric they espoused in defense of why public education should exist continued to resonate decades later as individual states created public school systems in their respective constitutions.

States' Purposes for Public Education

Since education is a power left to states, as a direct result of the federal constitution's Tenth Amendment, each states' constitution is filled with prose concerning the purpose and provisions surrounding its public school systems. To illustrate this point, four states' constitutional statements on public education are provided. The first case we will focus on is Massachusetts, where public education originated nearly two centuries prior to it being widely accepted by other states. Massachusetts' constitution, ratified in 1780 and primarily authored by John Adams, is the oldest working constitution in the world. Its constitution says the following about public education:

> Wisdom, and knowledge, as well as virtue, diffused generally among the body of the people, being necessary for the preservation of their rights and liberties... (Chapter V, Section II)

Following the path blazed by Massachusetts, states formed in the mid–late nineteenth century placed a similar democratic purpose on their public school systems. For instance, the state of Minnesota, who ratified their constitution in 1857, stated about public education:

> The stability of a republican form of government depending mainly upon the intelligence of the people, it is the duty of the legislature to establish a general and uniform system of public schools. (Article XIII, Section 1)

Arkansas, who ratified its constitution in 1874, said the following about its public education system:

> Intelligence and virtue being the safeguards of liberty and the bulwark of a free and good government, the State shall ever maintain a general, suitable and efficient system of free public schools and shall adopt all suitable means to secure to the people the advantages and opportunities of education. (Article XIV, Section 1)

California who ratified its current constitution in 1879, also parlayed a democratic purpose toward its public school system:

> A general diffusion of knowledge and intelligence being essential to the preservation of the rights and liberties of the people, the Legislature shall encourage by all suitable means the promotion of intellectual, scientific, moral, and agricultural improvement. (Article IX, Section 1)

As you can see, Jefferson and Rush's rhetoric carried on to other respective states. Clearly, school's purpose, at least in these four respective states, is intrinsically linked to the nation's democratic society. However, not all states employ rhetoric in their constitutions to describe the purpose of public schools. Some states like Arizona, Florida, or even Jefferson's Virginia, simply state the fact that public schools should exist. Other states, like Rush's Pennsylvania, state something to the effect that public schools will serve the general needs of their state (or, commonwealth, as they put it).

While many states are more explicit than others in their constitutional statements about the democratic purpose of their public schools, the prevailing rhetoric amongst the states is that public schools function with the primary purpose of fostering democratic citizenship.

"We Want It All"

In the mid 1980s, noted educational scholar, *John Goodlad* (1984), published an important book about school simply titled *A Place Called School.* The book emerged from extensive survey research conducted by the Institute for Development of Educational Activities, Inc. The results, though from long ago, reveal much about the public's expectations of its schools that resonate to contemporary America. In a survey of nearly 8,600 parents, Goodlad's research team concluded that the parents had four broad goals for schools: academic, vocational, socio-civic, and personal. These goals, arguably, remain the four primary aims of school that exist to this day.

The "personal" aim of school include two areas: intrapersonal development and interpersonal development. Intrapersonal development includes notions such as individual responsibility, self-actualization, expression, and other skills related with an individual's ability to succeed in life. For instance, the presence of television and the Internet makes it easy for individuals to choose entertainment over developing themselves intellectually, morally, or physically. A 2016 study from the U.S. Bureau of Labor Statistics reported that individuals, on average, participated in a little over 5 hours of leisure activities per day with television watching consummating over half of that time. Strategies schools employ to develop students' intrapersonal skills may include a pervasive curricular push for students to have a more well-rounded daily schedule by replacing some time watching television with, for instance, more reading and more social activities. Intrapersonal development may also include areas such as stress management and psychological health. Schools, therefore, need to address these particular areas with relevant curricular programs and counseling services.

Another area of "personal" aims of school is the interpersonal development of students. Individual growth does not exclusively mean that students should focus on their own individual growth and needs but should also entail an ability to collaborate and cooperate with others. Interpersonal development may be fostered by schools through strategies such as cooperative learning classroom exercises, extracurricular activities such as athletics, or academic/social clubs.

The socio-civic aim of the American public school, as we have seen, is articulated in many states' constitutions. Education for democratic citizenship requires schools to intentionally direct students toward habits and dispositions that are, in many ways, unnatural. Democracy, according to civic educator Walter Parker (1996), "does not arise spontaneously but in institutions—democratic institutions—and then only with difficulty" (p. 3). According to John Dewey (1916/2005), democracy extends beyond mere voting and toward a habit of living together in ways that propel society forward. This notion of living together as a core component of democratic citizenship runs contrary to what Ancient Greeks referred to as *idiocy*, or self-centeredness of individuals. Parker (2003) explained the nature of idiocy:

> Idiots do not take part in public life—do not have a public life. In this sense, the idiot is immature in the most fundamental way, his or her life fundamentally out of balance, ajar, untethered, and unrealized: The idiot has not yet met the challenge of "puberty," the transition to public life. (p. 3)

The unnaturalness of democratic citizenship brings a persistent challenge to the public school experience because it requires the public to extend outward rather than inward upon individuals' own self-interests. This may be a key reason why the public school continually finds itself in a perpetual identity crisis. The socio-civic aim of public school is most prominently on display in the social studies curriculum. Social studies education is a broad field that includes history, government, geography, economics, sociology, psychology, and other disciplines related to the study of society. A strong social studies curriculum should center around problem solving and decision-making with an emphasis on contemporary issues that prepare students with the knowledge, skills, and dispositions necessary to be effective democratic citizens. However, socio-civic development should not be exclusively housed within the social studies curriculum.

All subjects within the school curriculum should, in some way, intentionally develop students' civic skill set. For instance, a science teacher may direct students how they may get involved in policy-making as it relates to environmental issues and/or funding for science research. All curricular areas should take into consideration how the school equips students to be cooperative with one another, to deliberate over issues with one another, to treat one another with respect and dignity, and to be vigilant with assuring individuals who may be subjected to marginalization within the school community are protected and welcomed. Frankly, the opportunities for the entire school community to engage in democratic education are seemingly endless.

While the public does expect schools to serve personal and socio-civic goals of schools, these two areas often are afterthoughts in educational policy making in light of the public's interest in the other two goals of school: academic and vocational. The public has always demanded that the public school be responsive toward a rigorous academic curriculum, but a heavier emphasis emerged in the latter half of the twentieth century with the advent of the Advanced Placement® (AP) program initiated by the College Board. In 1952, the College Board, a nonprofit organization founded at the turn of the twentieth century with a purpose to make higher education more accessible for individuals, launched a pilot program of courses and tests in 11 subjects. The pilot program evolved into the increasingly popular AP program that exists today. Currently, nearly three dozen AP courses exist within six subject categories: arts, English, history & social science, math & computer science, sciences, and world languages & cultures. Participation in AP courses within the United States has multiplied nearly six and, in some instances, nine times, in a 20 year span between 1996–2016 (The College Board, 2016). It is customary for colleges and universities to provide credit for successful completion of AP course examinations, given at the conclusion of the course itself.

College credit for high school courses is alluring for many American families. At the turn of the 21st century, various states participated in the Post-Secondary Education Option (PSEO) where successful high school students could take college courses that simultaneously counts as high school course credit at little to no extra expense to families. Since the mid to late 1980s, Minnesota and Ohio, where the program is currently called College Credit Plus, are the two states who spearheaded this option with the purpose of providing rigorous course options for students as well as providing better academic preparation for students as they enter college. In many instances, high school students involved in PSEO take courses at the college or university offering the course, or at home online, rather than attending their local high school.

While college preparation has increased in importance for the American public school, federal policy initiatives over the last quarter of a century have reaffirmed the academic goal of the public school. In 1994, the U.S. Congress passed an act entitled Goals 2000: Educate America Act (1994). This act, commonly referred to as Goals 2000, created educational goals ranging from academic readiness to a drug-free school environment. Among its stated goals was the following: "By the year 2000, United States students will be first in the world in mathematics and science achievement" (Chapter 68, subchapter 1, para. 5). Goals 2000 was later replaced in 2001 by The No Child Left Behind Act (which we will learn more about in another chapter). These federal initiatives prioritized the academic purpose of school but also focused on the vocational goals of the public school. Take notice of the following statement in Goals 2000 (1994):

> By the year 2000, all students will leave Grades 4, 8, and 12 having demonstrated competency over challenging subject matter including English, mathematics, science, foreign languages, civics and government, economics, arts, history, and geography, and every school in America will ensure that all students learn to use their minds well, so they may be prepared for responsible citizenship, further learning, and productive employment in our Nation's modern economy. (Chapter 68, subchapter 1, para. 3)

School and preparation for "productive employment in our Nation's modern economy" indicates the significance that vocational preparation plays in the American public school experience.

While federal initiatives, such as Goals 2000 (1994), often mention citizenship as a goal of public school, their emphasis upon subjects such as math and science provide a telltale sign that vocational preparation is at the forefront of the public's mandate for public schools. The most recent national effort to create national goals surfaced in 2009 in the form of the Common Core Standards. The starting point in the development of the Common Core was the "college and career readiness standards" that demonstrate the academic and vocational interest that spearheaded the Common Core (we will learn more about the Common Core and standards-based movement in a later chapter).

Thomas Friedman, foreign affairs columnist for *The New York Times*, is well known for surmising that contemporary public education fails to prepare its students for an ever-changing and demanding workforce. In his bestselling book from over a decade ago, *The World Is Flat*, Friedman (2006) warned: "The American education system from kindergarten through twelfth grade just is not stimulating enough young people to want to go into science, math, and engineering" (p. 270). Bill Gates, founder of Microsoft, pushes education initiatives with a similar vocational motive as espoused by Friedman. Gates' philanthropic organization, The Bill and Melinda Gates Foundation, put forth the following goal for American education on its website (https://www.gatesfoundation.org/What-We-Do/US-Program/K-12-Education):

> The goal remains to ensure all students receive a K-12 education that equips them to succeed in college or career training program since a high-quality education is a proven path to prosperity and participation in the American Dream. (para. 5)

Gates' emphasis on the net result of education to place individuals on "a proven path to prosperity and participation in the American Dream" is not without its critics. For instance, noted education critic Jonathan Kozol (2005) is known to express concerns over the growing effect that corporate leaders, such as Gates, have on the school experience:

> Corporate leaders, when they speak of education, sometimes pay lip service to the notion of "good critical and analytic skills," but it is reasonable to ask whether they have in mind the critical analysis of *their* priorities ... In all the business-driven classrooms I have been observing in the past five years, plastered as they are with corporation brand names and with managerial vocabularies, I have yet to see the two words "labor unions." (p. 106)

Kozol's criticism illuminates the division that the public has pertaining to the goal of the public school. A central challenge for the American public school lies in determining its goals in lieu of the fact that these challenges, on occasion, may collide with one another.

The struggle for the purpose of public education exists still today, and perhaps always has. Jefferson and Rush's vision of public school as a garden of democratic citizenship, alone, was not enough for the public writ large to warm to the idea of paying for a public school system. It was not until later, around the 1830s, that the public became willing to pay for public education. The fact that this turn of events ran parallel with the emergence of the industrial revolution, and thus a market need for higher literacy rates, was not likely a mere coincidence.

Summary

The American Revolution brought forth a democratic political regime that emphasized that the powers of government derive from the governed. In the wake of the Revolution, several Americans (notably Thomas Jefferson and Benjamin Rush), pushed for public education in their respective states as means to assure that the new democracy could be successfully led by an educated public. Although their attempts proved futile in their respective states, Jefferson and Rush's defense of public education as citizenship preparation carried over many years later to the rhetoric used in many states' constitutional statements on their purpose for public education. However, while public education may have an overarching purpose of preparing students for democratic citizenship, the public expects the school to do many others things, most notably prepare young people for college and careers.

Reflective Exercises

1. What do you believe should be the goals of American public education? Come up with a list of these goals. Do any of these goals conflict with one another? Explain.
2. What are the knowledge, skills, and dispositions necessary for a person to be a democratic citizen?
3. If you were given the opportunity to create a new public school from scratch, what are some ways, in terms of programming and classroom practices, you may direct it to educate for democratic citizenship?
4. Why is democratic citizenship, as a goal for public education, often cast aside in favor of college and career readiness?

References

The College Board. (2016). AP score distributions—All subjects 1996–2016. Retrieved from https://secure-media.collegeboard.org/digitalServices/pdf/research/2016/2016-Score-Distribution-All-Subjects.pdf

Dewey, J. (2005). *Democracy and education.* New York, NY: Barnes & Noble. (Originally published in 1916)

Friedman, T. (2006). *The World is flat.* New York, NY: Farrar, Straus, & Giroux.

Goals 2000: Educate America Act, H.R. 1804, 103rd Cong. (1994). Retrieved from https://www.congress.gov/bill/103rd-congress/house-bill/1804

Jefferson, T. (1853). *Notes on the state of Virginia.* Richmond, VA: JW Randolph.

Kozol, J. (2005). *The shame of the nation: The restoration of apartheid schooling in America.* Portland, OR: Broadway Books.

Parker, W. (Ed.). (1996). *Educating the democratic mind.* Albany: State University of New York Press.

Parker, W. (2003). *Teaching democracy: Unity and diversity in public life.* New York, NY: Teachers College Press.

Rush, B. (1786). *A plan for the establishment of public schools and the diffusion of knowledge in Pennsylvania; to which are added, thoughts upon the mode of education proper in a republic.* Ann Arbor, MI: Text Creation Partnership. Retrieved from https://quod.lib.umich.edu/cgi/t/text/text-idx?c=evans;id no=N15652.0001.001

3

Teachers and School

It was the end of a typical cold winter day at Kennedy Elementary School. Melissa Kepler, a veteran first grade teacher at the school, was busily preparing her room for the forthcoming grade level meeting with her first grade colleagues. Melissa prepared a table with seats available for each of her colleagues. Soon, her three colleagues (Mrs. Latsch, Mr. Horner, and Ms. Smith) trickled in, each with a smile blazened on their face. Melissa's classroom was always pleasant to enter primarily because Melissa was always a pleasant person. Friendly yet demure, Melissa was beloved by students, parents, and colleagues alike. The teachers' task was to begin a curricular assessment of the effectiveness of their reading instructional strategies. They wanted to see if their combination of whole language and phonics was or was not successful in reaching all of their students' learning needs. Just as the meeting commenced, Belleview's principal, Mike Adams, hurried in the classroom. "Do you mind if I join you?" the principal asked. The group was caught by surprise since they weren't expecting a visitor

Paradoxes of the Public School, pages 23–39
Copyright © 2019 by Information Age Publishing

but they quietly permitted the principal to join them. For the next several minutes, the teachers discussed the advantages and disadvantages with their reading program and were beginning to garner a mutual understanding that they should keep the combination of whole language and phonics in place for the time being. "Wait a minute," the principal interjected, "We should be using a whole-language approach with all of our students." Melissa responded: "But, some of our students respond better to a phonics approach so that is why we decided on a reading program that allowed for more individualization of instruction." The principal immediately recoiled, "We cannot afford to waste any time on other strategies, the second grade employs whole language and it works for them. Therefore, it should also work for you. Our reading test scores must improve and whole-language is a tried and true approach for other teachers." Mr. Adams walked out of the room politely stating that he had another meeting to attend. The teachers were stunned. They took great effort to research and collaborate on collective best practices for their students. The teachers were left despondently staring at one another. Should they comply with their supervisor's request or should they do what they think was right? Melissa asked the group what they thought. Mrs. Latsch voiced the concerns of the group: "He is outright wrong, but I do not want to lose my job. If we do not comply to his request, we are likely out on the street next year since none of us have tenure." The teachers mumbled among themselves a general agreement with their colleague. Melissa was the elder teacher among the group, with 10 years of experience under her belt. All of the others were either in their second or third year of teaching. Melissa responded to the group: "I wish we could do something else, but I do not have any more power than each of you." The members walked out of the room with their shoulders stooped.

While the efforts of reformers, such as Thomas Jefferson and Benjamin Rush, to create a publicly-funded school system dissipated, the efforts of a reformer in Massachusetts in the 1830s were widely successful. This reformer, Horace Mann, spearheaded an effort that not only created publicly-funded schools in his state but also lifted school teachers as a bona fide profession. Mann's educational vision spread throughout the United States, which led historians to aptly name him as the "Father of American Education." There are numerous educational innovations that can be attributed to Horace Mann. This chapter focuses on Mann's professionalization of school teachers and the professional status of contemporary teachers. Unfortunately, as you will see, many current teachers can relate to something akin to what the teachers in our story from Kennedy Elementary School experienced, namely their professional judgement usurped by a supervisor. The challenges that Mann faced in the professionalization of teachers, albeit nearly two centuries in the past, remain today. At the center of this chapter will be an exploration of the following paradox:

Teachers gained professional status with the efforts of Horace Mann nearly two centuries ago, but are continually at risk of losing professional status.

The Whig Reformer

Horace Mann (1796–1859) was a prominent politician in Massachusetts at the time when then Governor Edward Everett asked him to become the secretary of the state board of education. It was the first position of its kind in the United States. Mann accepted the position and used it to earnestly fight for the improvement of public education throughout Massachusetts. Mann's vision for public education reflected the principles of the *Whig Party*, of which Mann belonged. Whigs believed that public policy, among other things, should focus on institution building (i.e., banks and government offices) and infrastructure (i.e., roads and canals) as a means to quickly modernize the American economy. Some prominent Whigs in the mid-19th century included Henry Clay and Abraham Lincoln. Mann's argument for a strong, centralized public school system that would instill school children with democratic skills and habits fit nicely with the Whigs' political platform.

Upon taking the helm of secretary of the Massachusetts state board of education, Mann initiated numerous educational reforms that eventually transformed American public education in ways that resonate with contemporary practices in public education. These reforms included the state standardization of the school curriculum, teacher preparation, building codes, and classroom practices. In fact, Mann's struggle to attain universal, publicly-funded education in Massachusetts paved the way for the creation of public education as we now know it throughout the nation.

Arguably, the most significant reform that Mann initiated was publicly funded education. However, Mann's success in doing what Jefferson and Rush failed to do should not be simply understood as the work of a lone individual. To the contrary, Mann's struggle for public education emerged at a time when the public writ large was more willing to support publicly funded education than they were at the turn of the 19th century. The historian Carl Kaestle (1983) asserted that the American public's turnabout in its views on public education was primarily due to shared commitments between a growing American working-class and middle-class reformers such as Mann:

> Working-class and middle-class educators shared the goals of morality, respect-
> ability, and self-improvement…These shared commitments, sometimes rein-
> forced by religious and ethnic identities that crossed class lines, produced an
> alliance in the 1820s and 1830s between American workingmen's groups and
> middle-class reformers in favor of tax-supported common schooling. (p. 141)

Kaestle's assertion that the commitments of "morality, respectability, and
self-improvement" blurred class-based boundaries and fueled the growing
support for public education. The *common school*, a term used for the first
wave of public schools in the 19th century, personified these shared commitments by creating a public space where a broad array of Americans would
gather together to form a garden where American democracy would, hopefully, be nurtured and grown. We will explore further about the democratic
mission of the common school, specifically the teacher, later in this chapter.

Mann believed that the teacher should be the leader within the garden
of democracy. In other words, Mann envisioned a teacher to be a professional with the public calling of nurturing democratic knowledge, skills,
and dispositions amongst society. The theme in this chapter is the professional status of teachers in the past and in contemporary times. We will be
using three signifiers of a profession: pay, education, and influence in the
workplace. First, however, let's explore who constitutes the teaching profession in terms of gender, race, and age.

Teacher Demographics

The emergence of the common school in the mid-19th century led to a transition in who became teachers. Prior to the common schools, many school
officials viewed men as superior teachers than their female counterparts
(Preston, 1993). This changed amidst an upper- to middle-class movement
in the early–mid-19th century historians call the *cult of domesticity* that lauded
women's innate knack for nurturing children, purity, and submissiveness to
authority. Leaders of this movement, such as *Catherine Beecher* (1800–1878),
stressed that females were best suited to be males because the domestic
sphere women dwelled in was compatible to the caring components imbedded in the teaching profession. In 1841, the Boston Board of Education
advanced the beliefs of Beecher and others by advocating for females to
enter the teaching profession: "That females are incomparably better teachers for young children than males, cannot admit of a doubt. Their manners
are more mild and gentle, and hence more in consonance with the tender-
ness of childhood" (Elsbree, 1939, p. 201). Later in this chapter we will explore how early teacher preparatory schools became destinations for young
women in 19th century America to venture out on their own as respected

professionals in an environment that offered little other professional opportunities for them. While we are closing in on two centuries since the initial feminization of the teaching profession, little has changed in terms of the dominance of female teachers in schools. In 2016, women made up 97.6% of preschool and kindergarten teachers, 79.8% of elementary and middle school teachers, 58% of secondary teachers, and 87.5% of special education teachers (Bureau of Labor Statistics, 2018). See Table 3.1 for the teacher demographics in terms of sex and race.

As you can see, the trend is greater concentration of women for the younger child served, with special education being largely a mixed bag of elementary and secondary level teachers. However, secondary teachers are also mostly women. In terms of race, the amount of African-American, Asian-American, and Hispanic-American teachers becomes disconcerting once compared to the amount of students in these racial categories.

By comparing Tables 3.1 and Figure 3.1, a dichotomy exists between the percentage of African-American/Hispanic-American teachers and students. This dichotomy promises to increase over the next several years

TABLE 3.1 **Teacher Distribution by Sex and Race**				
Teacher Level	**Women**	**African American**	**Asian American**	**Hispanic American**
Preschool and Kindergarten	97.5%	16.0%	4.0%	14.5%
Elementary and Middle School	79.8%	11.1%	3.3%	10.3%
Secondary School	58.0%	7.3%	2.6%	9.0%
Special Education	87.5%	8.5%	1.6%	7.6%

Source: Bureau of Labor Statistics, 2018.

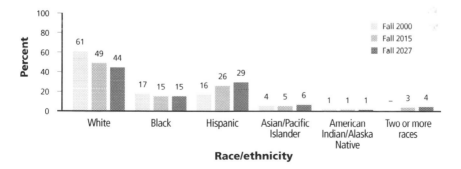

Figure 3.1 Percentage distribution of students enrolled in public elementary and secondary schools, by race/ethnicity. Fall 2000, 2015, and 2027. *Source:* National Center for Education Statistics, 2017.

TABLE 3.2   Distribution of Teachers by Race as it Relates to Socioeconomic Status (SES) of Schools

SES Level of Schools	White Teachers	African-American Teachers	Hispanic-American Teachers
Low Poverty	93.4%	1.9%	3.6%
High Poverty	75.0%	7.7%	11.1%

Source: National Center for Educational Statistics, 2008.

TABLE 3.3   Distribution of Teachers by Age

Average Age of Teachers	Median Age of Teachers	Age Category			
		Less Than 30 Years	30–49 Years	50–54 Years	55 Years or More
42.4	41.0	15.3	54.0	11.9	18.8

Source: National Center for Educational Statistics, 2012.

unless more African American/Hispanic Americans enter the teacher workforce. Recent research (e.g., Egalite, Kisida, & Winters, 2015) reveals that students who have race-congruent teachers perform better academically in school. Additionally, race-congruent teachers for students are speculated to offer positive role modeling opportunities.

Additionally, the percentage of teachers of a particular race in schools rises and falls with the level of socioeconomic status of the students in a particular school (see Table 3.2). For instance, 93.4% of teachers are White who work in low poverty schools (with less than 35% of students eligible for free or reduced lunch) as opposed to 75% of teachers being White in high poverty schools (with 75% or more of students are eligible for free or reduced lunch). These statistics are reversed when it comes to African-American (1.9% in low poverty schools; 7.7% in high poverty schools) and Hispanic-American teachers (3.6% in low poverty schools; 11.1% in high poverty schools).

While the vast majority of America's teachers are White females, they are also predominantly between 30 to 50 years of age. The average age of teachers is 42.4 years. As Table 3.3 displays, 15.3% of teachers are under 30 years of age, whereas 11.9% are in their early fifties, and 18.8% are in their upper fifties or older, respectively.

Teacher Preparation

While the demographics of teachers largely reflect the feminization of the teaching profession that took place in Horace Mann's era, the preparation of teachers also, to some degree, reflects Mann's desire for the professional preparation of teachers. However, the professional preparation of teachers has taken a turn of late that likely runs counter to what Mann envisioned for the teaching profession.

Colonial America did not have specialized preparation for its teachers. Those who taught usually had a broad liberal arts education and/or were preparing for a career in law or ministry. Teaching was perceived as a stopgap position for someone aiming to do something else with their professional life. By the early 19th century, however, an educator blazed a trail for specialized teacher training in the country. Emma Willard (1787–1870) founded the Troy Female Seminary in New York that sought to purposefully prepare teachers and she created a network of individuals equally committed to teacher preparation throughout the country (Fraser, 2007). Willard, along with Catherine Beecher, were feminists who saw teaching as an empowering profession for women. We saw the lasting impact that the feminization of teaching had upon the teaching profession, but Willard is significant because she paved the way for a formalized education of teachers that Horace Mann eventually used to systematically prepare teachers throughout Massachusetts. While Willard's Troy Seminary served as a pioneering model of teacher preparation in the early 19th century (it produced nearly 600 teachers between 1839 and 1863), Mann built upon this idea when he created a centralized system of *normal schools* in Massachusetts that became a model for much of the nation. Normal schools derive from the French word *école normale* which means to establish clear standards, or norms, for education. Mann used the normal school system in the mid-19th century to fuel the freshly minted common schools in Massachusetts. As the common schools spread across the nation, so did the concept of normal schools. Still today, many universities across the United States had their start as normal schools in the 19th century.

Mann's normal school model became the basis for modern day teacher education. Like schools of medicine, law, nursing, or divinity, schools of teacher education infuse benchmarks and acceptable research-based practices into their respective profession. In essence, professional schools protect, preserve, and improve the profession it serves and are the gatekeepers for *licenses* that assure individuals are qualified members of their profession. States determine their own teacher licensure guidelines and commonly rely upon schools of teacher education to prepare individuals to meet the licensure criteria created by the state legislature. Generally speaking, various levels of licensure exist for teachers usually in the form of temporary licenses (provisional) where an individual may get a short-term license (often 2 years in length) in an area where a teacher shortage exists or the customary more permanent license (professional) that usually needs to be renewed every 5 years. Once a teacher earns a license, she or he may seek to be employed by a school. If hired, the teacher will be provided a *contract* that serves as an agreement between the district and teacher. Beginning teachers usually receive what is called a *term contract* that will last between 1 and 2 years. At the conclusion of the term contract, the district decides whether or not it can or will renew its contractual agreement with the teacher. Experienced teachers, usually those who have taught for at least 5 years and have earned education credentials beyond the bachelor's degree, may be eligible to receive a *tenure contract* from their school district. A tenure contract is never up for renewal and becomes a "property right" for the teacher who holds it. A primary difference between the two types of contracts, in addition to their differences in duration, is that the burden of proof of wrongful dismissal is placed in the hands of the individual teacher holding a term contract whereas the burden of proof rests with the school if it believes that a teacher with a tenure contract should be terminated from its faculty. We will elaborate further on tenure contracts later in this chapter as we explore teacher unions.

Licensure requirements are the greatest influence on the curriculum of schools of teacher education. Most, if not all, contemporary teacher education schools provide coursework primarily rooted in instructional methods, educational psychology, historical and sociological foundations of education, special education, and multiculturalism. Diane Ravitch (2013), a contemporary scholar and advocate for public education, recently proposed that teacher education programs should provide intensive study in cognitive science, literacy, child development and adolescent psychology, sociology of the family and community, cultural diversity, special education, and the historical and political foundations of education. Additionally, Ravitch emphasized that teacher candidates should engage in extensive practice teaching with experienced mentors already in the teaching field. Most traditional schools of teacher education provide a curriculum similar to what Ravitch proposed. However, there is a growing trend of alternative routes to licensure where a teacher may bypass a traditional program of teacher education and take an alternative route.

In 2001, the U.S. Department of Education issued an educational reform called the No Child Left Behind Act (NCLB). We will learn more about NCLB in a later chapter. A significant feature of NCLB was its requirement for each classroom to be led by a highly qualified teacher. A highly qualified teacher, according to NCLB, is one who is trained in their particular subject matter and has obtained full state certification or has passed a state teaching licensing exam. However, nothing in the legislation

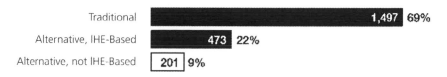

Figure 3.2   Number and percentage of teacher education providers, by provider type: 2014. *Source:* U.S. Department of Education, 2015.

mentioned preparation in a college or university-based teacher education program as a necessity for the qualification of teachers. Thus, alternative routes which bypass teacher education schools were latently legitimatized and the role of the schools of education became ambiguous in the qualification of teachers under NCLB (Cochran-Smith, 2002). Figure 3.2 refers to the contemporary numbers and percentage of providers by provider type. As you can see, nearly two thirds (69%) of teacher education providers remain schools of teacher education within institutions of higher education (IHE). These traditional routes involve a specific bachelor's degree associated with teacher education. Nearly one third of teacher education programs (31%) are categorized as an alternative route.

These alternative routes are typically created by states to alleviate growing teacher shortages. Often, the teacher enrolled in the alternative program is already teaching in a classroom. Therefore, a significant difference between traditional and alternative teacher education routes is the nature of the clinical experience. In a traditional program of teacher education, the teacher candidate participates in an extensive student teaching experience where she or he is closely supervised by an experienced teacher and a university supervisor. In an alternative program of teacher education, teacher candidates may instead participate in a mentorship or induction support as part of their program. Often times, the alternative, IHE based program is a graduate program for candidates who earned a bachelor's degree outside of education. An alternative, non IHE-based program is facilitated by, among other types of groups, nonprofit organizations, state agencies, and school districts.

Medical and law schools remain as the exclusive preparers for professionals in their respective fields. While traditional routes for teacher education remain the most dominant type of provider for teacher licensure, its dominance is nonetheless diminishing over the course of time. Some states, such as Minnesota, have recently deliberated over legislation pertaining to temporary teaching licensure where the candidate may only need to take a single course on education. Such reforms are typically born out of necessity rather than what was best for the teaching profession itself. It would be odd for the medical or legal profession to consider such alternative routes of professional licensure. Horace Mann emphasized that teachers, like other professionals, need the professional training that informs them how to understand the experiences, knowledge backgrounds, and various approaches from which her or his students approach learning, all of which make up the unique call of the school of teacher education. This professional call of the school of teacher education is gradually becoming less unique for teacher licensure in the contemporary era.

Teacher Pay

While educational preparation is central to the sturdiness of a profession, compensation is another earmark of a profession that can be used to signify its status in society. In Horace Mann's era, teachers were not well compensated and female teachers were compensated less than men. However, a turning point took place with the rise of teacher unions. At the turn of the 20th century, teacher dissatisfaction of their profession (including teacher compensation) paved the way for a collective effort by teachers to unionize. This movement was spearheaded by Margaret Haley (1861–1939), a sixth grade teacher from Chicago, Illinois. Haley, then a member of the Chicago Teachers Federation, focused her efforts on school reform and teachers' labor rights. Her tenacity and notoriety eventually led to a national labor movement on behalf of teachers. We will look at this movement in the next section, but Haley's labor activism for, among other things, teacher pay provides the backdrop for this particular section on teacher pay.

The teaching profession has long struggled for fair compensation. However, with the help of labor unions, teacher pay became competitive with other similar professions. However, the pay for teachers plateaued decades ago. In Table 3.4, you see the average annual teacher salary for particular years categorized into both current dollars and constant dollars.

TABLE 3.4 Estimated Average Annual Salary of Teachers in Public Elementary and Secondary Schools		
Year	Average Annual Teacher Salary (Current Dollars)	Average Annual Teacher Salary (Constant Dollars)
1969–1970	$8,626	$52,830
1989–1990	$31,367	$57,152
1999–2000	$41,807	$57,133
2012–2013	$56,383	$56,383

Source: National Center for Education Statistics.

Constant dollars takes inflation into consideration whereas current dollars does not. As you can see, teacher pay actually regressed over the past 2 decades. Whereas the salaries of registered nurses, for instance, have continued to climb.

Nurse salaries were once similar with teacher salaries. According to the Bureau of Labor Statistics, however, registered nurses made an average salary of $72,180 in 2016 which is a stark contrast to the average of $55,490 that teachers made in 2016 (Bureau of Labor Statistics, 2018). To further elaborate on how teacher pay fails to run parallel with pay in other professions, the Economic Policy Institute reported that public teachers' weekly wages (in constant dollars) amounted to $911 in 1980 as compared to $1,159 for college graduates writ large, making a difference of $248. By 2015, these differences were more stark: $1,092 for public teachers and $1,416 for college graduates, a difference of $324 (Allegreto & Mishel, 2016).

At the root of the status of a profession is the compensation of the professional. The statistical shifts point that the status of the teacher profession continues to decline. Some speculate that the decline in teacher pay is at the root of a growing shortage of teachers in many rural and urban areas in the United States (McKenna, 2015). The level at which teachers get paid in comparison to other similar professionals may determine the level of morale within the teaching profession. A sturdy profession has a high morale within it where its members are proud to be within the profession.

Teacher Influence

The third, and final, signifier of a profession that we will examine is the level of influence that members of the profession have upon the profession itself. Doctors, for instance, are provided with the necessary autonomy to examine, diagnose, and prescribe health care for patients. The doctors' autonomy to make such decisions lend tremendous credence toward valuing the individual doctor and the medical profession writ large. We expect doctors to know their speciality and be able to use that knowledge to make good medical decisions for patients. Likewise, teachers should be expected to know their specific subject matter and have the ability to transform that subject matter in such a way that the student can learn it. Teachers also must assess students' understanding of certain knowledge, skills, and dispositions and intelligently intervene on the students' behalf when they determine the student needs assistance in the learning process. In many ways, teachers are provided autonomy. Largely, the classroom experience (what we call the *microcurriculum*) is the teacher's domain. Or, that has traditionally been the case. The larger school experience (what we call the *macrocurriculum*) is not always part of the teacher's professional domain. In this section, we will explore how the teacher's influence is diminishing in both of these curricular domains.

Teacher influence is defined in numerous ways. For our purposes, we will define teacher influence as a teacher's ability to make decisions for their own profession, their students, as well as the school policy writ large. The most obvious means through which a teacher influences the classroom is through creating learning experiences that empower students to learn specified knowledge, skills, and dispositions that they, the teacher, determines to be necessary for the students' personal growth and the development of society. Prior to the close of the 20th century, teachers were provided great latitude on these ends. Teachers developed nearly all aspects of the school curriculum. In fact, teachers still have enormous influence upon the school curriculum in some of the world's highest performing school systems (Darling-Hammond et al., 2017). However, a trend emerged in the United States, near the end of the 20th century, that centralized power away from teachers. The rise of the standards movement near the close of the century offered a glimpse into what eventually emerged in terms of stymying teacher autonomy of the curriculum. According to political scientist Michael Lipsky (1980), teachers, as public servants, fall into the category of *street-level bureaucrats*. Street-level bureaucrats are individuals who work directly with the public and are therefore in the position of implementing governmental policies, regardless of the teachers' view of the policy measure. Teachers are accustomed to having their professional judgement infringed upon in the name of fulfilling policies of upper government officials. We will learn more about street level bureaucracy when we explore high stakes standardized testing movement in a later chapter.

As you will see in a later chapter, the accountability movement involved the emergence of a standards-based approach within many states at the close of the 20th century that sought to assure students were learning a curriculum broadly agreed upon by the states, and later the entire nation (we will further explore the standards movement in a later chapter). Beginning in the 1990s, each state adopted their own statewide curriculum standards, with Iowa being the last to do so in 2008. Currently, the nationwide Common Core State Standards Initiative has been adopted by 42 states, the District of Columbia, and four U.S. territories. Under state standards, schools and their teachers are held accountable by their respective states to fully address these standards in their curriculum. While these are minimum standards, teachers who seek to extend their curricular experiences beyond the limitations of the standards may feel pressured to not do so whenever some students struggle to master some standards when assessed by a singular standardized test. We will address the problems with such an approach in a later chapter.

There are also examples in recent educational policy where teachers are required to employ particular instructional strategies; despite the fact employing these strategies may counter their own professional judgement on how to best teach their own students. In 2001, NCLB prescribed the use of scientifically-based research (SBR) teaching methods. These SBR methods were often applied upon a randomized sample of students, taking little consideration into the myriad of variables associated with individuals' ability to learn at a given time. Policymakers who crafted NCLB were confident that its use of SBR in the classroom would greatly improve teaching. Yet, SBR ignored the local inheritance from which teaching derives. Many teachers, deemed excellent by their peers, students, and parents, are known to go against the averages and apply their own discretion with helping a particular student in whatever way best fits that particular student. For instance, some students may be better suited to learn how to read through a phonics-based approach while others may be better served using a whole language approach. The point is that while the averages may reflect the majority of students, a teacher must respond to the needs of all learners. The employment of SBR moved against this wisdom and became a force that sought to limit teacher's professional judgement.

Another area where teachers' influence is stymied has been the increased limitation of teacher unions. *Unions* are organizations that laborers join in order to collectively call for fair pay and practices from their employers as well as an outlet for laborers to seek to improve, as is the case with teachers, a profession writ large. In sum, unions represent the collective voice of teachers. The two primary unions are the National Education Association (NEA), which claims to have 3 million members, and the American Federation of Teachers (AFT), which claims to have 1.7 million members. These two unions have been around for over a century (NEA was founded in 1857 and the AFT in 1916) and remain the prominent union voices for teachers. The AFT began in the 20th century with a greater bend toward union activities with the NEA gradually acclimating toward union activity as the century progressed. The NEA feared that engaging in union activities may hinder teachers' professional status in the community. Prior to its turn toward unionization, the NEA was best known for forming the report of the Committee of Ten in 1892 and the Cardinal Principles Report of 1918, two pioneering attempts to standardize the high school curriculum (we will explore these two reports in a later chapter in this book). At the core of contemporary union activity is its ability to collectively bargain. *Collective bargaining* is laborers' ability to negotiate compensation and working conditions with their respective employer. The Universal Declaration of Human Rights, drafted by the United Nations in 1948, stipulates that "Everyone has the right to form and to join trade unions for the protection of his interests" (Article 23.4). The means through which a union seeks to protect its members interests is throughout collective bargaining. Marjorie Murphy (1990), labor historian, explained the impact that collective bargaining had upon the teaching profession:

> For elementary teachers, collective bargaining meant breaks from the constant pressure of being in front of the classroom for six hours; for high school teachers it meant time to prepare for classes; for junior high school teachers it meant relief from extra lunch guard duties. Teachers were no longer told arbitrarily when they had to appear at school and when they could leave; surprise faculty meetings after school disappeared; and administrators could no longer appear suddenly in a teacher's classroom. Teachers still had to report to school at a prescribed time, they still had to attend meetings, they still had to welcome in outsiders to their classes, but what changed was the arbitrariness, the complete absence of control on the job that teachers had incessantly complained of. (p. 209)

Since unions are the primary voices of the laborer as they seek to negotiate a contract with their employer, some states have *fair share* policies in place that help to protect labor unions by requiring employees to pay a fee to the union for representing their interests, which unions are bound by law to do so for all employees regardless of their membership status. However, as ideological perspectives against unions have arisen in the country in recent times, especially from wealthy corporate leaders such as Charles and David Koch, some states' fair share policies have been challenged at the national level. In *Janus v. American Federation of State, Council, and Municipal Employees Council 31* (2018), the U.S. Supreme Court heard a case from Illinois that claimed that the fair share policy in their state infringed on their freedom of speech. The plaintiffs believed that since they were required to pay contributions to their union and yet disagreed with some of the union's political stances, they indirectly supported stances they inherently disagreed with. The defendant asserted that none of the fair share funds go to support politics or political candidates. In a close 5–4 ruling, the Court ruled in favor of the plaintiffs in *Janus* stating that fair share policies were unconstitutional because it violates nonunion members' First Amendment protections of free speech and assembly. The case was a direct challenge to a key Supreme Court case *Abood v. Detroit Board of Education* (1977) that ruled union activity is legal in the public sector and that non-members may be required to pay their "fair share" of fees for purposes of collective bargaining and other contractual matters, but their funds may not be allocated for political purposes outside of this scope.

While recent court challenges threaten to usurp the power of teachers unions, government officials in some parts of the United States have asserted the power to dismantle teachers' collective bargaining power. The most prolific example of a state government stripping teachers of their collective bargaining rights was spearheaded in 2011 by Wisconsin governor Scott Walker and the Republican led Wisconsin state legislature through their passage of the 2011 Wisconsin Act 10. The passage of the act resulted in an election recall of Governor Walker in 2012, with Walker surviving the recall. The act was also challenged in the Wisconsin Supreme Court and was upheld, officially putting to an end the collective bargaining rights of teachers in Wisconsin for the time being.

Labor unions, including teacher unions, are lightning rods for public criticism, because of claims that they protect incompetent teachers and limit efforts to be fiscally responsible with school and state budgets. Proponents of teacher unions see that unions are the lone voice of teachers that assures teachers are treated fairly and are provided a work environment of respect by their employers.

Summary

In the 1830s, Horace Mann sought to uplift school teaching into a robust profession that would rise simultaneously with the rise of the common schools. This led to the emergence of schools of teacher education and a rise of women enrolling in the teaching force that remains to this day. The 20th century saw changes in school teaching that reflected Mann's vision of a rising profession. However, school teaching in contemporary times has been engulfed with a triad of forces that threaten school teaching's professional status. While schools of teacher education remain the primary means teachers are educated and licensed in the United States, these schools of teacher education are being bypassed in some states so teachers may be more efficiently licensed in schools where shortages exist. Teachers have also received lower pay in the last couple of decades than what they once did, while other professionals' pay rose. Finally, teachers have witnessed their influence challenged through various policies that both infringe on their professional judgment and limit their collective voice in their workplace and in the profession writ large.

Reflective Exercises

1. Do you think there is such a thing as a feminine and masculine sphere for teachers? If so, what is the difference between the two? If not, why not?
2. Do you think education schools adequately prepare teachers akin to medical and law schools do with their respective students? Explain your answer.
3. Why do you think teachers have been paid less money over the course of the last 2 decades?
4. Should teachers be allowed to collectively bargain? Explain your answer.

References

Allegretto, S., & Mishel, L. (2016). The teacher pay gap is wider than ever: Teachers' pay continues to fall further behind pay of comparable workers. *Economic Policy Institute*. Retrieved from www.epi.org

Bureau of Labor Statistics. (2018). *Household data annual averages: Employed persons by detailed occupation, sex, race, and Hispanic or Latino ethnicity*. Retrieved from: https://www.bls.gov/cps/cpsaat11.pdf

Cochran-Smith, M. (2002). What a difference a definition makes: Highly qualified teachers, scientific research, and teacher education. *Journal of Teacher Education, 53*(3), 187–189. https://doi.org/10.1177/0022487102053003001

Darling-Hammond, L., Burns, D., Campbell, C., Goodwin, A., Hammerness, K., Ling Low, E., . . . , Zeichner, K. (2017). *Empowered educators: How high-performing systems shape teaching quality around the world*. San Francisco, CA: Jossey-Bass.

Egalite, A. J., Kisida, B., & Winters, M. A. (2015). Representation in the classroom: The effect of own-race teachers on student achievement. *Economics of Education Review, 45*, 44–52.

Elsbree, W. S. (1939). *The American teacher: Evolution of a profession in a democracy*. New York, NY: American Book Company.

Fraser, J. W. (2007). *Preparing America's teachers: A history*. New York, NY: Teachers College Press.

Kaestle, C. (1983). *Pillars of the republic: Common schools and American society, 1780–1860*. New York, NY: Hill and Wang.

Lipsky, M. (1980). *Street level bureaucrats*. New York, NY: Russell Sage.

McKenna, L. (2015). America's teaching force, by the numbers. *The Atlantic*. Retrieved from https://www.theatlantic.com/education/archive/2015/09/americas-teaching-force-by-the-numbers/404590/

Murphy, M. (1990). *Blackboard unions: The AFT and the NEA, 1900–1980*. Ithaca, NY: Cornell University Press.

National Center for Education Statistics (2017). *Digest of education statistics: Enrollment and percentage distribution of enrollment in public elementary and secondary schools, by race/ethnicity and region: Selected years, fall 1995 through fall 2027.* Retrieved from: https://nces.ed.gov/programs/digest/d17/tables/dt17_203.50.asp?referer-raceindicators

Preston, J. A. (1993). Domestic ideology, school reformers, and female teachers: Schoolteaching becomes women's work in nineteenth-century New England. *The New England Quarterly, 66*(4), 531–551.

Ravitch, D. (2013). *Reign of error: The hoax of the privatization movement and the danger to America's public schools.* New York, NY: Vintage.

U.S. Department of Education, Office of Postsecondary Education. (2015). Higher Education Act Title II reporting system.

4

Race and School

Janet Grace was a 17-year-old junior at Mayfield High School. She excelled in the classroom and was active in the school, serving as president of the student council, and a member of the varsity basketball team. Mayfield was located in the suburbs of a large city and the student population was predominantly White. The most obvious difference between Janet and her classmates was that she was an African American. Janet's parents were well educated, her mother was a lawyer and her father was a history professor at a nearby college. Janet, along with her younger brother, were familiar with the culture and history of the African-American experience due to the guiding influence of her parents. This made it especially challenging for Janet in her U.S. history course, taught be Mr. Steven Maas, since African-American history was seldom referenced in class. For example, in teaching the American Civil War, Mr. Maas emphasized the tactical military strategies of the Northern and Southern forces with little attention paid to the cause of the war, the abolition movement, or the racist-fueled

Paradoxes of the Public School, pages 41–59
Copyright © 2019 by Information Age Publishing
41

terrorism that arose within the nation in the aftermath of the war. Janet viewed Mr. Maas to be a nice man who was not a racist, but seemed oblivious to the experience of her ancestors. In fact, Janet's peers seemed to be a lot like Mr. Maas in that they seldom read African-American literature or were conscious of issues related to race. However, things began to change in Ms. Gloria Lange's language arts class. Mrs. Lange, a tall, White woman with shoulder-length light brown hair, was in her first year of teaching. "Today, we are beginning a new unit on multicultural literature," Mrs. Lange announced to Janet's class. "In this unit, we will read two examples of African-American literature: A new and popular young adult novel called *The Hate U Give* by Angie Thomas and a classic novel called *Invisible Man* by Ralph Ellison." Janet was thrilled to hear this news, but she kept her composure throughout the day. "I can't wait to tell my dad," she continually repeated in her mind. Upon arriving home, Janet rushed in her house on the lookout for her dad. "Dad, Dad, guess what happened today!" Janet's father was in his home office grading papers when he heard Janet's enthusiastic shrieks. Janet found her father and the good news rolled off her tongue: "Our new language arts teacher is assigning us African-American literature from Angie Thomas and Ralph Ellison! Here are the books!" Janet's father glanced at the books and remarked with delight: "Those are tremendous books and I've recommended them to my students on numerous occasions." Father and daughter smiled at one another with delight. "What is the name of the teacher who assigned this?" "Mrs. Gloria Lange, but she just got married this summer. Her maiden name was Roberts," Janet replied to her father. With eyebrows raised in surprise, Janet's dad remarked: "She was in my history class 3 years ago."

The previous three chapters focused on the development of the American public school, beginning in the colonial era and leading up to the rise of Horace Mann in the 1830s. That historical analysis focused on inclusion of the mainstream population within the public school experience, paying no attention to the populations marginalized by American society. Individuals, much like Janet in our story, who are marginalized in the school because of race, are well familiar with their cultural heritage being left out of the school curriculum. This chapter focuses on populations marginalized because of race and their relationship with the public school because of this marginalization.

The public school is a direct reflection of American society—particularly the local communities from which the school derives and to which it directly serves. Sometimes school may take the lead with influencing society, as arguably was the case with desegregation in the latter part of the 20th century. Yet, much of the time, schools run parallel with its local society, taking neither a lead nor running behind local societal norms and values. This holds true with how the American public school addresses the issue of race. As with any public institution, if society discriminates based on race, then the public institution is more than likely to do the same. But, shouldn't the public school be different than other institutions? After all, we learned in Chapter 2 that the public school is widely held to be a democratic institution with the missional charge to serve our democratic nation. This brings us to the paradox that grounds this chapter:

The public school is supposed to intentionally imbed our society with democratic skills and dispositions, yet it has historically marginalized populations because of race.

America's Racial Idiosyncrasy

Understanding race and the United States' behavior surrounding it is no easy matter. Genetically speaking, race does not exist among humans (Harrison, 2010). Scientific research reveals to us that there is no more genetic differences between an African and a White European than there is between a White European and another White European. However, race as a social construct matters a great deal in the human experience. Race is a social construct that involves power, influence, and identity—all of which results in the formation of a particular culture. Race permeates throughout American society and *racism*, a belief that one race is superior to another, has a hold on the American people in an array of ways—sometimes unknowingly by the person holding the racist viewpoint. For instance, historian Matthew Frye Jacobson (1999) poignantly demonstrated how individuals arbitrarily affix racial labels by posing the following question: "Why is it that in the United States a White woman can have Black children but a Black woman cannot have White children?" (p. 1–2). Jacobson's inquiry reveals American's idiosyncrasies with regard to matters of race. These idiosyncrasies have been, and continue to be, very damaging to certain populations in the United States. *Ethnicity* is a construct closely associated with race, and individuals understandably confuse the difference between race and ethnicity. Generally, race refers to the physical differences whereas ethnicity refers to cultural differences. One can rightfully assert, for instance, that *ethnocentrism*, the belief held by an individual or groups of individuals that their ethnicity is greater than others, is closely aligned with race because marginalization of certain racial groups are targeted to something related with their cultural differences from the dominant group. While a significant difference between race and ethnicity is that there may be a myriad of ethnicities within a certain racial group, both are present in the sociological struggle between majority and minority groups. For our purposes of understanding the historically rooted relationship between race and school, we will understand racism and ethnocentrism to be intrinsically linked together, though possessing some different features. This chapter will explore the history of three populations marginalized within the American school experience because of America's racial idiosyncrasy: Native Americans, African Americans, and Latino Americans.

Native Americans

While the colonists gave birth to the United States in the 18th century, they were not the first inhabitants to this land. That designation belongs to Native Americans, who lived here long before Europeans knew that the Western Hemisphere even existed.

For centuries upon centuries, the North American continent was inhabited by a myriad of tribes, each of whom viewed themselves as stewards of land passed along to them by their ancestors with no need for a contract granting them the rights to the land. A sampling of some of these tribes and location were: the Navajo and Apache in the American Southwest; the Cheyenne and Sioux in the Great Plains; the Shawnee, Miami, and Cherokee in the Ohio and Mississippi Valleys; and the Choctaw and Seminole in the American South. These tribes had complete reign over the Western Hemisphere where they built strong communities to educate their children, who were taught significant economic, cultural, and spiritual lessons in an informal manner much akin to the best practices supported by contemporary research in the learning sciences. It is important to note that school as a formal institution was imported from Europe, not something that all societies and cultures believed was the best mode to channel education. The Native American lifestyle was disrupted and brutally destroyed beginning at the close of the 15th century when European ships landed on coasts throughout the Western Hemisphere.

Europe in the 15th century was filled with nations led by monarchs who had three primary motivations: gold, God, and glory. First, with gold, the monarchs sought ways to improve the economic conditions for their particular nation. Second, with God, they sought to spread their brand of Christianity. Third, with glory, they wanted to be bigger and better than the other surrounding nations. These three motivations, taken together, formed an imperialistic fervor that eventually led individual nations to seek alternate trade routes to propel their own ascent in the world. This imperialistic fervor merged with the rising technologies of maritime navigation to form the thrust behind what historians call: *The Age of Exploration*. It would be an understatement to say that the Age of Exploration had an impact on modern American culture. It resulted in a mass importation of the European population in the 16th and 17th centuries that directly affected all aspects of culture from the language we speak to the conception of how to educate children. The contemporary United States is predominantly an English speaking country primarily because the Italian navigator, John Cabot (1450–1500), discovered the North American continent for King Henry VII of England in 1497. Spanish is most prominent today along the Southwestern border of the United States, Mexico, and Central America primarily because the Italian navigator, Christopher Columbus (1451–1506), discovered the Caribbean region for King Ferdinand and Queen Isabella of Spain in 1492. Columbus was actually commissioned by Spain to discover a shorter trade route to Asia (which Europe called India at the time), Columbus thought he accomplished this feat leading Europeans to call the Natives "Indians," a popularized term that remains today. French is prominent in Canada primarily because Jacques Cartier (1491–1557), a navigator from then the Duchy of Brittany, discovered the Gulf of St. Lawrence region for King Frances I of France in 1534.

After the navigators fulfilled their mission for their respective monarchs, the European imperialistic fervor spread across the Atlantic Ocean onto the Western Hemisphere. This resulted in a significant period of *cultural hegemony* (the domination of one culture over diverse cultures within a particular society) that, arguably, still remains. The most notorious case of cultural hegemony involved the Spanish *conquistadors* who succeeded Christopher Columbus' voyage to the Caribbean. The conquistadors, a Spanish derivative meaning "conqueror," were professional warriors and explorers who pillaged Central America and Mexico with the goal of controlling territory and opening trade routes for Spain.

The colonists believed that the Native American society was inferior to the European society. As a result of this *ethnocentric* viewpoint, the Europeans sought to appropriate Native American resources, including land, for their own purposes. Both the Spanish and the English focused their efforts on what historians call *the Columbian exchange*, the large scale transfer of food and animals from Europe to the Americas. The Native American response was mixed. There are stories of harmony amongst the Europeans and Natives, as typified by the popular myths of the English pilgrims and the Native Americans in the 1620s. However, the overwhelming larger effect of the

Columbian exchange was absolute devastation to the Native American population. First, a plethora of diseases spread wildly across Native American society, killing millions of the population. Second, there were many efforts by Native Americans to resist the European takeover. For instance, several Native American tribes in New England united in 1675 to push European colonists off their land in what came to be known as *King Philip's War*. The result was a bloody loss for the Native Americans and enhanced resolve by the colonists to inculcate the Native American with both the English language and their brand of Christianity through educational efforts such as the opening of numerous schools to educate Native Americans throughout colonial America during the mid-18th century (Altenbaugh, 2003, p. 18).

King Philip's War was a prelude of things to come while the United States of America was still in its infancy. Much like the continual conflicts that arose within the North American colonies throughout the 17th and 18th centuries, conflicts between the United States government and Native Americans became commonplace in the 19th century. The United States government sought to expand territories under their mantra *Manifest Destiny*, a justification for the goodness and inevitability of American imperialism, that further antagonized Native Americans. The *Indian Removal Act of 1830*, spearheaded by U.S. President *Andrew Jackson* (1767–1845), was one prominent example how the United States government treated the Native Americans. The 1830 Removal Act was born out of the government's desire to appropriate land in the Southeastern United States for their own economic purposes and decreed that the Native Americans living on that land must relocate to territory west of the Mississippi River. This affected many tribes, most notably the Cherokee in 1838, as they each suffered thousands of deaths of members. The suffering of the Cherokee people in their 1838 trek was aptly called *The Trail of Tears*.

The United States government continually faced the dilemma of what to do with the Native American in face of its own political and economic ambitions since the Native Americans were so different in terms of religion and language than the prevailing majority of the U.S. population. Historian Richard Altenbaugh (2003) placed this ongoing conflict between the European Americans and the Native Americans over religion and language into historical perspective:

> Religion and language serve as the pillars of any culture. Alter either of these, and that culture will experience profound change, if not disappear altogether. The historical contest between dominant and subordinate cultural groups usually centers on these two elements. In lieu of physical eradication, the best way for a majority group to erase a subgroup's culture, or

to assert its authority over that subgroup, is to transform its religion or language, or both, through an education process. Conversely, the best strategy a minority group can use to preserve its culture is to protect its religion or language by resisting the dominant group's educational process or institution. (pp. 18–19)

Native American resistance led to continual surfacing of warfare between the government and Natives throughout the 19th century, resulting in a drain on the military budget of the U.S. government. This fiscal concern led the U.S. government to change course in how they approached their problems with Native Americans, and education stood front and center of their new plan.

At the close of the 1860s, the United States was recovering from a devastating civil war and new hope was on the horizon for the rebuilding nation. Out of this aura of hope came a new policy initiative addressing the Native American culture's resistance to the imperialistic impulse of the government. This new initiative centered around educating Native Americans in such a way that they become better assimilated to the predominant culture in the country and cease to be such a military threat to the government. This educational initiative focused on a network of federally operated schools that, according to Richard Altenbaugh (2003), had three primary purposes: (a) Native Americans are taught individualism and moved away from tribalism, (b) Native Americans are taught English in place of their native language, and (c) Native Americans are Christianized (p. 138). Among the strategies the schools employed to fulfill its purposes was to strip Natives of their tribal identity by cutting their hair short and clothing them in uniforms. The results were dramatic and photographs were often published to the comfort and delight of the general American public.

Native American children, though not required by law to attend the boarding schools, often went at the insistence of their parents who were often coerced by government officials who painted the schools as an opportunity for their child to succeed in life. At the time, Native Americans were experiencing poverty due to the years of disruption that land acquisition and forced removal brought. Many Native Americans lived on reservations provided for them by the U.S. government and the nature of their school experience depended on its relationship to the reservation. Some schools existed on the reservation and were either day schools or boarding schools. Others, such as the acclaimed school founded in 1879 in Carlisle, Pennsylvania, were off-reservation boarding schools. The founder of the Carlisle boarding school, an ex-Army officer named *Richard Pratt* (1840–1924), was the movement's most visible champion. Pratt articulated the boarding school movement's overarching philosophy, which was perceived at the time by many Americans as a humane effort to benefit both American society and the Natives themselves:

> A great general has said that the only good Indian is a dead one, and that high sanction of his destruction has been an enormous factor in promoting Indian massacres. In a sense, I agree with the sentiment, but only in this: that all the Indian there is in the race should be dead. Kill the Indian in him, and save the man. (Official Report of the 19th Annual Conference of Charities and Correction, 1892).

Pratt's phrase "kill the Indian, save the man" became the mantra of the boarding school movement and gained momentum throughout the latter years of the 19th century, as evidenced by rising amounts of federal expenditure on education for Native Americans. In the span of nearly a quarter of a century (1877–1900), federal spending on education for Native Americans jettisoned from $20,000 to $3 million per year. School enrollment for Native Americans in this same period climbed from 3,598 to 21,568. Eventually, with the help of a compulsory school law passed by the U.S. Congress in 1891, well over three-fourths of all Native Americans were enrolled in what was perceived by the mainstream American culture to be an "American" school (Adams, 1995; Altenbaugh, 2003).

While many Native Americans today choose to attend traditional public schools, remnants of the boarding school experience are ingrained in the psyche of many who lived through the boarding school experience as recent as the mid-20th century. A contemporary report from National Public Radio (NPR) on Indian boarding schools revealed how the boarding school experience continues to haunt individuals who attended them through, among other things, creating schisms within Native American families:

> In 1945, Bill Wright, a Pattwin Indian, was sent to the Stewart Indian School in Nevada. He was just 6 years old. Wright remembers matrons bathing him in kerosene and shaving his head. Students at federal boarding schools were forbidden to express their culture—everything from wearing long hair to speaking even a single Indian word. Wright said he lost not only his language, but also his American Indian name. "I remember coming home and my grandma asked me to talk Indian to her and I said, 'Grandma, I don't understand you,'" Wright says. "She said, 'Then who are you?'" Wright says he told her his name was Billy. "Your name's not Billy. Your name's TAH-rruhm," she told him. "And I went, 'That's not what they told me.'" (National Public Radio, 2008).

Another individual, Lucy Toldeo, a member of the Navajo tribe who attended a boarding school at the Sherman Institute in California in the 1950s explained the nature of the curriculum she was exposed to at the school:

> It wasn't really about education . . . Saturday night we had a movie, Do you know what the movie was about? Cowboys and Indians. Cowboys and Indians. Here we're getting all our people killed, and that's the kind of stuff they showed us. (National Public Radio, 2008)

The boarding school experience became the symbolic gesture of how mainstream American society treated Native Americans: a savage people who needed to be civilized.

Sadly, this racist and ethnocentric paradigm ran parallel with how the public school writ large addressed Native Americans. Many public schools used Native American themed mascots to represent their school. Often, these mascots nostalgically parodied Native Americans with a savagery that mainstream America could now embrace for its own use. Names such as "warriors" and "braves" became affixed into the lexicon of schools' identity and self-branding. Professional sports teams such as the Cleveland Indians and Boston (eventually Milwaukee, now Atlanta) Braves did the same thing at a regional and national level. Some schools went further and used the racial slur "redskin" label as their mascot, with universities such as Miami University in Ohio using the term until 1996 upon the urging of the Oklahoma-based Miami tribe for it to be changed. The current National Football league franchise in Washington, DC continues to use the "redskin" label despite numerous protests.

History courses in elementary, middle, and secondary schools usually addressed Native Americans as an antidote to the grand narrative of mainstream American culture. Only since the latter half of the 20th century has there been a greater emphasis on teaching the culture of Native Americans from their own perspective. However, Native American history still holds a secondary place in most history curricula in public schools. The Native people who once reigned over the Americas went from a group held in disdain by mainstream American culture to a group now who are largely ignored as another under-appreciated racial minority in American society.

African Americans

The plight of the African American is an outright tragedy in American history, but the resilience of the African American people is inspiration to all of humanity. Native Americans were not the only group affected by the

Columbian exchange of the 16th and 17th centuries. In fact, the genesis of the African American people is rooted in the imperialistic fervor made by the exchange. At the root of this genesis was slavery, more specifically: *chattel slavery.*

Slavery is an institution nearly as old as humanity itself. There are many forms of slavery. For instance, many civilizations who practiced slavery did so as either a form of payment to individuals or groups of individuals may give when mired in debt or, perhaps, slavery was a direct result of a military conquest where the victors could enslave the losers. With chattel slavery, however, the slave is a commodity that can be bought or sold. European powers, from the 16th until the 19th century, engaged in a large scale chattel slave trade enterprise that permanently stained what would eventually be the United States of America. This slave trade enterprise centered around a *triangular trade* between Western Africa, the Caribbean or North America, and Europe. This triangular trade involved hundreds of African slaves crammed in a large ship in insufferable conditions on the *middle passage* of the triangular trade between Africa and the Americas. The slaves were used by large-scale planters to plant and harvest cash crops, such as sugar or cotton, that was traded between the three players in the triangular trade.

The African slaves, stripped of any semblance of humanity, were subjected to terrorization and punishment from their owners. As a result, these slaves formed their own community that centered around their suffering. This culture consisted of, among other things, songs and stories passed on from generation to generation. As the colonies evolved into the United States of America, the Declaration of Independence's cosmic statement that "all men are created equal" did not yet apply to the African slave. In fact, slavery intensified after the American Revolution with the advent of the *cotton gin*, invented by Eli Whitney. The cotton gin, a byproduct of the industrial revolution, was an engine that could separate cotton seeds from the cotton plant, making cotton easier to produce. As a result, plantation owners demanded more slaves to pick the cotton that would result in the plantation owner accumulating vast amounts of wealth. The American South was the location of most slavery in the United States, primarily due to the temperate climate best suited for cotton production. Unlike the South, the economy of the American North was best suited for fishing and eventually manufacturing as the primary source of economic growth.

Southern states protected their economic interests by ensuring that African slaves remained subdued to the planters who owned them. For instance, in 1831, North Carolina's general assembly declared it illegal to "teach, or attempt to teach, any slave within the State to read or write" (State of North Carolina, 1831, p. 11). That same year, the state of Virginia and Alabama passed similar resolutions. Slave owners understood the liberating force of education and sought to immunize their slaves from experiencing what may lead them to question and rebel.

The expansion of the United States in the mid-19th century consistently unearthed tense relations between the country's regions. Northern states sought to have new western states free from slavery whereas the South sought to expand slavery in those areas. Meanwhile, *abolitionism,* a political movement to end slavery, was increasing in the country. Some notable abolitionists included former slave, Frederick Douglass (1818–1895), newspaper editor William Lloyd Garrison (1805–1879), and Sojourner Truth (1797–1883). The abolitionist movement raised fear among the South's political leadership and when *Abraham Lincoln* (1809–1865), an anti-slavery politician though not associated with the abolitionist movement itself, was elected U.S. president in 1860, many states debated whether or not to leave, or *secede,* from the nation itself. States in the deep South, beginning with South Carolina in December of 1860, declared their secession from the United States. These first few states sent their own ambassadors to plead wavering states, such as Kentucky and Virginia, to join their cause to maintain slavery (Dew, 2002). This split amongst the states over the issue of slavery led to the American Civil War (1860–1865) that resulted in approximately 750,000 deaths (Gugliotta, 2012).

Some African Americans fought in the Civil War, most notably the all African American 54th Massachusetts regiment, led by Robert Gould Shaw (1837–1863). As a result of actions taken by President Lincoln, such as the Emancipation Proclamation and later a push for the passage of the 13th Amendment, to secure freedom for African Americans, the Civil War resulted in the abolishment of slavery and eventually citizenship for African Americans. One of the most significant efforts made to help former slaves to adjust to free life was the *Freedman's Bureau,* passed in 1865 just before the close of the Civil War. The Freedman's Bureau, officially entitled the Bureau of Refugees, Freedmen, and Abandoned Lands, was a federal program that sought partnership between the government, religious missionaries, and the African-American community to form a series of offices, or bureaus, aimed at assisting former slaves with gaining employment and, most notably, acquiring an education to help them in free society. The Freedman's schools was the first effort by the U.S. government to empower African Americans with literacy skills. Eventually, funding for the Freedman's Bureau stopped in 1872, leaving African Americans to fend for themselves in a Southern society where hostility toward them had grown.

White supremacy, the belief of the superiority of European Americans, appeared in various forms in the United States after the Civil War. First,

President Lincoln, who initiated the Freedman's Bureau and took measures on behalf of African Americans, was publicly assassinated by a White supremacist on April 14, 1865. Second, the rise of domestic terrorist organizations in the South and later in the North, such as the Ku Klux Klan, sought to intimidate African Americans as a means to politically and culturally subdue them. Third, the socio-political culture in the South was significantly influenced by White supremacy. The post-war plan by the federal government to rebuild the South after the Civil War, called *Reconstruction,* further antagonized Southerners against African Americans because many Southerners blamed African Americans for the socioeconomic limitations the region experienced after the war. Once Reconstruction was officially lifted in 1876, Southern states began to pass a series of laws aimed at discrimination toward African Americans. These laws focused on limiting African Americans' access to public and private spaces, such as schools and restaurants, and served as the foundation for what became known as the *Jim Crow* South (Jim Crow is a derivative from a popular minstrel character earlier in the 19th century).

School policy amidst the Jim Crow South was fueled by White supremacy, leading to schools being deeply segregated by race. European Americans participated in the traditional public school experience whereas African Americans were not allowed to attend a predominantly European American school, even if the school may be nearby where they lived. African Americans were left to attend public schools set aside exclusively for them—usually in subpar conditions when compared to the European Americans' schools. This, of course, created significant educational inequality between the races and escalated the economic and political gap that existed between them. We will learn more about school segregation (and desegregation) in a later chapter. While African Americans faced marginalization amidst the public school system, they experienced terrorism within their communities. Mobs of citizens, usually but not exclusively in the American South, commonly used *lynching* (public hanging by a rogue group) as another method of intimidation and control against African Americans. Thousands of African Americans were lynched in the late 19th century.

The demise of the Freedman's Bureau signified that African Americans were without advocacy amongst political leaders at the turn of the 20th century. Amidst this isolation, two leaders emerged from within the African American community who brought differing visions on improving the plight of African Americans: *Booker T. Washington* (1856–1915) and *W. E. B. Du Bois* (1868–1963). Washington, a former slave, became the leader of the Tuskegee Institute in 1881. The Tuskegee Institute, in Tuskegee, Alabama, was a trade school for African Americans that became the base for Washington's movement to uplift African Americans by promoting economic entrepreneurship and a culture of artisanship in numerous trades. Washington's 1895 speech in Atlanta, known as "the Atlanta compromise," personified his accommodationist philosophy that African Americans should focus on sharpening their contribution to the economic landscape and that segregation would eventually fade away once African Americans proved their value to the predominant power structure driven by White supremacy. Washington, as a result of this moderate approach, was the benefactor of significant financial support for Tuskegee Institute from wealthy industrial capitalists such as Andrew Carnegie. On the other hand, W. E. B. Du Bois believed that Washington's approach was too moderate to adequately improve the plight of African Americans. Du Bois was a scholar in history and sociology who, in 1895, became the first African American to earn a PhD from Harvard University. While Du Bois was not opposed to the type of vocational education that Washington's Tuskegee Institute focused upon, he was opposed to Washington's accommodationist philosophy. Du Bois believed that African Americans needed to agitate more forcefully for the economic and political power they rightfully deserved. This agitation would happen, according to Du Bois, through the top academic tier (the "talented tenth," according to Du Bois) of African Americans filling economic and cultural positions of power throughout American communities. As a result, Du Bois inspired numerous African Americans to become doctors, lawyers, and university educators.

Both Washington and Du Bois viewed education as central to the improvement of conditions for African Americans at the turn of the twentieth century. However, they differed on the scope and intensity to which African Americans should challenge the predominant power structure in the United States at the time. African Americans' origin in the United States is borne out of the pain and suffering brought by slavery in a nation whose mission declared equality for all. The aftermath of the bloody Civil War left African Americans as the exposed target of White supremacists' vile and ruthless hate. This hate surfaced in numerous ways, including the racial segregation of the American public school. Like Native Americans, the historically rooted forces of racism continue to plague African Americans through a prolonged silence in the history curriculum of their story and situation. Also, like the Native American, they are degraded in popular culture, through such commercial figures as Aunt Jemima®, Mrs. Butterworth®, and Uncle Ben®, as individuals who lack intelligence and happily serve the interests of the predominant power structure.

Latino Americans

Just as Native Americans and African Americans faced intense marginalization in the United States throughout the 19th century, Latino Americans too faced a similar struggle with some distinctive twists. Latino Americans were of Spanish descent, whose population descended from the Spanish settlement during the Columbian exchange era. The primary area of focus in this particular section will be the Latino Americans in what is now the southwestern United States (i.e., Texas, New Mexico, and Southern California). Latino Americans lived in the Southwest Territory of North America since the 16th century, and as the United States began to expand its territory under the banner of Manifest Destiny, they too faced forces of White supremacy that took the form of *nativism*. Nativism, a movement by the inhabitants of a nation to protect their own interests against immigrants in the mid-19th century, has a prolonged historical root in American history. For instance, Roman Catholic immigrants faced intense nativism from an underground group of politicians, who were aptly termed the "Know Nothing" party because of their covert attempts to thwart the threat they believe immigrants posed (you saw some of this nativism play out in chapter one with the Philadelphia Bible riots of the 1840s). In 1855, this intense brand of nativism organized itself into a political party called the American Party that championed what it viewed as American culture. The party attracted nearly 21% of the popular vote in the 1856 Presidential election with former President Millard Fillmore (1800–1874) serving as its candidate.

American bred nativism customarily considered Protestants of European descent to be "American." Oftentimes, language posed as a significant feature among some factions of nativism as they insisted on individuals' use of English. Latino Americans in the southwestern territories were particularly vulnerable to the forces of nativism because they spoke Spanish, were Roman Catholic, and fell victim to White supremacy because of their darker skin color. As the United States gained the Southwest Territory of North America at the conclusion of the Mexican–American War (1846–1848), Latino Americans in those territories found themselves under nativist forces that sought to assimilate them into the predominant American culture. Schools in the territories were often used to strip Latino Americans of their ethnicity throughout the latter half of the 19th century. Texas even went so far, in this time period, as banning the speaking of Spanish in schools, which historian Richard Altenbaugh (2003) referred to as "a highly selective and prejudicial action since the legislature permitted the use of the German language in education for children of that ethnic group" (p. 144). Latino Americans were at their own disposal to learn English.

Some Latino-American children attended private schools that taught English in preparation for the public schools whereas other children did not attend school at all. The "Americanization" process, rooted in the 19th century, employed by the predominant culture over Latino Americans remains a contentious political and cultural contemporary issue.

Learning English was something the traditional public school expected Latino Americans to do on their own. However, for obvious reasons of economics and culture, many Latino Americans lacked the resources to become proficient in English. Contrary to contemporary public perception, past immigrants to the United States did not suddenly learn English through hard work and discipline. Rather, it took many immigrant families several generations to be proficient enough with their English speaking and steady enough economically to experience academic success in the American school experience. In 1974, the U.S. Supreme Court issued a landmark decision in the case *Lau v. Nichols* (1974) that altered how public schools address students' language needs.

Lau v. Nichols (1974) was a case that, interestingly, focused on a group of Chinese immigrant children who experienced a significant language barrier in their public school situated in San Francisco, California. In response to the children's families' request for help, the public school officials declared that all students enter their doors with some form of deficiency and it is not the school's responsibility to meet all of their students' needs prior to their school experience. In sum, the school mirrored its historically rooted practices by leaving English language learning exclusively in the hands of the families. The families took their concerns to court, and after experiencing disappointment with lower-court rulings in favor of the school's decision, the U.S. Supreme Court heard the case and ruled unanimously in favor of the families, stating that the school's stance violated section 601 of the Civil Rights Act of 1964 that stated:

> No person in the United States shall, on the ground of race, color, or national origin, be excluded from participation in, be denied the benefits of, or be subjected to discrimination under any program or activity receiving Federal financial assistance.

Although *Lau* focused on the language needs of Chinese immigrants, the case had significant implications for Latino Americans because it gave birth to English Language Learning (ELL) as a responsibility of the public school.

Several contemporary models of ELL exist in the school experience. Dual language forms of ELL became prominent in areas of the United States, such as states in the Southwest, where a large conglomeration of students from a particular native language tradition (Spanish, in the American Southwest's case) attend the same school. The most popular form of ELL is the transitional model where students are initially taught in their native language and are gradually taught in English. This transition from the native language to English may occur within a 2-year span or up until the sixth grade (Baker, 2011). The aim of the transitional model is not bilingualism, but rather a replacement of the native language with English. Another popular approach of ELL is the English as a second language (ESL) model used when not enough students from a singular native language tradition for a transitional model is feasible. In ESL, ELL students are typically pulled out of their mainstream education setting for special instruction in English for a part of the school day. The ESL classroom, therefore, becomes a resource for ELL students to work on their assignments in the regular classroom.

Neither ESL nor a transitional model aim toward bilingualism. Bilingualism requires teachers who are proficient in dual languages, which can be difficult to support in the United States where only about twenty percent of the population is bilingual (Grosjean, 2012). However, bilingualism as an aim of ELL is unpopular partly due to historically rooted nativist impulses still present in the United States.

The Challenge of Multiculturalism

This chapter focused on three groups of people who, because of their race, suffered through marginalization at various levels and continue to encounter marginalization in one form or another. The response of the American public school has largely been a mixed one in addressing the needs of marginalized populations mostly because the school itself emerges locally from society. The school is not immune from racism and nativism if the society, from which it springs, suffers from such things. The public school, however, must transcend above the racism and nativism of American society.

According to civic educator, James Banks (2009), the American public school has an enormous challenge: How do we unite our society while still allowing room for diversity to exist? Our society's answer to that question is central to how we address the issue of race going forward. Balancing unity and diversity is no simple matter. An overemphasis upon unity, through the assimilation of diverse individuals into a singular culture, can create a cultural hegemony that threatens to lift one culture over others. The story of Native Americans we saw in this chapter testifies to the dangers of an overemphasis of assimilationist forces. However, an overemphasis upon diversity, by empowering each cultural group control of the general curriculum, threatens to divide our society and stifle communication in our democracy. Rather than positioning the classroom as a field for turf wars between various groups, a balanced multicultural curriculum should permeate throughout the American school experience. Banks and McGee-Banks (2009) shared a multi-dimensional approach to address multiculturalism in the school experience that included the following characteristics:

- content integration,
- knowledge construction,
- equity pedagogy,
- prejudice reduction, and
- empowering the school culture.

Content integration entails teachers including examples from a variety of cultures into the cultural bias or predominant cultural assumptions present in the construction of the knowledge taught in a particular discipline under study. Equity pedagogy involves the teacher employing learning strategies that help facilitate the academic achievement of students from a particular marginalized population. For instance, rote memorization will likely not help students achieve academic success whereas activities that involve problem solving will perpetuate students' academic success. Prejudice reduction involves intentionally modifying students' racial attitudes by exposing them to perspectives from a variety of cultures and how certain attitudes contribute to further marginalization of individuals whereas other attitudes reduce further marginalization. Empowering the school culture involves examining the entirety of the school culture (i.e., curricular, extra-curricular, student–staff relationships, student–student relationships) and direct it to empower students from all racial and cultural backgrounds. The challenge for schools today remains preparing a curriculum that reflects these characteristics. This can be especially challenging in those communities where racism and ethnocentrism is especially strong.

The contemporary United States of America is a pluralistic society with democratic values. The public school, as we saw in Chapter 2, is charged with the mission of serving our democratic society. As we saw earlier in this chapter, race exists as a significant social construct. Racism was and is at the root of the marginalization of Native Americans, African Americans, and Latino Americans. White supremacy permeates throughout American history's policies and practices regarding individuals not included in the predominant culture—and will remain if the school is not persistently proactive in addressing this problem.

Reflective Exercises

1. What perceptions of Native Americans, African Americans, and Latino Americans did you have prior to reading this chapter? Where did those perceptions come from?
2. What are some ways that racism still exists in the contemporary United States?
3. How might your school experience be different today if you were from a marginalized race as opposed to if you were from the predominant race in our society?
4. What are some instructional approaches, in your own school experience, that may help reduce racial prejudice amongst students? Explain.

References

Adams, D. W. (1995). *Education for extinction: American Indians and the boarding school experience, 1875–1928.* Lawrence: University Press of Kansas.

Altenbaugh, R. J. (2003). *The American people and their education: A social history.* Upper Saddle River: NJ: Merrill.

Baker, C. (2011). *Foundations of bilingual education and bilingualism* (Vol. 79). Bristol, England: Multilingual Matters.

Banks, J. A. (2009). Diversity and citizenship education in multicultural nations. *Multicultural Education Review, 1*(1), 1–28.

Banks, J. A., & Banks, C. A. M. (Eds.). (2009). *Multicultural education: Issues and perspectives.* Hoboken, NJ: Wiley.

Dew, C. B. (2002). *Apostles of disunion: Southern secession commissioners and the causes of the Civil War.* Charlottesville: University of Virginia Press.

Grosjean, F. (2012, May 20). Bilinguals in the United States: Who are the millions of bilinguals in the U.S.? *Psychology Today.* Retrieved from https://www.psychologytoday.com/us/blog/life-bilingual/201205/bilinguals-in-the-united-states

Gugliotta, G. (April 2, 2012). New estimate raises Civil War death toll. *The New York Times.* Retrieved from https://www.nytimes.com/2012/04/03/science/civil-war-toll-up-by-20-percent-in-new-estimate.html

Harrison, G. P. (2010). *Race and reality: What everyone should know about our biological diversity.* Amherst, NY: Prometheus Books.

Jacobson, M. F. (1999). *Whiteness of a different color.* Cambridge, MA: Harvard University Press.

Lau v. Nichols (1974). 414 U.S. 563.

National Public Radio. (2008, May 12). *American Indian boarding schools haunt many* [Audio podcast]. Retrieved from http://www.npr.org/templates/story/story.php?storyId=16516865

Official Report of the Nineteenth Annual Conference of Charities and Correction. (1892), 46–59. Reprinted in Richard H. Pratt (1973), "The Advantages of Mingling Indians with Whites," *Americanizing the American Indians: Writings by the "Friends of the Indian" 1880–1900* (pp. 260–271). Cambridge, MA: Harvard University Press.

State of North Carolina. (1831). Act Passed by the General Assembly, Raleigh, NC. In E. F. Provenzo (Ed.). (2006). *Critical issues in education: An anthology of readings.* Thousand Oaks, CA: SAGE.

5

Reform and School

Tony Campbell was a social studies teacher candidate at a mid-tier public university. He was in his third year at the university and mired in the midst of his core block of teacher education courses. These course required Tony to become involved in two field experiences, each at a different high school placement. The first field experience was with Ms. Tara Schultz. Ms. Schultz was a stern veteran teacher who taught courses in world history and world geography. Tony visited her class in the mornings and occasionally helped Ms. Schultz by passing out papers or taking attendance. However, most of the time, Tony simply watched Ms. Schultz talk to the students or provide students "seat work" from the textbook. Questions were seldom posed by Ms. Schultz or by the students. However, the class was organized and the students were occupied, leading to few disciplinary issues among them. Whenever Tony was finished with his first field experience, he often walked out of Ms. Schultz classroom perplexed at the zombie-like expression he saw on her students' faces during class.

Paradoxes of the Public School, pages 61–73
Copyright © 2019 by Information Age Publishing

"History is so much fun," Tony thought to himself, "and those kids are not having any fun whatsoever."

The next day, Tony traveled to his other field experience with Ms. Tammy White. Ms. White was also a veteran teacher who taught U.S. Government and World History. As was customary, whenever Tony walked into Ms. White's classroom, he was met with a greeting from the veteran teacher and debriefed on the activities planned for the day. "Ok, Tony, today we're going to try out a simulation on how a bill becomes a law," Ms. White told Tony. "Great," Tony said, "What would you like for me to do?" Ms. White smiled at Tony and said, "Would you mind presiding over the Senate while I preside over the House of Representatives to make sure that each student is fully understanding their role? They were assigned their roles yesterday but it will help if one of us was there providing any help they may need." "Of course," Tony said, "I'd be glad to." The students walked into the classroom with smiles on their faces, greeting one another and their teachers as the bell rang, signaling the start of the class period. Ms. White welcomed the class and reminded the students of their roles in the simulation. The simulation commenced with a burst of energy from the students. Two-thirds of the class became the House of Representatives, frantically creating an education bill while the other third became the Senate, also frantically creating their own version of an education bill. Tony was quite impressed with the depth of conversations amongst the students as they composed their own bill. "They are learning what's in the textbook, but they're actually doing it rather than exclusively memorizing it," Tony thought to himself. By the end of the class, each chamber of Congress passed their own version of an education bill. Ms. White authoritatively spoke to the entire class: "Ok, tomorrow we're going to have you create a conference committee to create a singular bill out of these two bills. You will then vote on them in your respective chamber and, if approved, we will send it to the president of the United States." One student interjected and asked Ms. White the following question: "Who is our president?" Ms. White looked over to Tony and asked: "Mr. Campbell, would you mind serving as our president tomorrow?" The students cheered on Tony as a means to persuade him. "Sure," Tony replied.

Tony used the driving time from Ms. White's class back to the university to reflect on the past two days. He simply could not figure out what made Ms. Schultz and Ms. White such different teachers. "Why doesn't Ms. Schultz try different activities out?" Tony thought to himself.

The differences between Ms. Schultz and Ms. White may be unique to those two particular teachers, but more than likely, the differences among the teachers are indicative of a prevailing problem in a school, namely that some parts of the school are serving students better than are other parts. The American public school is an institution that serves a society that is in perpetual motion. It is a central component of our nation's infrastructure and, as we saw in Chapter 2, it serves a myriad of interests. Like any form of infrastructure, there comes a time when the institution of the school needs reform. Sometimes the public may see that the school does not adequately serve the academic needs of students. Perhaps economic leaders might desire for new skills imbedded in the labor market. Maybe our democracy is struggling with cohesiveness or cooperation. Perhaps the psychological and emotional needs of the public need to be better addressed. The public may also desire for more efficiency out of its tax dollars and perceive the school as an inefficient bureaucracy that needs to operate more efficiently and effectively. The school, as a public institution, may succumb to any of these concerns and rarely satisfies all of them in the eye of public opinion. The nature of public institutions, for good or bad, is that the public's expectations may seldom be fully satisfied. The school is particularly vulnerable to the contempt of the public because the school's purpose focuses on the growth of children. As we will examine more extensively in a later chapter, children's growth is dependent on a myriad of factors, many upon which the school has no control. This is one significant reason reforming school is a challenging endeavor.

The school has undergone numerous reforms. Some of these reforms, like updating technology use by teachers and students, are temporal and subject to consistent change. Other reforms, however, are more large scale and affect the nation's entire school experience. According to sociologist David Labaree (2012), the American public school has undergone four primary reforms in its existence: the common school movement, the progressive movement, desegregation, and the high stakes accountability movement. Labaree asserted that all but the common school movement have been unsuccessful. This book addresses all of these reforms and my judgement is that most (not all) reforms in school, though often wieldy and awkward, are too complicated to estimate as being either successful or unsuccessful. Perhaps no reform of the school is more complicated than the progressive movement of the late 19th and early 20th century and is the singular focus of this chapter. The central paradox in this chapter, therefore, is the following:

The progressive education movement was successful but also unsuccessful.

The Progressive Education Movement

In the years roughly between 1880–1920, the United States underwent a myriad of changes that came as a direct result of a rise in immigration and an expanding industrial economy that fostered an abnormal rise in urbanization. *The Progressive era* was when many Americans embarked on an endeavor to reform American life, particularly urban life, so to improve the livelihood of the American people. Many of the reforms were sparked by writers such as Upton Sinclair, whose 1906 novel, *The Jungle*, shed light on the despicable lives of factory workers and the challenges faced by immigrant families. Others, like Jacob Riis, a well-known photojournalist, published a book in 1890 entitled *How the Other Half Lives* that unveiled the impoverished living conditions families faced while in the midst of America's bustling cities. As these problems came to surface in the public's eye, reform crusaders such as the philosopher Herbert Croly and politicians such as Presidents Theodore Roosevelt and Woodrow Wilson, proposed and put into practice government-led reforms to remedy some of the nation's growing problems. Other prominent progressives were cultural figures such as Jane Addams, founder of inner city Chicago's Hull House, a settlement house for recent immigrants, who made it their mission to uplift the rising tide of immigrants toward success in the United States. At the crux of Addams' effort to support the new Americans in Hull House was a type of education that was both relevant and practical for them.

Progressive education was a significant reform movement within the larger Progressive era. Its influence upon the American public school experience is significant, to the say the least. Yet, strangely, the nature of the progressive education movement and the scope of its impact is a source of great debate among historians. The reason for this debate is that the progressive education movement was not a singular movement motivated by a singular focus. Rather, it was a series of movements, each with competing visions. As you will see, the uneven success of the progressive education movement depends largely upon what particular vision is under scrutiny. But first, prior to taking a close look at the particulars of the competing visions, let's first look at the model of education the progressive education movement was "progressing" away from.

Traditional Education

A surge of interest emerged in the late 19th and early 20th century toward *traditional humanism* as a means through which all children should learn (Kliebard, 2004). Traditional humanism depended largely upon an immersion into the liberal arts disciplines and was commonly associated with teaching strategies such as rote memorization. Rationalization for traditional humanism was rooted in the learning doctrine called mental discipline (Hlebowitsh, 2007). The doctrine of mental discipline, a theory espoused within the psychology field at the time, stressed that the human brain required training, or discipline, to rigorously exercise its potential ability. This training relied heavily on the traditional academic disciplines as the source of rigor. This doctrine of mental discipline was widely held and still advocated among those who promoted a classical education.

In 1893, the National Education Association funded an endeavor that became the first attempt in history to standardize the school curriculum. This endeavor resulted in the *Committee of Ten Report*, a curricular report that suggested what should be taught in the American public high school. It was chaired by Charles Elliot, president of Harvard University, and created by a committee whose members were largely in support of the doctrine of mental discipline. As a result, the Committee of Ten Report largely represented traditional humanism. It suggested four years of secondary education with core subjects, now commonplace in the school experience, such as foreign languages, physical sciences, English, history, and mathematics. High schools across the nation widely followed the curriculum proposed by the Committee of Ten report.

Also in the late 19th century, a surge of interest emerged in child development that contrasted with traditional humanism. This interest in the child's growth capacity and learning ability was influenced by the earlier contributions of *Jean Jacques Rousseau* (1712–1778), an 18th century French philosopher, whose 1762 book *Émile* put forth the notion that individuals were innately good and their corruption came at the hands of society. *Émile* influenced a wave of European thought on educational practices such as those promoted by *Johann Pestalozzi* (1746–1827), a Swiss educator whose writings and teaching stressed inquiry and sensory learning over memorization and recitation. After his death, Pestalozzi's work influenced teacher preparation and school practice throughout Europe and would eventually reach the United States through Horace Mann's push to improve the school system in Massachusetts. By the late 19th century, normal schools in the United States commonly integrated Pestalozzi's work into their own curriculum.

In conjunction with the rise of Pestalozzi's philosophy and practices in American schools of education, an effort in the scientific community to better understand childhood emerged. This effort, put forth by a myriad of psychologists, is aptly called *the child study movement*. The child study movement constituted an attempt by psychologists and educational leaders, alike, to ground instructional strategies in scientific research rather than rely on tradition or guesswork (Davidson & Benjamin, 1987). Perhaps the most well-known figure who emerged out of the child study movement was *G. Stanley Hall* (1846–1924), a psychologist whose landmark contribution to the movement was his study of teenagers simply entitled *Adolescence*, published in 1907. The central tenet behind Hall's body of work, as it relates to effect on school practices, was that the school curriculum should be differentiated so as to provide each child opportunity to fulfill their potential. We will further address Hall in a later chapter that explores the issue of curricular tracking in the school. Once the child study movement gained momentum, many educational leaders began a quest to improve the school experience. However, these leaders were split into two primary factions that differed in exactly how the school should be improved: pedagogical and administrative progressives (Tyack, 1974).

Pedagogical and Administrative Progressives

According to Labaree (2005), the pedagogical and administrative progressives were motivated by two different forces. The *pedagogical progressives* focused on teaching and learning in the classroom, and thus were motivated by the romantic outlook on childhood brought forth from the work of Rousseau and Pestalozzi. The *administrative progressives*, on the other hand, were motivated by utilitarianism that sought to improve the school experience for the majority of people. This section will focus on the nature of these two forces in the progressive education movement that, at times, opposed one another.

The pedagogical progressives, much like the progressive education movement writ large, were not a singular group with a cohesive goal. Rather, the pedagogical progressives had their own subgroups that, all too often, have been incoherently lumped together by popular criticism of the progressive education movement (i.e., Ravitch, 2001). These subgroups consisted of what we will call romantic naturalists and experimentalists. *Romantic naturalism* emphasized the self-educating powers of the child. Influenced heavily by Rousseau, romantic naturalism sought to empower children and free them from the cumbersome influence of institutions and adults. Teachers, according to romantic naturalism, were to facilitate the child's learning and provide opportunity for the child for self-expression and individual interest. *Experimentalism*, on the other hand, gravitated toward a democratic ideal of society that required a type of citizenship that emphasized social problem-solving, deliberation, and understanding. Experimentalists, similar to romantic naturalism, believed that a child's experiences should be the genesis of instruction. However, experimentalists did not agree with romantic naturalists that the child's interests should dictate the curriculum. Instead, experimentalists emphasized that teachers should direct the curriculum toward not only the child's interests, but also the needs of a democratic society.

Many individuals personified both forces of pedagogical progressivism. The next chapter will introduce some of those individuals. However, no pedagogical progressive was more prolific in his writings and better known in the eyes of the public than *John Dewey*. Dewey (1859–1952) was a prolific philosopher who emphasized education in his work. As you will see more explicitly in the succeeding chapter, Dewey was an experimentalist who fashioned the United States as a social democracy that necessitated reflective inquiry amongst its citizenry. As a professor at the University of Chicago in the late 19th century, Dewey founded a laboratory school that proved to be a prime example of pedagogical progressivism put into practice as it emphasized the interests of the child as well as the aims of a democratic society. Dewey is so influential that nearly all subsequent attempts at pedagogical reform, which almost always emphasize to teachers the need to first connect to children's current experiences, were at one time either conceived or promoted by him. However, while Dewey receives praise in schools of education, his ideas remain novel in the actual practice of teaching and learning (e.g., Cuban, 1993; Labaree, 2005). This is because of the administrative progressives' deep utilitarian roots interwoven in the evolvement of the American public school experience during the latter half of the 20th century.

The administrative progressives emerged as part of a larger movement in the United States called social efficiency. Social efficiency emphasized practicality and proper use of resources, talent, and time in the school experience (Knoll, 2009). This emphasis on practicality and efficiency rooted in reforms from the social efficiency movement emerged primarily out of economic necessity. As the United States, at the turn of the 20th century, became an industrialized society, a surge of interest in Frederick Taylor's theory of scientific management emerged. *Frederick Taylor* (1856–1915) was a mechanical engineer whose book *The Principles of Scientific Management*, published in 1911, paved the way for a scientific approach to create and divide work that maximized business' profit oriented goals. Taylor believed that a standardized system, led by managers and not workers, was central to business success. School leaders hopefully looked upon Taylor's work as a way to ensure that schools were maximizing time with children. Among the most prominent of these school leaders was a University of Chicago professor named *John Franklin Bobbitt* (1876–1956). Bobbitt was explicit in his comparison of the school to the industrial factory: "Education is a shaping process as much as the manufacturing of steel rails" (Bobbitt, 1913, p. 11). As a result, Bobbitt personified the implications of Taylor's work: to standardize the curriculum so that learning outcomes for students were specifically stated and clearly observed when met. Often, the learning objectives that Bobbitt sought were set at a mechanistic, at times perfunctory, level. For instance, here are some objectives Bobbitt (1921, p. 609) proposed for a reading program:

> You will be ready to undertake A-1 reading when you can do the following things:
>
> 1. When you are spending at least 60 minutes a day on reading and phonetics.
>
> 2. When you know at sight 100 words from the list of 125 flashcards chosen from the main list.
>
> 3. When you can use any of the 100 words in sentences with the following word phrases: "This is"; "I see"; "We have"; "I can"; "We can"; "Can you"; "Have you"; "I like"; "We like: a, the, an."

In another book, Bobbitt (1916, p. 28) asserted the amount of school books students should read at a particular grade level:

> A fifth, sixth, seventh, or eighth-grade student ought to be able to read all the materials supplied his grade, both reading texts and all kinds of supplementary reading, in 40 or 50 hours. He ought to do it easily in six weeks' work without encroaching on recitation time.

For administrative progressives, like Bobbitt, students' learning experience could be scientifically analyzed and improved. At the center of this rise in popularity of scientific management in school reform was the new standardized test (or, objective test, as it was called then).

No single individual personified this interest in applying objective tests to the school experience than *Edward Thorndike* (1874–1949). Thorndike was a renowned psychologist at Columbia University's Teachers College in the early 20th century. Just as John Dewey became a living symbol of pedagogical progressivism, Thorndike became the most prominent figure among the administrative progressives primarily due to his extension of standardized tests as a means to measure "anything and everything relevant to education—mental capacities, changes in behavior, and even the aims of education" (Lagemann, 2002, p. 59). Thorndike's work became popularized through a series of textbooks that primarily focused on the use of tests as a means to measure learning outcomes. The work of Thorndike, and other testing advocates, revolutionized the use of standardized achievement tests in American schools. As a case in point, between 1917 and 1928, nearly 1,300 achievement tests were created in the United States; by 1940 that figure rose to 2,600 (Monroe, 1950). By the 1930s and 1940s, a multitude of objective tests were available that aimed to assess anything from intelligence, personality, or vocational aims (Reese, 2005). The utilitarian goals of the administrative progressives became closely associated with the standardized test, as we will learn more about in a later chapter.

Retrospective and Contemporary Assessment

In the late 20th century, historian Ellen Condliffe Lagemann (1989, p. 185) provided the following poignant estimation of the progressive education movement:

> I have often argued to students, only in part to be perverse, that one cannot understand the history of education in the United States during the 20th century unless one realizes that Edward L. Thorndike won and John Dewey lost.

Lagemann's estimation is a correct one. As we will see more closely in a later chapter, Thorndike's interest in testing and the administrative progressives' overarching interest in measuring specific, often mechanistic, learning outcomes became the mantra of the contemporary high-stakes, academic standards-based, accountability reform of schools. So, if one was to assert whether or not the progressive education movement was successful, it could rightfully be said that the administrative progressives were successful in their attempt to reform the school in their mold. However, if success of the administrative progressives' reform is translated to mean that it improved the school experience—then, that estimation should be held in question. Again, we will further examine the contemporary high stakes accountability movement later in this chapter. Now that we concluded that Thorndike's social efficiency-oriented vision of the school experience prevailed, where does that leave John Dewey's legacy?

To say that John Dewey "lost" is not inaccurate. However, it may not be accurate to say that John Dewey's pedagogical progressive movement failed to affect the school experience. To the contrary, the pedagogical progressive movement had some significant influence on the school experience. Yet, that influence is persistently under threat by those who advocate social efficiency and even those who advocate for traditional humanism. As a case in point, in 1918 the NEA published its *Cardinal Principles Report of Secondary Education*, which became misinterpreted and often misapplied over time. In contrast to the discipline dominant report two decades earlier from the Committee of Ten, the Cardinal Principles Report suggested that the secondary school experience should revolve around seven general objectives, or principles. These principles were: (a) health, (b) command of fundamental processes, (c) worthy home-membership, (d) vocation, (e) citizenship, (f) worthy use of leisure, and (g) ethical character (National Education Association, 1918). Some scholars (e.g., Krug, 1964; Labaree, 2005) assert that the Cardinal Principles Report was a document produced to diffuse social efficiency aims such as vocational and intrapersonal habits. However, the Cardinal Principles Report actually reflected more of the pedagogical progressives' thrust to teach subject matter in a transformative way that fits students and society's needs. Historian William Wraga (2001, p. 515) put it this way:

> What the CRSE (Cardinal Principles Report) called for, in effect, were new ways of treating subject matter—specifically, of treating subject matter not exclusively as an end in itself, but as means to other ends, and of organizing curricula in a more coherent fashion than possible in a fragmented, compartmentalized approach by focusing all courses on the seven unifying objectives.

While the Cardinal Principles Report possessed characteristics that resembled aims of the pedagogical progressives, the school experience is continually resistant to embrace their pedagogical reform effort. Sociologist David Labaree (2005, p. 278) surmised the nature of the typical American classroom today:

> Instruction in American schools is overwhelmingly teacher-centered; classroom management is the teacher's top priority; traditional school subjects dominate the curriculum; textbooks and teacher talk are the primary means of delivering the curriculum; learning consists of recalling what texts and teachers say; and tests measure how much of this students have learned. What signs there are of student-centered instruction and discovery learning tend to be superficial or short-lived. We talk progressive but we rarely teach that way. In short, traditional methods of teaching and learning are in control of American education.

Labaree's assertion that pedagogical progressive reforms are superficial or short-lived is a death blow to the progressive education movement. However, these reforms continue to surface. For example, the contemporary concept, espoused primarily by educational theorist Luis Moll (e.g., González, Moll, & Amanti, 2006) that teachers should connect subject matter with students' preexisting "funds of knowledge" is clearly a reconceptualization of the type of progressive education advocated a century ago by John Dewey. Research (e.g., Schul, 2012) in the use of emergent digital technologies consistently point that they should be used to promote constructivism, which is modern educational psychology's term for pedagogical progressives from long ago. The new assessment of teacher candidates that currently dominates the discourse of teacher education, *edTPA®*, holds teacher candidates accountable for having the necessary skills to teach subject matter using inquiry methods rather than recitation. While administrative progressivism continues to be a prevailing reform in the American school experience, pedagogical progressivism remains a resurfacing reform still in search of more advocacy amongst school practitioners, school leaders, and policy makers.

The next two chapters will branch from this exploration of the pedagogical and administrative progressives. Chapter 6 focuses on the relationship between pedagogy and school, which includes analysis where the pedagogical progressives fit in this relationship. Chapter 7 focuses upon the relationship between efficiency and school, with close attention paid to two reforms inspired by administrative progressives: the adoption of the Prussian school model and curricular tracking.

Summary

Attempts at reform of the American school experience have been historically unsteady. The progressive education movement at the turn of the 20th century personifies this unsteady nature of school reform. While the movement collectively sought to move the school experience away from the grips of traditional humanism, the movement was split in how it should do so. One faction of the movement, the administrative progressives, was influenced by social efficiency and sought to scientifically mold the school experience into an industrial business model that was specific with its objectives and efficient with producing those objectives. Contrary, the pedagogical progressives were influenced by a romantic desire to connect subject matter to students' lives and to simultaneously improve society. The administrative progressives' reforms evolved toward the wave of high stakes testing and standards-based accountability that dominates the contemporary landscape of school The pedagogical progressives' reforms persistently rise and fall in search of more advocacy in the school experience.

Reflective Exercises

1. List some school reforms in your lifetime. Categorize those reforms as better fitting with the purposes of administrative progressives or pedagogical progressives.

2. Why do you think Dewey "lost" and Thorndike "won" the battle to reform school?
3. Contrast traditional humanism with progressive education. Which approach do you think best serves students and society? Explain.
4. Did the progressive education movement rid the school experience of traditional humanism? Explain your answer.

References

Bobbitt, J. F. (1913). *The supervision of city schools: Some general principles of management applied to the problems of city-school systems.* Twelfth Yearbook of the National Society for the Study of Education, Part I. Bloomington, IL: Public School Publishing Co.

Bobbitt, J. F. (1916). *What the schools teach and might teach* (Vol. 4). Survey committee of the Cleveland foundation.

Bobbitt, J. F. (1921). A significant tendency in curriculum-making. *Elementary School Journal, 21*(8), 607–615.

Cuban, L. (1993). *How teachers taught: Constancy and change in American classrooms, 1890–1990.* New York, NY: Teachers College Press.

Davidson, E. S., & Benjamin, L. T. (1987). A history of the child study movement in America. In J. A. Glover & R. R. Ronning (Eds.), *Historical foundations of educational psychology. Perspectives on individual differences* (pp. 41–60). New York, NY: Springer.

González, N., Moll, L. C., & Amanti, C. (Eds.). (2006). *Funds of knowledge: Theorizing practices in households, communities, and classrooms.* New York, NY: Routledge.

Hlebowitsh, P. S. (2007). *Foundations of American education.* Dubuque, IA: Kendall-Hunt.

Kliebard, H. M. (2004). *The struggle for the American curriculum* (3rd ed.). New York, NY: Routledge Kegan.

Knoll, M. (2009). From Kidd to Dewey: The origin and meaning of 'Social efficiency.' *Journal of Curriculum Studies, 41*(3), 361–391.

Krug, E. A. (1964). *The shaping of the American high school, 1880–1920.* Madison: University of Wisconsin Press.

Labaree, D. F. (2005). Progressivism, schools and schools of education: An American romance. *Paedagogica Historica, 41*(1–2), 275–288.

Labaree, D. F. (2012). *Someone has to fail.* Cambridge, MA: Harvard University Press.

Lagemann, E. C. (1989). The plural worlds of educational research. *History of Education Quarterly, 29*(2), 185–214.

Lagemann, E. C. (2002). *An elusive science: The troubling history of education research.* Chicago, IL: University of Chicago Press.

National Education Association. (1918). *Report of the Commission on the Reorganization of Secondary Education*. U.S. Bureau of Education Bulletin 35, 7–16. Washington, DC: Government Printing Office.

Monroe, W. S. (1950). *Encyclopedia of educational research*. New York, NY: Macmillan.

Ravitch, D. (2001). *Left back: A century of battles over school reform*. New York, NY: Touchstone.

Schul, J. E. (2012). Compositional encounters: Evolvement of secondary students' narratives while making historical desktop documentaries. *Journal of Social Studies Research, 36*(3), 219–244.

Reese, W. J. (2005). *America's public schools: From the common school to 'No Child Left Behind.'* Baltimore, MD: The Johns Hopkins University Press.

Tyack, D. (1974). *The one best system: A history of urban education*. Cambridge, MA: Harvard University Press.

Wraga, W. G. (2001). A progressive legacy squandered: The Cardinal Principles report reconsidered. *History of Education Quarterly, 41*(4), 494–519.

6

Pedagogy and School

As was customary each morning, an aroma of freshly brewed coffee permeated the teacher's lounge at Eldora Middle School. Teachers who had free periods came in and out each morning to get their cup of mocha and sit down to "shoot the breeze" with one another. Mark Miller and Steve Klapper were two such teachers who happened to be best of friends. They were both social studies teachers and enjoyed their morning time together to discuss issues and ideas instead of the customary gossip that often rolled off the tongues of other teachers. They worked hard and were both well respected by students and colleagues alike. Anyone who observed Mark and Steve converse can almost predict what they would talk about. Here's an example of a typical conversation between the two:

Mark: I think that our schools should position students to critically think on issues pertinent to our times.
Steve: I'm not disagreeing with you on that, but I think that our students

Paradoxes of the Public School, pages 75–89
Copyright © 2019 by Information Age Publishing
All rights of reproduction in any form reserved.

need to first have a robust amount of background knowledge on our history and culture. These students do not know much beyond their own lives; it is our job to cultivate their minds. They will not be equipped to critically think if they have no background knowledge on the ideas for them to think about.

Mark: But, don't you think the students will get that background knowledge in the midst of problem-solving on current issues? Shouldn't their curiosity first be aroused prior to their exposure to rigorous subject matter so they would be more likely to understand that knowledge when they do encounter it? Plus, we want our students to be lifelong learners who see patterns in what they learn so that they can learn for themselves outside of school.

Steve: You're an idealist, Mark. I've heard all this before, but there is no more sure way to spark students' minds than expose them to the ideas beforehand. Frankly, our students don't know what they don't know. It is my job to first teach them what they don't know.

In Chapter 5, we saw the rise of the pedagogical progressives at the turn of the 20th century. This group challenged the entrenchment of traditional humanism with the school curriculum. Of course, as we saw, the pedagogical progressives encountered the simultaneous rise of the administrative progressives. While the pedagogical progressives may not have dominated the landscape of educational policy reform as the would have liked, they nonetheless became central in the preparation of teachers. *Pedagogy* refers to the teaching of children and *pedagogues* are the teachers of children. While it is essential to acknowledge the effect that the administrative progressives have on the practice of teachers, as we will see in the next chapter, teachers' classroom practices, to some extent, are influenced by the philosophical orientation of the teachers who practice them. Despite the coldness that may be associated with analyzing school, as if its characteristics are always predictable with predictable effects, the school experience, by and large, is a human experience. School is essentially a gathering place for students and their teachers—all of whom are people with their own mind and a certain agency to make their own decisions about teaching and learning.

This chapter focuses on the philosophical underpinnings of teachers' pedagogical decision-making. While the pedagogical progressives made significant contributions to teachers' pedagogical orientations, they are not alone in this endeavor. However, the pedagogical progressives brought fresh focus on the role of pedagogy in the school experience. Teachers are influenced by a myriad of philosophies. The philosophical differences between Mark and Steve in our story are not unique to them, and are representative of genuine philosophical differences that may exist among excellent teachers under the same school roof. As you will see, there are philosophies that fall upon the conservative tradition of education whereas other philosophies align more closely to a radical tradition. One teacher may employ both traditions at different times, depending upon the pedagogical intention of that teacher. Therefore, the central paradox of this chapter is:

Teachers are often labeled as having one philosophy or another, but many times a teacher may simultaneously employ multiple teaching philosophies that may or may not appear to be at odds with each other.

The Practice of School Teaching

There is a difference between being a teacher and being a school teacher. Teachers exist anywhere there is communication between people. A school teacher, however, exists in a certain context with certain curricular expectations and restraints. For instance, a school teacher is provided with a group of students in a class, usually without a prior relationship and in a compulsory fashion for the students, and provided a specific time and place where they are supposed to meet. School teachers are also usually expected to fulfill certain requirements in a curriculum that are interconnected with other coursework the students take.

While school teachers operate under unique circumstances, one school teacher may operate differently from another. School teachers perform at various levels, depending upon their ability to make emergent decisions that interconnect the three curricular sources: the nature of students, the knowledge represented in the subject matter, and the aims of society writ large (Tanner & Tanner, 1995). There are three performance levels of teachers, according to Tanner and Tanner (1995), that exist to help describe the teaching and learning experience provided by the classroom teacher. These three levels are: imitative-maintenance, mediative, and creative-generative. See Table 6.1 for analysis of these three performance levels. Teachers at the imitative-maintenance level rely primarily on a scripted curriculum, often leaning heavily on a textbook or some other resource that provides subject matter and classroom activities for students. Teachers at this level seldom, if ever at all, connect to the three sources of curriculum development. Teachers at the mediative level tend to be able and willing, on occasion, to adjust their curriculum to better connect to the three curricular sources. However, mediative teachers usually work in a somewhat restricted curriculum, either by their choice and/or by external factors such as limitations placed upon them by administrators usually out of a desire to quickly fulfill high-stakes accountability measures placed upon them. Teachers at the creative-generative level represent the highest performance level of a teacher. Creative-generative teachers gravitate toward positioning students to solve problems posed to them and to construct an understanding of the subject matter in a way that is meaningful to them. These teachers usually exhibit a strong capacity to connect the three curricular sources. It must be stressed that these performance levels are not meant to be a hierarchical growth model for teachers. In other words, a teacher does not need to begin at imitative-maintenance to eventually reach creative-generative. The goal for all teachers should be to perform at the creative-generative level, with an understanding that some teachers may be limited by either experience, skill, or school policies.

A teachers' pedagogical philosophy does not necessarily foretell the performance level of the teacher. Rather, teachers from a variety of philosophical orientations may successfully perform at the creative-generative level. The best teachers, arguably, are the ones who select the best attributes of multiple philosophies to forge their own philosophical underpinning. Teachers who do so suggest to others that that they are reflective and committed to their craft. Some scholars of education begin with antiquity in their analysis of teaching philosophies. While this is not a poor practice by any means, it would not necessarily serve us best as we seek to ultimately examine the landscape of the contemporary American public school experience. What follows is an analysis of the predominant teaching philosophies that exist among teachers in the United States. It is not the purpose of this chapter to rank one philosophy as superior to another. In fact, I suggest that all of these philosophies may be enacted by creative-generative teachers. Instead, this chapter will systematically analyze these philosophies in separate categories, providing possible strengths and weaknesses of each

TABLE 6.1 Analysis of Teacher Performance Levels		
Imitative Maintenance	**Description**	**Connection to Three Curricular Sources: Learner, Subject Matter, Society**
Imitative Maintenance	Relies on scripted curriculum	Seldom
Mediative	Sporadically adjusts curriculum	Occasionally
Creative-Generative	Problem-centered classroom; teacher consumes and applies theory and research	Usually

Radical	Progressive	Conservative
Social Reconstructionism	Romantic Naturalism	Perenialism
Post-Modernism	Experimentalism	Essentialism
		Discipline-Specific

Figure 6.1   Teaching philosophy continuum.

philosophy. The reality of teaching, as the paradox of this chapter suggests, is that these philosophies do not exist separately in a vacuum as this analysis suggest. Rather, one teacher may possess multiple philosophies with one possibly being more dominant than another.

Figure 6.1 represents a continuum of the teaching philosophies that we will use throughout this chapter. While these philosophies are categorized with terms similar to those used to describe political philosophies, it is important to note that the two need not be synonymous with one another. For example, a political radical could feasibly have a conservative teaching philosophy. The focus of the remainder of this chapter is devoted to understanding this continuum.

The Conservative Tradition

The conservative tradition is rooted in traditional humanism (which we looked at in the previous chapter). However, with the rise of progressive education, advocates for traditional humanism focused on preserving a cultural tradition. Conservatives perceive that a body of knowledge is under siege and would be lost in culture without a concerted effort to conserve it. They advocate for a subject-centered curriculum that places a heavy emphasis on reading. Three primary subgroups exist among conservatives: *perennialism, essentialism,* and *discipline-specific.*

Perennialists tout the benefits of a classical curriculum that emphasizes study of principles as opposed to a litany of facts. The argument here is that the application of principles is always relevant in the human experience whereas the relevance of facts are not. The two most high-profile perennialists of the 20th century were *Robert Hutchins* (1899–1977) and *Mortimer Adler* (1902–2001) who co-founded the *Great Books Foundation*® in 1947. Both men believed that American public education was too focused on electives and vocational training rather than developing students' minds. Their position was that schools, at both the elementary and secondary level, should expose

- Homer: Iliad, Odyssey
- The Old Testament
- Aeschylus: Tragedies
- Sophocles: Tragedies
- Herodotus: Histories
- Euripides: Tragedies
- Thucydides: History of the Peloponnesian War
- Hippocrates: Medical Writings
- Aristophanes: Comedies
- Plato: Dialogues
- Marcel Proust: Remembrance of Things Past
- Bertrand Russell: The Problems of Philosophy; The Analysis of Mind; An Inquiry into Meaning and Truth; Human Knowledge, Its Scope and Limits
- Thomas Mann: The Magic Mountain; Joseph and His Brothers
- Albert Einstein: The Meaning of Relativity; On the Method of Theoretical Physics; The Evolution of Physics
- James Joyce: 'The Dead' in Dubliners; A Portrait of the Artist as a Young Man; Ulysses
- Jacques Maritain: *Art and Scholasticism*; *The Degrees of Knowledge*; *The Rights of Man and Natural Law*; *True Humanism*
- Franz Kafka: The Trial; The Castle
- Arnold J. Toynbee: A Study of History; Civilization on Trial
- Jean Paul Sartre: Nausea; No Exit; Being and Nothingness
- Aleksandr Solzhenitsyn: The First Circle; The Cancer Ward

Figure 6.2 Selections from Mortimer Adler's suggested reading list. *Source*: Adler & Van Doren, 1972.

students to a pre-selected curriculum featuring literature widely regarded as being historically significant writing. In Figure 6.2, you see some of the books Adler deemed worthy of inclusion on a list of significant pieces of literature. Perennialism remains prominent in the contemporary landscape of American education. Some universities, charter schools, and homeschool programs feature a perennialist flavored curriculum that differentiate it from the traditional public school. Former Secretary of Education, William Bennett, showcased his perennialist colors with the publication of the popular *Book of Virtues* that emphasized classic pieces of literature intended to teach children ethical virtues he deemed to be universal.

Perennialists generally believe that a curriculum should be universal and that all people are, more or less, the same in their need to be mentally prepared through critical analysis of classic literature. Essentialists, on the other hand, look more closely at the needs of modern democracy when comprising a curriculum. The difference is subtle, as there is much more in common between the two subgroups than there are differences. However, differences do exist. Essentialists, like perennialists, are grounded in traditional humanism's doctrine of mental discipline. Unlike perennialists, essentialists place less emphasis on the universality of certain selections of literature. The most high profile essentialist in the mid-20th century was *William Bagley* (1874–1946) who was concerned with the rise of progressive education, particularly Romantic Naturalism. Bagley (1907) believed that a curriculum should conserve a body of knowledge necessary "when knowledge shall be needed in the constructive solution of new and untried problems" (p. 2). The role that a body of knowledge plays in the sustenance and growth of a democracy is an integral feature of essentialism. For instance, during the Cold War era in the mid-20th century, the United States sponsored an academic discipline-centered curriculum focused on science and mathematics to thwart the imperialistic threat that the Soviet Union posed to the nation and world at that time. A popular modern version of essentialism exists in *Core Knowledge Foundation®*, a group that provides suggestions to schools regarding how they may improve their curriculum. The group was formed by *E. D. Hirsch* (b. 1928), whose book *Cultural Literacy*, first published in 1987, stressed that American students lacked knowledge about American culture and history and provided suggestions as to what knowledge was necessary in contemporary American society. Hirsch's group sought to fill the nation's knowledge gap by providing a series of texts and curricula that, quite frankly, many schools and teachers found to be helpful.

Advocates of perennialism and essentialism point out students who experience their curriculum learn a robust body of knowledge that would not otherwise be provided in the traditional school curriculum. Critics of these two subgroups of the conservative tradition point out the cultural bias they employ to select their curriculum. Perennialists are commonly criticized for developing a curriculum filled with authors who are predominantly White and European. Essentialists, particularly E. D. Hirsch, provide a more multicultural flavor to their curriculum than perennialists, but are still vulnerable to the criticism of a general bias in selecting the worthiness of a particular set of knowledge.

The third subgroup, discipline-specific, diverts from perennialists and essentialists in many ways. Foremost, advocates for the discipline-specific approach are less interested in forming a particular body of knowledge to be transmitted to students and are more interested in how students learn the body of knowledge. In sum, the discipline-specific approach emphasizes positioning students into the role of the practitioner of a particular discipline. For instance, a science teacher should position students to conduct scientific experiments; history teachers should position students to play the role of the historian; literature teachers should position students to play the role of a literary critic. The widely held belief of this approach is that there is a type of thinking unique to a particular discipline. For instance, mathematicians think mathematically; scientists think scientifically;

and historians think historically. The genesis of this approach sprouts from the advent of new approaches to teach history. In the 1960s and 1970s, history education underwent a reform entitled "The New Social Studies" that, among other things, positioned students to solve problems. A significant contribution to this reform was the inclusion of primary sources in history classrooms as a means to teach and learn history. This resulted in a series of curricular packets, such as *JackDaws®*, used widely in history classrooms across the country. However, it wasn't until the turn of the 21st century that the use of primary sources became a preferred method in history education. The work of Stanford professor *Sam Wineburg* (2001) on the concept of historical thinking fostered a framework for history teaching and learning that eventually became accepted in many states as an achievable goal for students of history. Historical thinking entails the critical analysis of the purpose, intent, and effect of a particular primary source within a particular era of time. This approach diverts from the then customary approach to teach history as a compilation of facts, concepts, and generalizations and moves toward students playing the role of historian and to actually construct their own historical narratives. Although this approach existed in other disciplines, the marketing success of historical thinking as an educational framework paved the way for other disciplines to successfully promote their own disciplinary approaches into the teaching and learning of their own subject matter such as mathematical thinking (Schoenfield & Sloane, 2016) or scientific thinking (Kuhn, 2011).

Placing the disciplinary-specific approach on our philosophy continuum is no easy matter. Whereas the approach is not necessarily akin to perennialism and essentialism, it nonetheless stresses the learning of subject matter, albeit in an innovative fashion. The discipline-specific approach, however, does not belong in the progressive tradition since the approach is less concerned with contemporary issues and the developmental stages of children than they are with positioning students toward a particular type of disciplinary thinking. Advocates of the disciplinary-specific point out that students learn to think critically and to construct their own knowledge. Critics, however, point out that this approach positions students to dwell within a professional discipline they likely will never belong to in their lifetime, and that the critical thinking skills students learn from this approach are seldom applied to contemporary problems and issues. In many ways, the discipline-specific approach stands alone in its own category. However, because of its tendency to approach subject matter devoid of paying attention to contemporary issues and eliciting social skills, it has a unique place within the conservative approach.

The Progressive Tradition

As we saw in Chapter 5, progressive education diverted from traditional humanism. The movement sought to position the child at the forefront of curriculum development. This section focuses on the two primary subgroups of the progressive tradition: romantic naturalism and experimentalism.

Romantic naturalists garner their philosophy around the central tenets espoused by Jean-Jacques Rousseau that children should be left unpolluted by society's impulse to control and condition them for their own purpose. We saw, in the previous chapter, how Johann Pestalozzi carried this child-centered mantel across Europe and changed the nature of teacher preparation. Two figures, strongly influenced by Pestalozzi, created primary school curricula that became the organic representation of romantic naturalism: *Friedrich Froebel* and *Maria Montessori*.

Friedrich Froebel (1782–1852) was a German educator who advocated for privileging students' innate gifts and ability through such individual activities as drawing, painting, dancing, and drama. Froebel initiated the concept of "kindergarten," which means where children grow, as a place set us aside for his psycho-motor concept of learning. Froebel's primary goal was for children to discover themselves through the act of play.

Maria Montessori (1870–1952) was an Italian educator who built upon Froebel's ideas but emphasized the learning environment of the child. Montessori concluded that many children who experienced failure in school did so because they were in a poor learning environment rather than possessing an inept biological nature. Montessori formed a model of pedagogy, today referred to as the "Montessori method," that included games and the use of didactic materials as a means to privilege students' sensory skills. The Montessori method is currently employed by many private and public schools across the United States. According to the North American Montessori Teacher's Association (NAMTA), an advocacy group for Montessori schools, there are approximately 4,500 Montessori schools in the United States. Table 6.2 juxtaposes the nature of traditional education practices with those of the Montessori approach. The romantic-naturalist influence on the Montessori approach can be easily identified. For instance, an emphasis on student choice and their development highlights the uniqueness of the Montessori approach. Additionally, teachers in the Montessori approach act more as facilitators rather than the dominant voice over the whole class.

While romantic naturalists emphasize the child's ability and interests, the experimentalists seek to adhere more closely to subject matter and

TABLE 6.2 Traditional Education Practice Versus Montessori Education Practices

Same age groups	Mixed age groups
A certain block of time allotted for each subject, all students work on the same subject at the same time	Uninterrupted work cycles, students choose when and for how long to work on each activity, many subjects are integrated
Adult-centered; teacher controls the classroom and enforces discipline	Child-centered; a carefully prepared environment encourages students to practice self-discipline
Focus on the product use tests and grades	Focus on the process, do not use tests or grades
Students are expected to be within the norms of what is average for their grade level	Students have the opportunity to advances academically at their own pace, without limits

Source: Lilard & Else-Quest, 2006.

society's democratic aims. At the heart of *experimentalism* is the notion that subject matter should be connected to students' experience in such a way that it fosters a new understanding of their experience and a propulsion toward better understanding of future experiences. At the forefront of the origins of this approach within the progressive movement stood John Dewey. Dewey, whose background we saw in the previous chapter, was a renowned philosopher who studied education in the midst of the progressive education movement. Unlike the romantic naturalists who believed that children should learn freely, experimentalists, like Dewey, asserted that the teacher was "an intellectual leader of a social group" (Dewey 1933/1989, p. 337) who must not only be a master of subject matter but also of the students' intellectual responses to the subject matter. However, unlike advocates of the conservative tradition who believed that the subject matter should be taught on its own authority, experimentalists believed that "the teacher should become intimately acquainted with the conditions of the local community, physical, historical, economic, occupational, and so forth, in order to utilize them as educational resources" (Dewey 1938, p. 40).

The unique characteristic of experimentalists is that they seek to branch out the scientific method of inquiry to social settings (this is why they are called experimentalists, but others prefer the name "reflective inquirers" or "social meliorists" to describe the same thing). According to this approach, a teacher should pose a problem to students (i.e., Why is there war?) and allow them space to formulate hypotheses of their own. The teacher should then position students to collect data to verify their hypothesis (i.e., have students study different wars and their causes). Teachers should then allow students to create broadly applicable statements called generalizations (i.e., wars are caused by economics). Students, with the new found generalization, have new knowledge that they could apply to subsequent experiences of war. This approach, according to experimentalists, should be employed with the teaching of nearly all disciplines of subject matter.

The thrust behind experimentalists' vision of teaching and learning is that school should usefully serve the interests of the students and society by making the subject matter intellectually applicable to current times. Dewey (1933/1989) explained his concerns with a school curriculum that failed to be intellectually relevant:

> Pupils are taught to live in two separate worlds, one the world of out-of-school experience, the other the world of books and lessons. Then we stupidly wonder why what is studied in school counts so little outside. (p. 325)

Advocates of experimentalism state that it is a fluid philosophy well suited for a democracy because it privileges posing problems as means for new understanding. Critics of experimentalism (e.g., Lippman, 1922), however, point out that experimentalism unreasonably expects the public to engage in intellectual activity that often falls far beyond their capacity to understand.

Radical Tradition

The progressive tradition challenged tenets of traditional educational practices and produced a constructive curricular foundation for the public school to adopt. The radical tradition, to the contrary, weighs in with significant challenges to society and school while yielding little tangible curricular foundation for the school. However, the significance of the radical tradition should not be dismissed. It is through the critical eye of the radical tradition that the school becomes more responsive to the needs of marginalized populations and more aware of injustices upon which the school may align itself. This section will focus on two subgroups within the radical tradition: social reconstructionism and postmodernism.

Social reconstructionism was born as a direct challenge to socioeconomic disparity in the 1920s and 1930s. *George Counts* (1889–1974) was an educational theorist who contrived social reconstructionism as a means to channel his collectivist vision of the United States into a reality. According to Counts, American institutions such as the public school supported the centralization of economic power into the hands of the wealthy. For instance, Counts asserted that most school boards consisted of men from middle to upper class families. Unlike the experimentalists who sought to foster reflection amongst the citizenry, Counts envisioned a bolder, more forceful curriculum that positioned students to challenge economic injustices with the eventual aim of creating a socialist state. Counts (1932) was frank and public with his radical vision of education that must

> emancipate itself from the influence of the (ruling upper classes), face squarely and courageously every social issue, come to grips with life in all of its stark reality, establish an organic relation with the community, develop a realistic and comprehensive theory of welfare ... and become less frightened than it is today at the bogeys of imposition and indoctrination. (pp. 9–10)

Counts' assertion that schools should adopt an educational format that boldly imposes a socialist perspective on to students was unsurprisingly met with challenges that his vision to force a perspective onto students ran contrary to the democratic aims of society. Counts (1969) countered this challenge by declaring that the school already imposed a form of group-think upon the citizenry:

> We must realize that whenever choices are made in the launching of a program values are involved. This is obviously true in shaping of the curriculum, the selection of textbooks, the giving of grades, the organization of social activities, the construction of a school building, the hanging of pictures and paintings on the walls of a schoolroom, and in the selection of a teacher ... The big question therefore is not whether we should impose anything on the child in the process of education but *what* we should impose. In the swiftly changing world of the twentieth century we must certainly examine our cultural heritage critically in the light of the great and inescapable realities of the present age and the trends toward tomorrow. What this means, in my opinion, is to present to the younger generation a vision of the possibility of finally fulfilling the great promise of America expressed in the Declaration of Independence. (p. 188)

While Counts' vision for schools as agents of a socialist state never came to fruition, it did perpetuate a new paradigm within the landscape of educational thought called *critical pedagogy*. Advocates of critical pedagogy, such as the renowned Brazilian educator *Paulo Friere* (1921–1997) and contemporary scholars *Michael Apple* (b. 1942) and *Peter McLaren* (b. 1948), mirror Counts' belief that teaching is an inherent political act, devoid of neutrality, and that teachers should seek to emancipate oppressed individuals by awakening their students' critical consciousness. Friere (1982), for instance, articulated a critical stance against the Brazilian educational system that he asserted was responsible for the sustainability of the country's oppressive governmental regime. Friere called this educational system *"banking education"* because it focused on teachers "depositing" facts into students' minds and later asking for "withdrawals" of those facts with little to no reflection or critical questioning involved. As a result, according to Friere, the government could maintain its power because the citizenry were taught to be passive and quiet and who generally lacked critical thinking skills that would directly challenge it.

In addition to social reconstructionism, postmodernism is a subgroup within the radical tradition that challenges societal and school norms that are representative to them of the domineering power of the wealthy or majority. While social reconstructionism stresses replacing one political order for another one, postmodernism is more focused on decentering assumptions and practices that pervade the school experience. Such assumptions and practices, under the overarching title of modernism, may include a firm reliance on rational thinking, scientific progress, and the reliability of social labels. Postmodernists often challenge these assumptions and practices, rooted in the values of Western civilization, as being racist, ethnocentric, elitist, or patriarchal. Postmodernism emphasizes that school leaders should view school through the eyes of the *latent curriculum.* The latent curriculum, sometimes referred to as the "hidden" curriculum, consists of the subject matter and practices within the entire school curriculum that implicitly reveal certain rules, values, or norms not necessarily explicitly addressed by the school curriculum, but arguably equally effective and, at times, more effective than the explicit curriculum. The latent curriculum could address positive behaviors. For instance, a teacher who seeks to teach students the love of reading may purposefully carry a book to and from school in hope that students take in a value of the importance of reading. Postmodernists, however, emphasize the negative messages that emanate from the latent curriculum. Often, these messages reveal forms of racism, sexism, or other forms of marginalization of individuals. As a case in point, schools provide many labels on students regarding their perceived academic ability such as gifted or learning disabled. A postmodernist is very concerned with such labels and makes a concerted effort to eliminate them from the school experience because of the latent messages of inequality and inhumanity that the labels emit. *Jonathan Kozol* (b. 1936) is a well-known education critic who occasionally reveals his postmodern colors. Kozol, a former teacher, devoted his entire literary career toward shedding light on economic and racial inequality he saw imbedded within the school's latent curriculum. For example, Kozol (1967) unveiled the bigotry of his colleagues and the subpar educational practices toward poor African Americans at the Boston-based school where he spent his first year as a high school English teacher. Advocates of postmodernists, like Kozol, state that they propel the school experience toward improvement and foster a critical awareness of the latent curriculum. Critics of postmodernism state that its quest to investigate schools exclusively for their faults amounts to a propaganda campaign against the school that promotes a public distrust of an institution that contributes to society in a general positive manner.

Summary

When teachers craft their lessons and share them with their students, they are engaging in pedagogy. Teachers' pedagogy is influenced by an underlying philosophy of education. This chapter focused on a continuum of teaching philosophies that flavor a teacher's pedagogy, ranging from the conservative to the progressive to the radical. Teachers who seek to be creative-generative in their craft may fit anywhere on this philosophical continuum. Teachers may exclusively identify with a particular philosophy on the continuum but, more often than not, gravitate toward some philosophies and combine them to fit their own personality, skills, and predilections.

A significant difference between the conservative and progressive tradition is its emphasis on subject matter as opposed to the nature of the learner. Conservatives generally emphasize cultural transmission through a sturdy curricular experience with subject matter. Progressives, on the other hand, place an emphasis on the development on the child and their growth as a whole child. A split within the progressive tradition reveals that not all progressives believed that the nature of the learner should be the sole emphasis of the curriculum. While romantic naturalists emphasize, almost exclusively, upon the child's interests and abilities, the experimentalists placed additional emphasis upon the need to gravitate the curriculum toward subject matter and the aims of democracy. The radical tradition provides a critique of schools and their role as a tool of the powerful to sway society toward their own interests and as a means to sustain the marginalization of some populations.

Reflective Exercises

1. Consider your favorite teacher(s) in your own school experience. Why were they your favorite? Where would you place them on the philosophy continuum and why?
2. Which of the philosophical traditions have primary control of the contemporary public school curriculum?
3. John Dewey is heavily promoted in teacher education programs. However, an argument is often made that Dewey is seldom practiced by teachers in the classroom. If this is true, why? If this is not true, why not?

4. George Counts contended that schools indoctrinate students to support those who are already economically and politically powerful, therefore teachers should counter this indoctrination by politicizing their classroom against the powerful. Do you agree or disagree with Counts' points? Explain.

References

Adler, M. J., & Van Doren, C. (1972). *How to read a book.* New York, NY: Simon and Schuster.

Bagley, W. (1907). *Classroom management.* New York, NY: Macmillan.

Counts, G. S. (1932). *Dare the schools build a new social order?* New York, NY: The John Day Co.

Counts, G. S. (1969). Should the teacher always be neutral? *The Phi Delta Kappan, 51*(4), 186–189.

Dewey, J. (1989) *How we think: A restatement of the relation of reflective thinking to the educative process.* In J. A. Boydston (Ed.), *John Dewey: The later works 1925–1953, volume 8: 1933* (pp. 105–342). Carbondale, IL: Southern Illinois University Press. (Originally published in 1933)

Dewey, J. (1938). *Experience and education.* New York, NY: Free Press.

Friere, P. (1982). *The pedagogy of the oppressed.* New York, NY: The Continuum.

Kozol, J. (1967). Death at an early age: The destruction of the hearts and minds of negro children in the Boston public schools. New York, NY: Houghton Mifflin.

Kuhn, D. (2011). What is scientific thinking and how does it develop? In U. Goswami (Ed.), *The Wiley-Blackwell handbook of childhood cognitive development* (2nd ed.; pp. 497–523). Hoboken, NJ: Blackwell. https://doi.org/10.1002/9781444325485.ch19

Lillard, A., & Else-Quest, N. (2006). The early years: Evaluating Montessori education. *Science, 313*(5795), 1893–1894.

Lippman, W. (1922). *Public opinion.* New York, NY: Harcourt, Brace.

Schoenfeld, A. H., & Sloane, A. H. (Eds.). (2016). *Mathematical thinking and problem solving.* New York, NY: Routledge.

Tanner, D., & Tanner, L. (1995). *Curriculum development.* New York, NY: Macmillan.

Wineburg, S. (2001). *Historical thinking and other unnatural acts: Charting the future of teaching the past.* Philadelphia, PA: Temple University Press.

7

Efficiency and School

Fourteen-year old Johnny Sumner was a polite boy who worked very hard in school. Despite his effort, Johnny struggled to achieve good grades in his eighth grade math class. Mr. Tom Sims, the math teacher, taught the class in a hurried manner. The custom in the class was Mr. Sims sitting at his desk with an overhead projector at his side, busily writing down formulas and showcasing his ability to solve those problems. The entire eighth grade class followed along with Mr. Sims, writing as fast as they could. At the conclusion of each week, Mr. Sims gave a written exam on the math exercises covered during the week. Johnny could not manage to keep up with his classmates and he began to panic. One afternoon, after school, Johnny came home from the bus and went straight to his room and closed the door—without giving his customary greeting to his mother. Johnny's mom knew something was wrong and went to see what was wrong with her son. She found him sitting on his bed with tears raining down his red cheeks. "What's wrong, Johnny? Did something happen at school today?"

Paradoxes of the Public School, pages 91–102
Copyright © 2019 by Information Age Publishing
All rights of reproduction in any form reserved.

Johnny wiped his eyes with his shirt sleeve and amidst his sad wheezing, Johnny told his mom everything: "I got an F today on my math test, and I really tried. I just can't keep up in class. Mr. Sims goes too fast for me." Johnny's mother responded with a question: "How are the other students doing in class?" "Not as bad as me," Johnny replied, "I got the worst grade in the class." While disappointed, this came as no surprise to Johnny's mom since she recently had a parent–teacher conference with Mr. Sims, who shared his own concerns about Johnny's performance but offered no advice outside of his need to work harder in preparation for the weekly tests. Knowing that contacting Mr. Sims would not help, Johnny's mom called the school and scheduled a meeting the next morning with Mrs. Alice Grimes, the principal.

Upon meeting Mrs. Grimes, Johnny's mother kindly shared her concerns about her son: "Mrs. Grimes, I came here to talk to you about Johnny. He is really struggling in Mr. Sims' math class and it's bothering him. Mr. Sims told me he needs to work harder, but he is working as hard as he can. He simply cannot keep up the pace in the class. Frankly, Mrs. Grimes, I don't know what to do." Mrs. Grimes sat back in her chair in a moment of thought and asked Johnny's mom a question: "Do you think that Johnny should take the intermediate math class with Mrs. Rhodes instead of the general class with Mr. Sims?" Johnny's mom responded, "Well, I had that thought but it will take him away from his friends and I am afraid that it could hurt his chances to go to college if he cannot succeed at math. I don't think the intermediate math will challenge him enough." "It looks like the general math is too challenging for Johnny," Mrs. Grimes replied. "Do you have another section of general math that Johnny could take, I think another teacher might be able to help him out?" Johnny's mom inquired. "I'm sorry, but we're a small school and Mr. Sims is our only general math teacher. So, that is not an option." said Mrs. Grimes.

While Chapter 6 stressed the role that the pedagogical progressives played in shaping how we envision the craft of teaching, this chapter focuses upon the role that the administrative progressives played in shaping how we organize and operate school. As we saw earlier in Chapter 5, the administrative progressives successfully reformed the public school toward utilitarian purposes that emphasized efficiency. There have been many efforts to change the public school to make it more efficient, most recently being the rise of high-stakes standardized testing. However, this chapter is historically grounded in the early 20th century and two significant changes took place at this juncture that reflect, arguably better than any other change, the role that efficiency plays in the American public school experience: school organization and curricular tracking.

The nature of change is that, over time, it becomes fixated as a conventional practice. This chapter will shed light on the changes brought forth by the factory school model that, while not a model most conducive to a child's growth and development as a reflective person, nevertheless became an accepted way to conduct the school's educational mission. As a result, students like Johnny Sumner often get cast aside in a system designed to be efficient but not necessarily effective in meeting his academic needs. Likewise, curricular tracking is a widely conventional practice that results in a widespread disparity in the quality of educational experiences provided to some children as opposed to others. The paradox that grounds this chapter is as follows:

> When schools adopt changes in the name of efficiency, they often originate as good ideas but, once in place, they appear to go bad when it comes to providing a quality educational experience for children.

School Management and Organization

It is a common misnomer to believe that an institution's structure and organization exists in a vacuum. In other words, some people believe that institutions operate in a certain manner because that is how they are supposed to operate. It is paramount that we reflect on the role that human choice, in the midst of historical context, played in how school functions.

By the turn of the 19th century, the American public school was shaped by nationalism and industrialism. As we saw in Chapter 2, public education was pushed by several leaders as a means to support a freshly minted democratic nation. The United States was not alone in this endeavor to push for public education as a means to foster nationalism. In fact, much of Europe was also embroiled in a wave of nationalism (stemming from the end of the Napoleonic Wars) where individual nations sought to form their own social cohesion and propel their nation toward economic prosperity. Frankly, the public school made a lot of sense to these nations. In the United States, Horace Mann fought for publicly funded education in the 1830s at a time when both labor groups and middle-class reformers saw the benefits of mass public schooling. Therefore, the historical backdrop of the advent of the American public school is that it emerged simultaneously with other Western nations to serve political and economic interests.

As we saw in Chapter 5, the administrative progressive movement emerged by the turn of the 20th century with a heavy emphasis on utilitarian school reforms in mind. These reforms meshed well with the overarching wave of interest in social efficiency that swept the nation at the time. Reformers such as Frederick Taylor promoted a system of factory management that placed an emphasis on efficiency in labor and production. This system of factory management meshed well with the formal education system that our nation inherited from English colonists. If you recall from Chapter 1, the English colonists sought to promote social cohesion and foster mass literacy amongst their children, and deemed formal schooling as the best means to accomplish those goals (see the Massachusetts Law of 1647). This system deviated from the informal approach of delivering education that Native Americans practiced. Unlike the formal approach of schooling, Native Americans relied heavily on families and communities to comprehensively educate their children. In contrast, schools since the colonial era would forever resemble how other institutions managed themselves. For instance, there is a board overseeing an entire school district, a head district administrator (superintendent) serving as the equivalent to a chief executive office (CEO) of the school district, and there are mid-level managers (principals) overseeing individual schools within the district. This group consists of the primary authority figures who oversee the school system, including policy measures as well as the performance of faculty and staff to deliver the educational experience (product) to students (customers). This administrative group is held accountable to the public at the local and state level and, in some areas, the federal level. Whether or not they actually provide an educational experience is debatable, and has been a contested source of debate for quite some time.

The Prussian Straw-Man

While the administrative progressives pushed school reforms that corroborated with a larger wave of social efficiency, many critics of education claim that the modern school system was actually shaped by a *Prussian model* from the turn of the 19th century. Prussia, now part of modern-day Germany, was a military power in Europe in the early 19th century. The general narrative surrounding the critics' claim is that the Prussians created a school system to serve its military and economic interests. The Prussian model of schooling, therefore, emphasized docility and obedience to authority. Although scholarship is lacking to fully substantive these claims, they nevertheless have a life of their own in contemporary criticism of the American public school (e.g., Brooks, 2012; Gatto, 2009; Khan, 2012). These criticisms point out that the Prussians fostered a *factory model of schooling* that brought about age-based education, a prescribed curriculum for each age group, and architecture that stressed uniformity that still exists. In sum, the school functions much like a factory according to this criticism. While these claims may have some shade of truth behind them, those who make the claims often do so while proposing a reform of their own that they believe to be an improvement over current practices of the contemporary school experience. However, these critics seldom mention common educational practices of the late 19th century that, while not usually associated with the factory-model of schooling, are viewed as antiquated and subpar by today's standards. As a case in point, the *Lancaster method* (often referred to as the monitorial system) positioned the teacher to select student "helpers" to teach a particular lesson to other students. Critics of the contemporary school experience who chastise its use of the factory-model of schooling also fail to mention that school does not always function as a factory. For instance, teachers are provided leeway to be creative-generative and to foster meaningful lessons for students and students are usually provided opportunity to be creative and to play. Of course, the argument can be made that the factory-model system limits the creative freedom of teachers and students. But, the point here is that creative freedom seldom exists in a true factory model, so the analogy may not be always helpful in understanding the complex nature of school. Therefore, the employment of a villainous Prussian school model may merely be a simplistic straw-man argument aimed to challenge the very real limitations of school to actually deliver an educational experience to students. The cold reality is that mass education is much more challenging than mass schooling.

Despite the flaws behind critics' seemingly fallacious argument against Prussia's sinister-like influence on schools, many thoughtful and insightful points about the limitations of school exist within their argument. Many critical voices of school organization emerged in the 1960s and 1970s that employed the latent curriculum as a lens to uncover problematic issues with how schools operate. As the public school embraced Frederick Taylor's concept of scientific management, often called *Taylorism*, school administrators envisioned themselves more as business executives and managers and less as educational philosophers (Callahan, 1964). This transition, according to several educational critics, reinforced a preexisting issue with school: It emphasized schooling over education. Table 7.1 provides a simple analysis of some characteristics that separate schooling and education. While the characteristics of schooling will inevitably be different from education, the aim of schools should nonetheless strive to focus on promoting the characteristics of education within the limited school structure. Critics, such as Callahan (1964), assert that it became more challenging to promote education in schools once Taylorism depersonalized the relationship between

TABLE 7.1 The Nature of Schooling as Opposed to Education		
Analytical Category	**Schooling**	**Education**
Pace	Time-oriented	Lifelong
Structure	Formally prepared	Open-ended
Knowledge	Separated by disciplines	Comprehensive
Growth	Externally directed by teacher	Internally directed through inquiry

leadership and students. As a result, according to these critics, schools that foster a personalized experience between leadership and students would be a noteworthy exception. *Jules Henry* (1904–1969), a noted anthropologist, questioned the role and effect of authority throughout the school environment in what he called a "vulnerability system." Henry (1966) argued that fear of punishment permeated throughout the school experience because those closest to the educational mission of the school, teachers and students, were vulnerable to managers overseeing them. The result, according to Henry, was that student inquiry was stifled out of fear that it would disrupt the structure and order of the school.

Henry's theory of the vulnerability system is especially applicable with the implementation of *compulsory schooling*. Compulsory schooling is the legal requirement that students must attend school. The first compulsory school attendance law was in Massachusetts in 1852. The argument here is that students are more vulnerable in a system that they must attend, sometimes against their wishes. After all, there are few compulsory actions placed upon citizens in the United States: School falls in the category of paying taxes and male registration for the selective service. *Ivan Illich* (1926–2002), a scholar and social activist, made some of the most forceful arguments against the compulsory nature of schooling. Illich (1970) asserted that authentic learning happens casually and that school structure impeded upon this casual phenomenon. In fact, Illich foresaw the possibilities of social networking, spurred by digital technologies, decades before the advent of the Internet. He proposed that, in place of formalized schooling, libraries use computer programs to match individuals' academic interests so they can jointly explore that interest.

The administrative progressives built upon a model of schooling introduced to America by the English colonists. Schools essentially exist as synthetic creations to propel individuals, and society as whole, toward being educated. Efficiency, more so than education, was a central aim of the administrative progressives when they sought to shape the public school closer toward a business model than it had before. Figures from the pedagogical progressive movement, most notably Maria Montessori, devised schools that they believed fostered an environment more conducive to learning than what children would otherwise experience in a traditional school experience shaped by the administrative progressives. The struggle to make school centered more on education, rather than cold efficiency, remains to this day. However, as you will see with curricular tracking, attempts to meet students' learning needs while still satisfying a school experience shaped by the administrative progressives, may produce damaging results.

Curricular Tracking

In order to understand the promises and pitfalls of curricular tracking, it is necessary to re-familiarize ourselves with G. Stanley Hall. Hall, as you may recall from Chapter 5, was a renowned psychologist known for his leading role in the child study movement of the late 19th century. Hall's work, in many ways, represented the school's need to meet the curricular needs of the learner. The child study movement exhibited research-based facts proving that children function at various academic, emotional, and social levels. Therefore, schools should adjust instruction toward the ability level of the student. This notion is reflective of the pedagogical progressives' interest in the teaching and learning of students. The administrative progressives, however, focused on efficiency in school management and organization. Hall believed that children should learn in an academically homogenous setting to fit their curricular needs. This idea, spurred by the administrative progressives, of forming homogeneous learning groups is the basic premise behind curricular tracking. Hall essentially served as a bridge between the pedagogical progressives and the administrative progressives in the area of meeting curricular needs of students.

Hall's beliefs on homogenous learning groups sprouted from his adherence to *social Darwinism*, a belief in the biological determination of the human race. In sum, social Darwinists, like Hall, assert Charles Darwin's evolutionary theory of natural selection and its concept of the "survival of the fittest" applies to the worthiness of individual humans. Therefore, Hall (1904) believed that the Committee of Ten's recommendation in 1893 for a standardized curriculum in the high school, devoid of recognizing individual differences, was especially wrong-headed because, as he put it, it ignored "the great army of incapables" (p. 510). *Curricular tracking* was born out of this struggle, spearheaded by Hall, to create efficiently organized learning experiences unique to particular groups.

The primary aim of curricular tracking is to create a homogenous instructional target for the teacher. The hope imbedded within tracking is that a child's learning needs are met and that high achievers are not "dragged down" by a teacher's tendency to meet the academic ability of the lowest achievers in a classroom setting. Curricular tracking, therefore, involves sorting students into instructional groups based upon a series of judgements of students' academic performance such as a test score or a recommendation of a teacher. Perhaps the most helpful way to understand tracking is to define it as *between* class grouping. This means that students identified at one academic level are literally in different classes than their peers identified at another academic level. This type of sifting and sorting is more typical in the high school curriculum, but can occasionally be found in certain elementary settings. The grouping within a tracked system manifests itself in two different ways within the school curriculum. One way is through wholesale curricular tracking where an entire district tracks the students to take all subjects (i.e., English, math, science, social studies) at a particular ability level. The other way tracking may be manifested in the curriculum is a subject-specific approach where students, for example, may take an advanced level English course but a general level Math course. As you can see in Figure 7.1, the courses are separated for each identifiable academic level (basic, intermediate, general, and advanced). In this curricular structure, it is difficult for a student to move from one level to another in the midst of a year and in some cases, with particular linear-based subjects such as math, throughout their entire schooling experience.

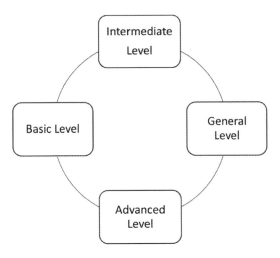

Figure 7.1 Curricular tracking as between class grouping.

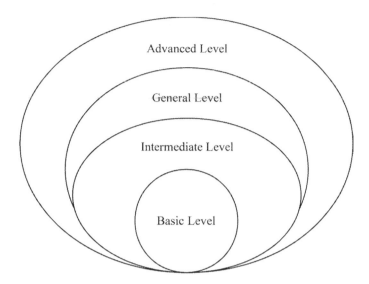

Figure 7.2 Ability grouping as within class grouping.

Ability grouping is an instructional approach that is widely practiced in schools, particularly but not exclusively at the elementary level, and is sometimes mistaken for curricular tracking. Put simply, ability grouping can best be defined as *within* class grouping. With ability grouping, students within a class are identified at a particular academic ability level and are grouped accordingly. A teacher may teach the whole class together but will allot time in class to meet with particular ability groups to assist them with certain skills such as reading. As you can see in Figure 7.2, the ability levels are housed within the same larger circle, much like ability groups are housed together within the whole class. Unlike curricular tracking, mobility between ability groups is fluid. For instance, it is feasible and often desired that a student in an intermediate level group may advance to a general level group at some point in the class. Teachers who perform ability grouping par excellence do so discreetly, without fanfare in the class that one group is advanced over another.

Criticisms of Tracking

Tracking, while a widespread conventional practice in school, is riveted with public criticism. Much of the criticism pointed against tracking revolve around the fear that it perpetuates the social Darwinist perspective on humanity that G. Stanley Hall, the leading pioneer for curricular tracking, believed. Jeannie Oakes, a notable professor of education at UCLA, conducted exhaustive examinations of curricular tracking and concluded that it undeniably produced disparate educational experiences. In her renowned book *Keeping Track: How Schools Structure Inequality,* Oakes (2005) contrasted interesting results from questionnaire data taken from students at various curricular tracks. An example of a question asked was: "What is the most important thing you have learned so far in this class?" Table 7.2 provides a sampling of Oakes' results to this question. As you can see, the data results consistently revealed that students in higher tracks employed critical inquiry and analysis in their coursework whereas those in the lower tracks took away views that their coursework was either useless or it reflected mostly fact-based knowledge or data entry skills that they either had to memorize or mindlessly perform. Using this type of data, Oakes proceeded to form conclusions on the disparity of the learning experiences for each curricular track (see Table 7.3 for a listing of these conclusions). Oakes also noted, among other things, that students in high tracks were more likely to have qualified and experienced teachers and were more apt to be in an engaging and friendly classroom atmosphere than their peers in low tracks.

Oakes is not alone with her criticisms of tracking. For instance, some critics of the practice (e.g., Burris, 2015) claim that curricular tracking stratifies the school experience in such a way that students are increasingly segregated by social class and race. Popular culture also weighs in on tracking. In the highly acclaimed political documentary, *Waiting for Superman* (Beck et al., 2011), tracking is portrayed as a morbid practice that entraps students away from living out their potential. Curricular tracking, like the so-called "factory-model" structure of the school, has few outspoken allies but persists as a convention on the school experience. Often times, efficiency is a more compelling justification of a practice than is educational equity in the American school experience.

TABLE 7.2 Answers to the Survey Question: "What is the Most Important Thing You Have Learned so Far in This Class?"

High-Track	Low-Track
Greek philosophy. Renaissance philosophy, humanities. How to write essays and do term papers. The French Revolution. HISTORY! —Social Studies (Junior High)	A few lessons which have not very much to do with history. (I enjoyed it). —Social Studies (Junior High)
Learned to change my thought processes in dealing with higher mathematics and computers. —Math (Senior High)	Really, I have learned nothing. Only my roman numerals. I knew them, but not very good. I could do better in another class. —Math (Senior High)

Source: Oakes (2005, pp. 67–72).

TABLE 7.3 Grouping-Related Differences in Learning Opportunities	
High-Group Advantages	**Low-Group Disadvantages**
Curriculum emphasizing concepts, inquiry, and problem solving	Curriculum emphasizing low-level facts and skills
Stress on students developing as autonomous thinkers	Stress on teaching students to follow rules and procedures
More time spent on instruction	More time spent on discipline or socializing
More active and interactive learning activities	More worksheets and seat-work
Computers used as learning tools	Computers used as tutors or electronic worksheets
More qualified and experienced teachers	More uncertified and inexperienced teachers
Extra enrichment activities and resources	Few enrichment opportunities
More engaging and friendly classroom atmosphere	More alienating and hostile classroom atmosphere
Hard work a likely classroom norm	"Not working" a likely classroom norm

Source: Oakes (2005, p. 228).

Summary

As the American public school expanded at the turn of the 20th century, to include more students, the administrative progressives spearheaded reforms designed to foster an efficient system designed to deliver educational services to the public. When schools adopt reforms that aspire toward efficiency, the quality of an educational experience may be sacrificed. This chapter addressed two such reforms: the structure and organization of the school to mirror the management suggestions of Frederick Taylor, and the implementation of curricular tracking.

The structure and organization of school implemented by administrative progressives built upon the formal structure put in place centuries earlier by the English colonists. Eventually, it relied heavily on compulsory student attendance, pace, and an unrelated schedule of coursework that did not necessarily foster critical inquiry or an overall enjoyment of learning amongst students experiencing it.

Curricular tracking is a practice aimed at providing an educational experience that meets learners' needs while also assuring that low-achieving students do not drag down high-achieving students in the comprehensive school system. It provides a homogenous instructional target for teachers to focus their attention on. Critics of tracking assert that it produces a disparate educational experience between high-achieving and low-achieving students. Critics also warn that tracking, unlike in-class ability grouping, entraps students onto a particular track for the remainder of the school experience, regardless of the students' potential to rise in ability level.

Reflective Exercises

1. How, if at all, do public schools and factories mirror each other in their structure and organization? Explain.
2. Is the conventional public school the best means to deliver education to the public?
3. What is your experience with curricular tracking? How about the experiences of others you may have known?
4. How might schools better meet learning needs of students?

References

Beck, C., Guggenheim, D., Kimball, B., Chilcott, L., Strickland, B., Roland, E., . . . Legend, J. (2011). *Waiting for "Superman"* [Documentary film]. Hollywood, CA: Paramount Home Entertainment.

Brooks, D. (2012, March 22). The relationship school. *New York Times.* Retrieved from https://www.nytimes.com/2012/03/23/opinion/brooks -the-relationship-school.html

Burris, C. C. (2015). *On the same track: How schools can join the twenty-first-century struggle against resegregation.* North Palm Beach, FL: Beacon Press.

Callahan, R. E. (1964). *Education and the cult of efficiency.* Chicago, IL: University of Chicago Press.

Gatto, J. T. (2009). *Weapons of mass instruction: A school teacher's journey through the dark world of compulsory schooling.* Gabriola Island, Canada: New Society.

Hall, G. S. (1904). *Adolescence: Its psychology and its relations to physiology, anthropology, sociology, sex, crime, religion, and education* (Vols. I & II). New York, NY: D. Appleton.

Henry, J. (1966). Vulnerability and education. *Teachers College Record, 68*(2), 135–145.

Illich, I. (1970). *Deschooling society.* New York, NY: Harper and Row.

Khan, S. (2012). *The one world schoolhouse: Education reimagined.* New York, NY: Twelve.

Oakes, J. (2005). *Keeping track.* New Haven, CT: Yale University Press.

8

Freedom and School

Emmanuel Smith was the new language arts teacher at Cedar High School. He was tall, articulate, and brash in his commentary on social issues. He believed that it was his responsibility, as a teacher, to foster social and political consciousness amongst his students. At the start of the school year, Emmanuel assigned students in his high school American literature class a series of pieces from the collected works of W. E. B. Dubois, the noted African-American scholar and activist from the early 20th century. The assignment of these readings fostered great interest amongst the students, leading one of them, Kayla Chiles, to write an editorial in the school newspaper entitled "America Oppresses the Poor." It was an essay that focused on how the American economic and political system favors the wealthy and perpetuates the impoverished conditions of too many Americans.

The phone rang one morning in the office of Al Kushton, Cedar High School's principal. The call was from an irate parent who read the newspaper and threatened to contact school board members about the "un-American"

Paradoxes of the Public School, pages 103–118
Copyright © 2019 by Information Age Publishing
All rights of reproduction in any form reserved.

activities promoted in the school. Mr. Kushton called Kayla into his office and found out that Emmanuel Smith's class served as an inspiration for her new found political views. At the conclusion of that day, Mr. Kushton called Emmanuel Smith into his office. Mr. Kushton started the conversation by stating to Emmanuel: "I hear that you're responsible for this editorial in the newspaper." Emmanuel's eyebrows raised in surprise. "What do you mean?" Emmanuel replied. "Kayla told me that she's getting these anti-American ideas from your class," Mr. Kushton said. "Well, I want my students to critically think on important issues of our day—and yes, challenge conventional thought. I do not see how that is un-American," Emmanuel responded. "Ok, I heard enough. We're here to teach our students how to be good Americans. I'm hearing from parents who are outraged about what you're doing in class. Teach the curriculum given to you and do not include any controversial political opinions. Your class is not the place for such things!" Mr. Kushton demanded. Emmanuel was stunned. He politely walked out of the office and back to his classroom with the following questions racing in his mind: "What just happened? What do I do now?"

Our story about Emmanuel Smith's dilemma resonates with the threats to some teachers' freedom that exist today. Emmanuel's experience with public pushback and censorship from school administration harkens us back to the 1930s when the teaching profession experienced a form of radicalization and later a widespread effort to thwart teachers' freedoms. During the 1930s, the United States was mired in a cataclysmic economic depression. By 1930, for instance, nearly 4 million people were unemployed. A mere year later this number doubled to 8 million (Browers, 1969). From 1929–1932, 15% of all American banks failed (Lind, 2012). This economic collapse, to some, signaled the downfall of American capitalism and the beginnings of an inevitable communist revolution similar to the one Russia had as it transitioned toward becoming the Soviet Union over a decade earlier. Some signs pointed to this happening in the United States such as the fact that "100,000 Americans applied for six thousand job openings in the Soviet Union" (Lind, 2012, p. 270). As always, the events in society affected the school. A group of Progressive educators, spearheaded by George Counts as their intellectual leader, sought to persuade American teachers to reach for political power and push the nation toward a socialist revolution. As we saw in Chapter 6, this context became the groundwork where social reconstructionism was planted.

Individuals and groups with sympathy toward socialist ideals, often called collectivism, was not uncommon nor hidden in the 1930s. As a case in point, from 1929 to 1934, the American Historical Association organized a commission to study and improve social studies education. The commission consisted of membership of individuals well known for their collectivist stance on society, most notably George Counts and the noted historian Charles Beard, who were not shy about sharing their perspective to other educational leaders (Schul, 2013). Yet, events within the American political landscape changed the course of the country toward an adamant fear and disavowal of communism. The United States and Soviet Union, once allies during World War II, became fierce enemies beginning in the 1940s. Any inkling toward support of communist ideas became cast in the eyes of society as a form of betrayal toward the United States and a danger to individual liberty throughout the nation. This fear percolated into the formation of watchdog groups such as the House of Representatives' Un-American Activities Committee. Individuals in the media, academia, and entertainment fields were closely scrutinized for harboring communists in their midst. The American public school also felt the heat from this scrutiny. Some teachers and school curriculum fell victim to this nationwide purge of communist sympathy.

The American public school has been anointed by the public as the caretaker of the nation's democracy. It is the site where the public expects individuals to be taught critical inquiry, problem-solving, deliberation, and tolerance of others' differences. Yet, the public school is also anointed by the public as the caretaker of national ideals, moral character, and general good stewardship of American culture. These expectations often collide with one another, leading dueling factions to arise that challenge the role of school in preserving freedom. This chapter examines the lines within this complex collision, particularly as it relates to rights of teachers and students and the battle for what should or should not be included in the school curriculum. The central paradox of this chapter, therefore, is as follows:

The public expects the school to be a laboratory of democracy yet also expects it to preserve social order and morality.

Teacher Freedom

The American public school operates as a decentralized system in that its schools are locally controlled with state oversight. This means that the values and expectations of specific local communities matter a great deal in determining the amount of freedom that a teacher may have within that school. While a teacher's freedom, both at a personal and professional level, is intrinsically bound within the context of local communities, there are nonetheless certain guidelines that are generalizable for understanding teacher freedom throughout the country. It is important that teachers know these general guidelines so that they can be cautious in their practices and know when to seek additional professional advice. This section takes a look at those guidelines that govern teachers' behavior and, when possible, we will examine legal precedent that reinforce those guidelines.

Teaching is an extremely moral profession (Labaree, 2004). Teachers are caretakers of children and the professional expectation is that they are moral, wise, and benevolent when caring for children. We already saw in Chapter 1 that teachers fall under the legalistic guidelines of *in loco parentis*, or "in place of parents," which means that teachers have the legal authority to compel students, in some cases, against their will. For instance, teachers may assign students homework or may assign a punishment to the student. As a result, like a parent, teachers need to care for the well-being of her or his students. It is for this reason, for example, that a teacher should never engage in a romantic relationship with any of their students. Doing so is a breach of trust between the community and teacher and grounds for punishment or dismissal of the teacher.

Since states pay considerable attention and money toward its public schools, it is customary for them to declare a code of ethics for teachers. These codes provide guidelines that states expect teachers to follow. Figure 8.1 provides an example of one such code of ethics created for teachers to adhere in the state of Minnesota. If you notice in the Minnesota code, there is an emphasis upon teachers' benevolence toward students, teachers' use of power, teachers' compliance to state laws, and professional behavior of the teacher toward colleagues and students. However, these guidelines are broad and open to interpretation.

While the code of ethics primarily focuses on the teacher's behavior in the classroom, how they wield power, and professionalism with colleagues and students, it does not sufficiently address guidelines surrounding the personal behavior of the teacher outside the parameters of the school. For instance, can a teacher frequent bars or gain extra employment as a stripper? This is a matter that separates the teacher from many other professions. As a case in point, a business person can frequent a bar without giving it much thought that his job would be on the line. The teacher, on the other hand, needs to consider some factors before engaging in behavior that might be shunned by a local community. The overarching umbrella idea that governs what is illegal teacher behavior is called *conduct unbecoming*. Conduct unbecoming is used as a legalistic idea to make a case against

A. A teacher shall provide professional education services in a nondiscriminatory manner.

B. A teacher shall make reasonable effort to protect the student from conditions harmful to health and safety.

C. In accordance with state and federal laws, a teacher shall disclose confidential information about individuals only when a compelling professional purpose is served or when required by law.

D. A teacher shall take reasonable disciplinary action in exercising the authority to provide an atmosphere conducive to learning.

E. A teacher shall not use professional relationships with students, parents, and colleagues to private advantage.

F. A teacher shall delegate authority for teaching responsibilities only to licensed personnel.

G. A teacher shall not deliberately suppress or distort subject matter.

H. A teacher shall not knowingly falsify or misrepresent records or facts relating to that teacher's own qualifications or to other teachers' qualifications.

I. A teacher shall not knowingly make false or malicious statements about students or colleagues.

J. A teacher shall accept a contract for a teaching position that requires licensing only if properly or provisionally licensed for that position.

Figure 8.1 Code of ethics for Minnesota teachers (2017).

a teacher that he or she engaged in unprofessional behavior, especially as it relates to moral issues. Conduct unbecoming as a concept of action for dismissal of a teacher for reasons of immorality that relies heavily upon whether there is a discernible *nexus* between the the teacher's private behavior and her or his performance in the classroom (Schimmel, Stellman, Conlon, & Fischer, 2014). The interpretation of whether or not a personal behavior of a teacher affects her or his classroom performance is widely open for interpretation. The easiest applications of conduct unbecoming involve a criminal offense, such as a felony. Such offenses qualify as *prima facie*, or face value evidence, of an unfitness to teach. If the behavior involves violent or otherwise harmful actions toward children, the teacher is more than likely at risk of being dismissed. However, many other behaviors depend heavily upon the context of that behavior within the scope of the local community. For instance, attending a bar is likely no problem and a singular instance of public intoxication likely would not be grounds for dismissal (Schimmel, Stellman, Conlon, & Fischer, 2014). However, frequenting it daily and exhibiting severe public intoxication, especially on school nights, could fall under grounds for dismissal if the public had knowledge of this fact. To highlight the importance of context in this regard, a health teacher would likely be more susceptible than an English teacher in this situation since knowledge of the teacher's alcohol abuse demonstrates a lack of integrity whenever he or she taught future health lessons. Likewise, a teacher who works a side job as a stripper would be more vulnerable to dismissal if the public knew it, especially students under her or his care since some communities may deem the behavior as a distraction for students. The general rule of thumb in these often difficult areas to navigate is that teachers have the right to a private life as long as their actions do not negatively affect classroom performance.

The scope of what constitutes a negative effect on classroom performance is particularly difficult to understand. In 1949, in the midst of the Cold War between the United States and Soviet Union, the state of New York passed the *Feinberg Law*. The law made it illegal for a teacher to "advocate, advise, teach, or embrace" the overthrow of the United States government. This law aimed particularly at communists such as Irving Adler, a successful high school math teacher, who joined the American Communist Party in 1935. After nearly sixteen years when he began his teaching career, Adler was subpoenaed to testify in front of a Senate subcommittee investigating the influence of communism on the nation's schools (Hevesi, 2012). Eventually, Adler was dismissed by his school district and challenged the dismissal in court. The case found its way to the U.S. Supreme Court in 1952. The court upheld the Feinberg Law in a 6–3 ruling in the case *Adler v. Board of Education of the City of New York* (1952) stating:

> A teacher works in a sensitive area in a schoolroom. There he shapes the attitude of young minds towards the society in which they live. In this, the state has a vital concern. It must preserve the integrity of the schools. That the school authorities have the right and the duty to screen the officials, teachers, and employees as to their fitness to maintain the integrity of the schools as a part of ordered society, cannot be doubted. One's associates, past and present, as well as one's conduct, may properly be considered in determining fitness and loyalty. (para. 24)

While in the midst of the Cold War, the *Adler* case expanded the proximity of conduct unbecoming toward a teacher's political affiliation. Therefore, an individual's constitutional rights of assembly, imbedded in the First Amendment, are narrowed once that person becomes a teacher. However, over a decade later in 1967, the U.S. Supreme Court reversed *Adler* in the pivotal case *Keyishian v. Board of Regents* (1967) declaring, in a 5–4 decision, that the Feinberg Law was unconstitutional. Because of *Keyishian*, many teachers, once dismissed, were reinstated (Hevesi, 2012).

Another well-known case that helps us to understand the proximity of a teacher's freedom is *Pickering v. Board of Education* (1968). The case involves a teacher who wrote an editorial criticizing school officials for their financial decisions in the operation of the school district where he was employed. The district dismissed the teacher, asserting that the teacher's comments posed a detriment to the entire school district since they undermined the school official's authority. The Supreme Court ruled on behalf of the teacher stating that teachers may comment on matters of public interest unless such speech limits the operation of the school and/or the classroom performance of the teacher. The court found no evidence in *Pickering* to justify limiting the teacher's speech. However, a more recent Supreme Court case *Garcetti v. Ceballos* (2006) may have implications that limit teachers' speech. In *Garcetti*, the Court ruled that a government employee's speech is not protected when it involves commentary on their professional duties. In other words, an employee, such as a teacher, may comment on matters of public opinion as long as it does not hinder the performance of the school or the teacher. Therefore, the employee may not comment on matters known exclusively to those within the professional ranks of the organization under scrutiny.

While teachers' sharing of personal views is protected as long as it does not hinder the operation of school or the classroom, what are the boundaries of a teachers' academic freedom in the classroom? As usual, these boundaries are drawn at the local level and may vary depending upon the locality of the school. We saw in Chapter 1 that a teacher may not endorse a particular religion in the classroom. We also saw that states require teachers to teach subject matter (see Figure 1.1) without suppression or distortion. Yet, how may a teacher address political issues in the classroom? Generally, teachers may not politicize the classroom and endorse particular candidates. However, even this is not always easy to navigate. The 2016 candidacy and election of U.S. President Donald Trump challenged some teachers' professional ethics and responsibility. The Trump candidacy involved numerous statements widely criticized as racist, sexist, and generally profane. Many teachers found it difficult to remain politically neutral when they found so much of Trump's candidacy to run contrary to their own classroom's commitments to diversity and inclusivity (Christensen, 2016). It remains a daunting challenge for teachers to create an environment of inclusivity and diversity while also fostering free thought and speech amongst students.

While contemporary times pose new challenges to teachers' academic freedom, the past reveals that teachers' academic freedom has rarely been without some public dispute. Perhaps the most important Supreme Court case that explores a teacher's freedom as it relates to their performance in the classroom is *Parducci v. Rutland* (1970). This case involved a high school English teacher who assigned to her junior class the novel *Welcome to the Monkey House* by Kurt Vonnegut. This assignment led the high school principal to dismiss the teacher because of its content. The teacher challenged the dismissal and the Court sided with her asserting that the school officials failed to demonstrate how the assignment was inappropriate reading for high school juniors or that it disrupted the operation of the school.

At first glance, it may appear that the *Parducci* case put an end to censorship of literature in schools. It did not. *Censorship*, the suppression or prohibition of literature or media, occurs at the local level and originates from parents' expecting teachers to respect their prescribed sense of morality or otherwise appropriate approaches toward schooling. Of course, often as a means to avoid a schism in a community, schools are known to appease some concerned community members who seek to censor literature used in schools. One of the most infamous instances of widespread censorship of literature involved the incremental removal of Harold Rugg's social studies textbook series in the 1940s. *Harold Rugg* (1886–1960) was a professor at Columbia University Teachers College who created a series of social studies textbooks that reflected much of the experimentalist philosophy espoused by progressive educators of the time, such as John Dewey. The textbook series, entitled *Man and His Changing Society*, was widely used in the 1920s and 1930s by high school social studies courses. However, amidst the Cold War, the textbook series came under attack by groups who argued the book promoted ideas, such as socialism, contrary to what they perceived to be American ideals. These critics wrongfully labeled Rugg a communist and many of them never read any of the books they placed under scrutiny (Evans, 2004). Eventually, local school boards throughout the nation banned the series from their schools. Rugg even went on a personal crusade to advocate for his textbook series in front of numerous school boards to no avail (Evans, 2007).

The fate of Rugg's textbooks mirrors the history of many other works of literature in the public school. The American Library Association (ALA) records instances of censorship in pockets of local school communities throughout the nation. Table 8.1 displays a sampling of classic works of literature as well as recent literary works censored, as recorded by the ALA.

Most of the literature censored sprouted from community concerns about the use of language and explicit sexuality. However, some books are viewed as politically dangerous. As a means to understand the variety of

TABLE 8.1 Classic and Contemporary Literature Censored	
Classic Literature Routinely Censored	**Contemporary Literature Under Censorship (2015–2016)**
Catcher in the Rye (J. D. Sallinger) *The Grapes of Wrath* (John Steinbeck) *Of Mice and Men* (John Steinbeck) *To Kill a Mockingbird* (Harper Lee) *The Color Purple* (Alice Walker) *Ulysses* (James Joyce) *The Lord of the Flies* (William Golding) *1984* (George Orwell) *Invisible Man* (Ralph Ellison) *The Adventures of Huckleberry Finn* (Mark Twain)	*The Perks of Being a Wallflower* (Stephen Chbosky) *This Book is Gay* (James Dawson) *Extremely Loud and Incredibly Close* (Jonathan Safran Foer) *Glass* (Ellen Hopkins) *The Kite Runner* (Khaled Hosseini) *The Namesake* (Jhumpa Lahiri) *The Glass Castle: A Memoir* (Jeanette Walls)

Source: American Library Association (www.ala.org)

reasons local schools may have for censuring literary works, Figure 8.2 provides the American Library Association's list of the top ten most challenged books in 2016 along with the reasons for the challenges. As you can see, censorship remains a threat to teachers' academic freedom. Community interests play a role in the classroom curriculum. Unless the teacher is willing to challenge censorship in a court of law, and risk alienation as a result, many teachers succumb to doing what the school and community demands.

Student Freedom

We just saw how local communities' expectations placed upon schools as a means to preserve social order and morality curtails teachers' freedoms. This is so because teachers are charged with the primary role of delivering the school's educational mission. The primary benefactor of the school's services, the students, are those the local community seeks to shape morally. Students' freedoms within a school are different than a teacher. For one, the teacher is an employer of the school while the student is compelled by law to attend school. It may appear, at first glance, that students have no rights in the school whatsoever because of the compulsory nature of school. This is not the case. This section delves into the legal parameters of students' freedom in school.

It is customary for schools to regulate student behavior for the purpose of teaching morality and securing a safe environment. For instance, it is commonplace for schools to form a dress code that prohibits vulgarity, promotes illegal behavior such as underage drinking, and that may be deemed sexually provocative. This does not mean, however, that students are completely stripped of their rights. For instance, we saw in Chapter 1

1. *This One Summer* **written by Mariko Tamaki and illustrated by Jillian Tamaki**

   Reasons: Challenged because it includes LGBT characters, drug use and profanity, and it was considered sexually explicit with mature themes.

2. *Drama* **written and illustrated by Raina Telgemeier**

   Reasons: Challenged because it includes LGBT characters, was deemed sexually explicit, and was considered to have an offensive political viewpoint.

3. *George* **written by Alex Gino**

   Reasons: Challenged because it includes a transgender child, and the "sexuality was not appropriate at elementary levels."

4. *I Am Jazz* **written by Jessica Herthel and Jazz Jennings, and illustrated by Shelagh McNicholas**

   Reasons: Challenged because it portrays a transgender child and because of language, sex education, and offensive viewpoints.

5. *Two Boys Kissing* **written by David Levithan**

   Reasons: Challenged because its cover has an image of two boys kissing, and it was considered to include sexually explicit LGBT content.

6. *Looking for Alaska* **written by John Green**

   Reasons: Challenged for a sexually explicit scene that may lead a student to "sexual experimentation."

7. *Big Hard Sex Criminals* **written by Matt Fraction and illustrated by Chip Zdarsky**

   Reason: Challenged because it was considered sexually explicit.

8. *Make Something Up: Stories You Can't Unread* **written by Chuck Palahniuk**

   Reasons: Challenged for profanity, sexual explicitness, and being "disgusting and all around offensive."

9. *Little Bill* **(series) written by Bill Cosby and illustrated by Varnette P. Honeywood**

   Reason: Challenged because of criminal sexual allegations against the author.

10. *Eleanor & Park* **written by Rainbow Rowell**

    Reason: Challenged for offensive language.

Figure 8.2   Top ten most challenged books in 2016. *Source*: American Library Association (www.ala.org)

that students' exercise of religion is protected as long as it does not lead to a disruption or create a situation that is otherwise pedagogically unfeasible. However, as is the case with teachers, the line between student freedom and a school's desire to secure order and promote morality is often difficult to navigate. Fortunately, the Supreme Court weighed in on some of these issues to provide some guidance regarding the nature of students' freedoms.

Perhaps the most significant case for the security of students' constitutional rights is *Tinker v. Des Moines Independent School District* (1969). In this case, students in a Des Moines school district devised a plan to wear black armbands to school as a form of protest of the U.S. involvement in the Vietnam War. Upon hearing of this plan, school officials quickly created a policy prohibiting students from wearing such armbands. A group of five students, comprised of four siblings and their friend, violated the policy and wore the armbands anyway. This led to the school's suspension of the students. The family of the children claimed that their constitutional right of free speech was violated and challenged the school in a court of law, eventually making it to the U.S. Supreme Court. In a 7–2 decision, the Supreme Court ruled in favor of the children. The Court determined that mere discomfort did not qualify as a disruption in the school. The majority opinion of the court in this case included the following statement regarding students' constitutional rights in school:

> In our system, state-operated schools may not be enclaves of totalitarianism. School officials do not possess absolute authority over their students. Students in school, as well as out of school, are "persons" under our Constitution. They are possessed of fundamental rights which the State must respect, just as they themselves must respect their obligations to the State. (*Tinker v. Des Moines Sch. Dist.*, 1969, para. 27)

Tinker assured that students possess constitutional rights of speech and expression. In the case of the Tinker children, the speech did not cause a disruption nor was it vulgar or otherwise dangerous to the school population.

Two significant Supreme Court cases emerged in the 1980s that curtailed the generous allowance of students' freedoms set by *Tinker*. The first of these cases, *Bethel School District v. Fraser* (1986), focused on student expression. The case involved a high school student who was suspended from school for presenting a campaign speech at a school assembly that was riddled with sexual innuendo. The response from the student audience, among whom were students as young as 14, was predictably boisterous with some making graphic sexually referenced gestures. Still, others in the crowd appeared uncomfortable and embarrassed (Imber, Van Gell, Blockhuis, & Feldman, 2013). Despite being advised ahead of time by teachers to not give the speech and that the school already had a disciplinary rule regarding student use of obscenity, the student who gave the speech still claimed that the school violated his First Amendment right to free speech. The Supreme Court disagreed and decided on behalf of the school. While the Court ruled that the speech under question in *Bethel* was not necessarily disruptive, it was vulgar and thus legally vulnerable to censorship by school officials. The Court provided the following statement explaining their decision:

> The process of educating our youth for citizenship in public schools is not confined to books, the curriculum, and the civics class; schools must teach by example the shared values of a civilized social order. Consciously or otherwise, teachers—and indeed the older students—demonstrate the appropriate form of civil discourse and political expression by their conduct and deportment in and out of class. Inescapably, like parents, they are role models. The schools, as instruments of the state, may determine that the essential lessons of civil, mature conduct cannot be conveyed in a school that tolerates lewd, indecent, or offensive speech and conduct such as that indulged in by this confused boy. (para. 29)

In this decision, the school highlighted the moral nature of the public school experience, stipulating that schools are unique public institutions regarding the parameters of freedom provided its inhabitants. Unlike a government writ large, a school is designed to inculcate morality and civility amongst youth and may, if necessary, punish student behavior that threatens this moral mission of the school.

The second case we will examine is *Hazelwood v. Kuhlmeier* (1988). In *Hazelwood*, a high school principal did not allow for the publication of two articles in the school's student newspaper. The censored articles focused on teen pregnancy and the effect of divorce on teenagers. They contained stories from students in the school, whose names were changed to protect their identity. The principal believed that the articles, which featured references to sexual activity and birth control, were inappropriate for widespread distribution in the school. The students who authored the articles claimed that their First Amendment rights of free press were violated and, after receiving resistance to their concerns from the administration, sought litigation on the matter. The case eventually made it to the Supreme Court with the decision given to the school district. The Court asserted in the decision that "educators do not offend the First Amendment by exercising editorial control over the style and content of student speech in school-sponsored expressive activities so long as their actions are reasonably related to legitimate pedagogical concerns" (*Hazelwood School District v. Kohlmeier*, 1988, para. 36). It is important to note that the school newspaper of interest in *Hazelwood* did not have circulation outside of the school environment where it could be read by the general public. In this case, the newspaper was intrinsically tied to the school curriculum through two journalism courses. However, if the newspaper was a student-centered newspaper, not tied to the school curriculum, it would experience more constitutional protection.

The scope of student freedom is not limited to merely speech. One of the most fundamental freedoms guaranteed to the American citizenry is protection from unreasonable searches and seizures. The Fourth Amendment of the U.S. Constitution provides this protection:

> The right of the people to be secure in their persons, houses, papers, and effects, against unreasonable searches and seizures, shall not be violated, and no Warrants shall issue, but upon probable cause, supported by Oath or affirmation, and particularly describing the place to be searched, and the persons or things to be seized.

However, as is the case with freedom of speech, students' protection from unreasonable searches and seizures is not as stringent as those in the general public. Students' Fourth Amendment rights were clarified by the U.S. Supreme Court in the monumental case *New Jersey v. TLO* (1985). In this case, a high school teacher suspected two female students were violating school policy by smoking in the school's restroom. The teacher took the two students to the vice-principal's office. One of the girls admitted guilt whereas the other, a 14 year old female named TLO in court documents, offered no such admission. The vice principal took TLO's purse and, upon searching, came across a pack of cigarettes and rolling paper. While this evidence alone confirmed TLO's guilt of violating school smoking policy, the rolling paper raised further suspicion and led the vice principal to continue searching the purse. The search resulted in the finding of some marijuana, a wad of money, and an index card listing names of students in debt to TLO, and a pipe, among other things (Perisco, 1998). Eventually, TLO confessed guilt to police but once the school took punitive measures against her, she claimed that her Fourth Amendment rights were violated since the search was conducted without a warrant to justify it. According to the Fourth Amendment, a search warrant may be issued only with probable cause and may only be conducted in a specific area for a specific person or thing. TLO challenged the case in a court of law, eventually being heard by the U.S. Supreme Court. The high court disagreed with TLO. The Court concluded that a school should not be expected to attain a warrant every time it seeks to protect the learning environment. With that stated, the Court believed that students in a school should maintain some level of Fourth Amendment protection, albeit less stringent than experienced by the general public. Therefore, the Court decided in *TLO* that schools may conduct searches and seizures of students upon the basis of reasonable suspicion. This means that the school cannot rely on rumors or an inkling that a student may be engaging in illegal behavior. Rather, the school must have pertinent evidence that would lead one to reasonably conclude a student's guilt. With the situation brought forward in *TLO*, the teacher's accusation, the admission of guilt of one of the students, along with TLO's denial, it was reasonable for the vice-principal to conduct the search of the purse. If the search resulted only the finding of cigarettes, any further search would be unreasonable. However, the initial search led to the finding of new evidence (i.e., rolling paper) that provided evidence for the second, more exhaustive search of the purse. While searches may be conducted by school officials without warrant, its requirement for a search to be based on reasonableness must take into consideration contextual factors such as the students' age, the degree of seriousness of the issue, and the nature of the search (Thomas, Cambron-McCabe, & McCarthy, 2009). Therefore, generally a physically intrusive search demands a higher standard of suspicion. For instance, the theft of two dollars should not be cause for a strip search of a student.

Summary

Schooling in the United States is a moral endeavor. The public expects schools to serve the dual role of being a laboratory of democracy as well as the safeguard of morality and social order in a local community. These two expectations naturally clash whenever contentious issues arise within the scope of a teacher's academic freedom or students' freedom of speech or security. Rather than existing as a pure democracy, the school experience offers teachers and students limited freedom. Teachers' private behavior, for example, must not lead to a disruption in the school experience. Teachers generally have freedom to choose teaching methodologies, curriculum materials, and topics as long as these choices fall within the school's educational mission, is appropriate for the age level and maturity of students, and they do not cause a disruption within the school environment. The local communities, from which schools emerge, may find curricular materials offensive and seek to censor them. Usually teachers comply with the school's request so to avoid litigation and possible alienation in the community.

Students have the constitutionally protected freedom of speech so long as it does not lead to a disruption or violates the moral mission of the school with its vulgarity or offensiveness. Schools may edit the school press, for pedagogical purposes, if it is tied to the school curriculum and exists exclusively within the parameters of the school. Schools may also reasonably search a student without a warrant as long as there is evidence that he or she is practicing behavior that is against school policy.

Reflective Exercises

1. Reflect on the following scenario: A teacher is arrested for dealing drugs in his local community. What should the school do with this teacher upon knowing about this incident?
2. Irving Adler was dismissed from his teaching job in the midst of an anti-communist frenzy during the Cold War years. The Supreme Court later ruled that schools may not dismiss teachers for their political affiliation. However, what if the teacher is known to be a member of a racist and terrorist organization such as the Ku Klux Klan? Does the school have legal grounds to dismiss the teacher in this instance?
3. Look at the list of challenged books in Figure 8.2. Do you think any of these challenges are justified? Would it be constitutional to ban a teacher from using any of the books? Explain.
4. What do you think constitutes a disruption in the learning environment? Consider these scenarios when answering this question: A student wearing a shirt that states "God hates gays"; a student wearing a shirt that states "God loves gays"; a student giving a campaign speech that claims their school engages in racial discrimination, leading to an uproar among school officials, teachers, and students.

References

Adler v. Board of Education of the City of New York. 342 U.S. 485 (1952). Retrieved from the FindLaw database. https://caselaw.findlaw.com/us-supreme-court/342/485.html

Bethel School District vs. Fraser, 478 U.S. 675 (1986). Retrieved from Findlaw database. https://caselaw.findlaw.com/us-supreme-court/478/675.html

Bowers, C. A. (1969). *The progressive educator and the depression: The radical years.* New York, NY: Random House.

Christensen, J. (2016, April 15). Teachers lounge: Teaching in the age of Trump. *PBS Newshour.* Retrieved from https://www.pbs.org/newshour/education/teachers-lounge-teaching-politics-in-the-age-of-trump

Code of Ethics for Minnesota Teachers. (2017). 8710.2100 of Minnesota Administrative Rules in the Office of the Revisor of Statutes.

Evans, R. W. (2004). *The social studies wars: What should we teach the children?* New York, NY: Teachers College Press.

Evans, R. W. (2007). *This happened in America: Harold Rugg and the censure of social studies.* Charlotte, NC: Information Age.

Garcetti v. Ceballos (2006). 547 U.S. 410

Hazelwood School District v. Kohlmeier, 484 U.S. 260 (1988). Retrieved from Findlaw database. https://caselaw.findlaw.com/us-supreme-court/484/260.html

Hevesi, D. (2012, September 27). Irving Adler, teacher fired in red scare, dies at 99. *New York Times.* Retrieved from https://www.nytimes.com/2012/09/27/books/irving-adler-author-of-science-and-math-books-for-the-young-dies-at-99.html

Imber, M., Van Geel, T., Blokhuis, J. C., & Feldman, J. (2013). *Education law.* Abingdon, England: Routledge.

Keyishian v. Board of Regents (1967). 385 U.S. 589.

Labaree, D. F. (2004). *The trouble with ed schools.* New Haven, CT: Yale University Press.

Lind, M. (2012). *Land of promise: An economic history of the United States.* New York, NY: Harper Collins.

New Jersey v. T.L.O. (1985). 469 U.S. 325.

Parducci v. Rutland (1970). 316 F. Supp. 352 (M.D. AL).

Persico, D. A. (1998). *New Jersey VTLO: Drug searches in schools.* New York, NY: Enslow.

Pickering v. Board of Education (1968). 391 U.S. 563.

Schimmel, D., Stellman, L. R., Conlon, C. K., & Fischer, L. (2014). *Teachers and the law.* New York, NY: Pearson Higher Ed.

Schul, J. E. (2013). Ensuing dog fight: The AHA commission on the social studies' testing controversy. *Journal of Educational Administration and History,* *45*(1), 1–27.

Thomas, S. B., Cambron-McCabe, N. H., & McCarthy, M. M. (2009). *Public school law: Teachers' and students' rights.* New York, NY: Pearson.

Tinker v. Des Moines Sch. Dist., 393 U.S. 503 (1969). Retrieved from https://www.law.cornell.edu/supremecourt/text/393/503

9

Segregation and School

Natasha Heyward, a senior at Lincoln High School, is the star student and athlete in her class. Lincoln is an urban school in the heart of the American South. Natasha, an African American, plans to attend Tuskegee University, one of the nation's most acclaimed historically Black universities, once she graduates from Lincoln. Natasha's decision did not come easy for her since her father encouraged her to attend the nearby public university. Unlike Natasha's school experience at Lincoln where she was surrounded exclusively with African American peers, her father attended a very racially diverse Lincoln High School in the 1980s. Lincoln's student population has been entirely African American for nearly a decade. However, Lincoln was more racially diverse when Natasha's father attended. "College is a time of growth and I think it is helpful to be surrounded by people who can relate with what it is like to be Black in America," Natasha told her father on one weekend car ride after visiting Tuskegee. "Well, I can understand that," her father responded, "but I'm afraid things are going back the way your grandparents had it, where we were separated. I know from experience that it is nice to be around a lot of White people when you're in school because that prepares you for real life. But, if you want to go to Tuskegee—I will support your decision. It's an excellent school with a tremendous history." Natasha smiled. "Daddy, I don't want things to go back the way Grandpa had it, but I'm not in charge of that. You taught me to be proud to be Black, and I am." With his hands holding the steering wheel and staring at the windshield, Natasha noticed a tear rolling down her father's cheek. "Natasha," her father said with a smile, "I'm so proud to be your Daddy."

While the United States was mired in the midst of the Cold War during the mid-20th century, the issue of race loomed over the country liked a dark cloud. In fact, the issue looms over us to this day as you can see in the dialogue between Natasha and her father. This chapter is a continuation of Chapter 4's exploration of the African American experience in the United States as it relates with the public school. As we saw in Chapter 4, the African American experience began with slavery up through the Civil War of the 1860s. The American Civil War represents a turning point for African Americans since the means of their marginalization turned from outright slavery toward a discriminatory system called segregation. *Segregation* is the separation of individuals for a particular reason, in this case because of race. Racial segregation in U.S. history is a byproduct of the racist paradigm of White supremacy. Racial segregation was put in place by a population who identified themselves as White as a means to preserve their self-identity by excluding individuals because of race. In other words, since it was illegal to enslave African Americans, White supremacists pushed for separation of the races out of their deeply rooted fear that the White race was threatened of being "polluted" by a Black race. The net result of segregation was further marginalization of African Americans as a means to strip them of their political and cultural power.

There are two primary types of segregation: *de jure* and *de facto*. De jure segregation means it occurred "by law" in that laws were created to ensure the separation of African Americans from the predominant population that identified themselves as White. These laws mostly existed in the southern section of the United States due to its past with slavery and the heightened interaction between races that did not necessarily exist in the northern section of the country. De facto segregation means it occurred "by practice" in that while segregationist laws did not exist but the culture nevertheless practices a separation of the races. These two types of racial segregation in the United States are intrinsically related with one another.

For instance, if a law was suddenly eliminated that once forced separation of individuals from one another for a lengthy period of time, the individuals who were once under that requirement would more than likely continue the practice of separation due to the psychological and cultural habits shaped by the law. This chapter examines the nature of racial segregation in the United States and the desegregation effort of the mid-20th century. We will also explore how racial segregation is actually on the rise amongst the contemporary American public school system. The central paradox of this chapter is as follows:

Racial segregation became illegal in 1954, yet racial segregation is on the rise in contemporary times.

Separate but Equal

As we saw in Chapter 4, the years after the Civil War brought new challenges for African Americans. While the Thirteenth Amendment forbade slavery, free African Americans faced a cultural backlash, primarily from the American South, that sought to marginalize them in odd and cruel ways. This backlash resulted in the rise of terrorist organizations such as the Ku Klux Klan, voter suppression, and Jim Crow segregation. These practices occurred at the state and local levels of the United States, with little intervention from the federal government to protect the freedoms and rights of African Americans. By the latter years of the 19th century, the African American community and their advocates were primed to challenge the practice of racial segregation. A Supreme Court case emerged in 1896, called *Plessy v. Ferguson* (1896), that many African Americans hoped would alter the landscape of racial segregation.

The *Plessy* case involved a challenge to a law based in Louisiana that required racial segregation within railroad cars. The plaintiff in the case, Homer Plessy, was a man classified "Black" by state law and was required to sit in the area of the car designated for those classified as "non-White." In an orchestrated event, Plessy was arrested and proceeded to challenge the segregation law on the grounds that it violated his rights of equal protection under the law guaranteed by the Fourteenth Amendment of the U.S. Constitution. The case went to the Supreme Court whose decision upheld segregation, but with a new twist. The Court ruled that states and local communities may employ segregationist practices without violating the Fourteenth Amendment as long as the separate facilities or services are equal.

This created the infamous *separate but equal doctrine* that emboldened those who favored racial segregation and made it more challenging for its critics to thwart its practice since equality of facilities or services is often difficult to determine. *Justice John Harlan* was the lone dissenter of *Plessy* among the Court who foresaw the civil rights challenges that the new doctrine created:

> Our constitution is colorblind, and neither knows nor tolerates classes among citizens. In respect of civil rights, all citizens are equal before the law . . . What can more certainly arouse race hate, what more certainly create and perpetuate a feeling of distrust between these races, than state enactments, which, in fact, proceed on the ground that colored citizens are so inferior and degraded that they cannot be allowed to sit in public coaches occupied by white citizens? That, as all will admit, is the real meaning of such legislation. (Plessy v. Ferguson, 1896, para. 51)

Justice Harlan envisioned a perpetuation of hatred and discord amongst races in the aftermath of the *Plessy* ruling. The disparity of conditions between White and Black school was apparent to many African Americans. Yet, the struggle to ensure equality within the segregationist system proved fruitless for the African American community (Patterson, 2001). In 1954, however, racial segregation took a dramatic turn with what has become arguably the most significant Supreme Court case in the history of the United States.

Brown v. Board of Education

The story surrounding *Brown v. Board of Education* (1954) is filled with drama and its aftermath is often simplistically misunderstood by contemporary students who are taught that this pivotal case ended segregation once and for all. Those who believe in this simplistic relay of the story often overlook the years of struggle by African Americans and their advocates to not only ensure that the *Brown* decision was enforced but also that the de facto segregation inculcated by nearly a century of de jure racial segregation was undone. The *Brown* case can best be understood as the beginning of a long struggle that, as you will see, still remains. This significant case began with an effort by the National Association for the Advancement of Colored People (NAACP) to shed light on situations that may lead to legal challenges to racial segregation in the United States. The frustration experienced by the Brown family from Topeka, Kansas proved to be a prototypical situation that the NAACP could use in its quest. The Brown's frustration centered around their young daughter, Linda, who was required by state law to attend elementary school at a "Black" school several miles away while the "White" public elementary school was nearby the Brown's home.

Linda's father, Oliver Brown, believed that this practice was unjust and unconstitutional, especially since the trek to and from the "Black" school was hazardous for Linda Brown. After experiencing resistance from the public school district to accommodate the family's needs, Oliver Brown (Linda's father) collaborated with other families, to be the plaintiffs the NAACP used to challenge the nation's racial segregation system (Patterson, 2001). *Thurgood Marshall* (1908–1993), an established civil rights lawyer at the time, served as the attorney who argued the case on behalf of the Browns and the other families in the case. Rather than challenge the standard of equality set forth under *Plessy*, Marshall argued that the entire concept of separation was in violation of the equal protection clause of the Fourteenth Amendment of the U.S. Constitution. In other words, Marshall used *Brown* to challenge the entire system of racial segregation in the United States (Patterson, 2001). This risk proved successful once it reached the U.S. Supreme Court as the justices unanimously ruled in favor of Brown, overturning *Plessy* and its separate but equal doctrine that remained in place nearly a half century. The opinion of the Court mirrored Justice Harlan's dissent in *Plessy* stipulating that "in the field of public education the doctrine of 'separate but equal' has no place. Separate educational facilities are inherently unequal" (Brown v. Board of Education, 1954, para. 31). The moment that the Court's decision was made public was akin, for the African American community, to the official release of the Emancipation Proclamation in 1863: a grand cause for celebration. However, the reality is that *Brown* only eliminated de jure segregation. A long and difficult struggle awaited those who sought true racial integration of the American school experience.

It was clear that the U.S. Supreme Court hoped that culture, and likely the other branches of government, would act to end racial segregation once the *Brown II* (1955) ruling declared that schools must integrate "with all deliberate speed." These were hollow words with ambiguous meaning. With little advocacy from government or the culture, the African American community would once again bear the burden of fighting for their own civil rights. The most high profile attempt by the African American community to push for the enforcement of *Brown* was the 1957 integration of Arkansas' Central High School by the *Little Rock Nine*. The Little Rock Nine was a high profile integration attempt that became a symbolic battleground pitting segregationists against civil rights activists' push toward desegregation (Ravitch, 1983). The situation began with little publicity as the Little Rock school board decided it would incrementally integrate its school system, beginning with nine African American students enrolling in Central High School. The situation escalated to a symbolic showdown once Arkansas Governor Orval Faubus defied the school board and the Supreme Court, when he ordered the state's National Guard to the school to ensure that the students did not attend the school (Ravitch, 1983). A meeting between Governor Faubus and U.S. President Dwight Eisenhower resulted in an agreement that Faubus would allow for the students to attend the school and release the National Guard. The start of the 1957 school year for Little Rock Central High was unlike any other as mobs of White supremacists flocked to the school to protest and block the students from attending school. The situation became very dangerous and caught the attention of the entire nation. Eventually, U.S. President Dwight Eisenhower federalized the Arkansas National Guard and sent additional federal troops to the high school to ensure the enforcement of *Brown* in the school. The NAACP coordinated its efforts to support the students as they went through the difficult trial of enduring hostility from many of their classmates and the community writ large.

The nine students involved in the Little Rock Nine incident are etched in the lexicon of American History as heroic figures who stood against tyranny. This is true. It is important for us to note that these nine students were ordinary individuals attempting to perform the ordinary task of merely attending public school. However, the extraordinary resistance against these students shed light on the extraordinary effort it took to fight the effects of racism ingrained in American society and, as a result, the American public school system. A larger effort, one that involved federal legislation and the Supreme Court to protect African Americans' civil rights, was brewing in the late 1950s and 1960s.

The American Race Experiment

The school desegregation effort was central to the larger American Civil Rights movement. The movement's leader, *Martin Luther King Jr.*, (1929–1968) was persistent in persuading the politically powerful to address discrimination that beset the African American community. The goals of the Civil Rights movement was generally consistent with President *Lyndon Johnson's* (1908–1973) ambitious political agenda to curtail poverty and discrimination across the United States (we will focus more on Johnson's political agenda in our next chapter). In 1964, the U.S. government took a significant step in addressing this discrimination with the passage of *The Civil Rights Act of 1964*. The primary purpose of this act was to ban discrimination in public places, including but not limited to schools, and to ensure voting rights for all individuals. It empowered individuals to file suits against discriminatory practices to the Attorney General of the United States. This significant litigation emerged at the same time as the U.S. Supreme Court took a dramatic, and controversial, turn toward putting an end to segregation rather than distantly standing pat and watch the detrimental effects of the Court's past decisions that had previously empowered and emboldened segregationists.

The country relied heavily on free choice of local and state governments as a vehicle for desegregation through much of the 1960s. This appeared to be a plodding path, too slow for many advocates for desegregation. In 1968, the U.S. Supreme Court heard a case, *Green v. County School Board of New Kent, Virginia* (1968), that challenged the freedom of choice path to desegregation (Ravitch, 1983). The case involved a school district in New Kent, Virginia with a distinctive "Black school" and "White school" with very little racial integration since the *Brown* decision nearly 14 years earlier. The *Green* case is significant because, with it, the Court devised a plan for desegregation that affected school districts throughout the nation. The plan required local school districts to achieve a concept the Court called *unitary status* with regard to the racial mixture within their respective schools. Unitary status, simply put, means that the racial demographics of schools must be in unison with the racial demographics of the entire school district (Hlebowitsh, 2007). For instance, if a school district has a twenty percent African American population, then each school within that district must possess a twenty percent African American population. Unitary status involved student, faculty, and staff demographics. Achieving unitary status amongst students proved to be challenging for districts, particularly with a rise of "White" families moving out of urban areas and toward more suburban outlets (a phenomenon widely called "White flight"). Some creative efforts were made by school districts to achieve desegregation goals and to help put an end to White flight, such as the creation of *magnet schools* with a specially devised curriculum or school design that sought to attract non-minority students (i.e., "Whites") to a school environment otherwise dominated by minority students (i.e., "Blacks"). The desegregation effort employed a variety of strategies. Perhaps the most controversial, and yet most successful in achieving measurable results, was the busing of students to achieve racial balance amongst schools within a district. The Supreme Court weighed in once again on the issue of desegregation when it ruled in the case *Swann v. Charlotte Mecklenburg Board of Education* (1971) that busing students across wide geographic areas within a district was an appropriate means to achieve the desegregation goal of unitary status. Figure 9.1 reveals the dramatic statistical shift of racial balance that occurred in the American South after this multi-faceted approach to desegregation took effect in the late 1960s through the 1970s. Notice the dramatic change that occurred beginning in 1964 (Civil Rights Act) and continued to rise in 1968 (*Green* case). In many ways, the graph in Figure 9.1 represents a

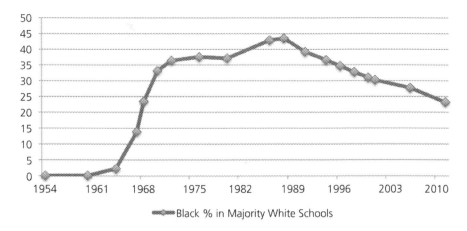

Figure 9.1 Percentage of Black students in majority White schools in the South (1954–2011). *Source:* U.S. Department of Education, National Center for Education Statistics, Common Core of Data (CCD), Public Elementary/Secondary School Universe Survey Data. Data prior to 1991 obtained from the analysis of the Office of Civil Rights data in Orfield (1983).

positive and hopeful story of how the United States, through the means of the public school, made improvements in race relations. The fact that so many "White" and "Black" children were spending days together, including eating and playing together, is a significant step forward from the era of Jim Crow that existed in the not too distant past. Unfortunately, the story is by no means simplistic nor as positive as first glance may imply.

By and large, the African American community sought to end the segregationist system that had so long dominated their lives. However, the effect of desegregation on the African American population was not completely positive. To begin with, many high quality African American teachers and administrators, were displaced or became increasingly vulnerable to the "White" school board members who controlled their jobs (Fairclough, 2004). Contrary to popular opinion of the time, the African American teachers were generally more educated and higher qualified than their White-Caucasian peers (Goldstein, 2014). Additionally, the elimination of many "Black" schools in favor of the practice of busing students across districts rose in prominence, led many members of the African American community to forlorn the community schools whose teachers privileged the culture of the students in school curriculum. A *community control movement* arose within the African American community in the late 1960s that sought reform to allow a more local flavor to schools within a district. The most well-known example of the community control movement in action was in the *Ocean Hill-Brownsville* school district in Brooklyn, New York. Ocean Hill-Brownsville was a school with nearly 95% African American or Latino student population with two-thirds of the teachers White-Caucasian. By 1968 the school was widely viewed as unruly (Goldstein, 2014). Individuals associated with *Black nationalism,* a movement within the African American community that asserted "Black" people should develop and maintain a Black national identity, advocated for the school to be decentralized and controlled by the local community. The mayor of New York City, *John Lindsey* (1921–2000), declared that the school would become one of three schools in New York neighborhoods under "community control." As the Ocean-Hill school sought to bring more African American and Latino teachers to its faculty, and subsequently ousted a group of White-Caucasian teachers without due process, the United Federation of Teachers led a school-wide strike that lasted 2 months (Goldstein, 2014). Under pressure from the powerful teachers' union, the New York state legislature eventually adopted a moderate school decentralization plan that did away with local control of schools. The community control movement was viewed by its critics and potential supporters outside the local community as merely a vehicle for Black nationalism to supercede its own interests of racial separation over the democratic notion of public schooling (Ravitch, 1983). The movement's supporters, however, saw it as another failed attempt for African Americans and Latinos to create a positive and uplifting school experience for their children who experienced continual marginalization from the hands of the political and economic stronghold of society.

Resegregation

Desegregation was challenging and burdensome for many school districts. Achieving unitary status was no easy matter for districts and gained increasing unpopularity amongst some portions of the African American community who longed for their own neighborhood schools. Decisions from the Supreme Court began to reflect the society's hesitation to continue the effort. In 1974, the Supreme Court heard an important case, *Milliken v. Bradley* (1974), that dealt with busing as a means for desegregation. The case focused on whether interdistrict busing may be used to achieve desegregation in a racially homogenous school district in urban Detroit. It was an opportunity for the Court to expand upon its earlier ruling in *Swan* that opened the door for the use of intradistrict busing to desegregate schools. However, the Court decided that it would not impinge upon the sovereignty of local school districts by requiring it to employ interdistrict busing unless it was shown that each district deliberately segregated their respective districts from one another. The latter instance would infer that de jure segregation took place, upon which the Court interpreted it proper to intervene.

As you can tell from Figure 9.1, the desegregation effort proved successful in the 1970s and 1980s with connecting people of different races in the school experience. This success, along with the unpopularity of districts' efforts to achieve unitary status, paved the way for another significant Supreme Court case: *Board of Education of Oklahoma City v. Dowell* (1991). This case posed the important question: Once a school district achieves unitary status in its racial composition, is it still required by the Court to continually fulfill unitary status? The Court ruled "No" in a 5–4 decision stating that supervision by federal courts is a temporary measure to remedy past discrimination. As a result of the *Oklahoma City* case, states were free to pass their own legislation freeing districts from compliance to the *Green* case once they achieved unitary status. The statistical shift in Figure 9.1 demonstrates the significance of this case. A downward slope of "Blacks" in majority "White" schools in the American South began roughly around the 1991 ruling of *Oklahoma City*. The aftereffect of this Court ruling is telling of the contemporary phenomenon of desegregation: The American public school can, once again, be characterized as a largely racially segregated institution.

Statistical analysis of students' exposure to other races further reveals the rise in segregation. Table 9.1 displays the percentage of "Black" students attending schools classified as "minority" schools, or predominantly "non-White" schools. The data in Table 9.1 reveals a similar trend we saw in Figure 9.1 in the American South. Segregation was high in 1968, with "Blacks" making up 76.6% of the population of "minority schools." This phenomenon took a dramatic shift by 1988 with "Blacks" only representing 56.5% of the population of "minority schools." By 2011, the situation

TABLE 9.1 Percentage of Black Students in 50–100% Minority Schools				
	1968	1988	2001	2011	Change From 1968–2011 (% Change)
South	76.6	56.5	69.8	76.8	−4.1 (−5.1)
Border	71.6	59.6	67.9	73.2	1.6 (2.2)
Northeast	66.8	77.3	78.4	79.4	12.6 (18.9)
Midwest	77.3	70.1	72.9	73.7	−3.6 (−4.7)
West	72.2	67.1	75.8	82.4	10.2 (14.1)

Source: U.S. Department of Education, National Center for Education Statistics, Common Core of Data (CCD), Public Elementary/Secondary Universe Survey Data. Data prior to 1991 obtained from the analysis of the Office of Civil Rights data in Orfield (1983).

regressed to a percentage higher than 1968. Outside of the American Midwest, where change in race distribution in schools did not dramatically alter, the entire nation experienced a similar shift.

There are primarily two likely reasons behind the parallel statistical shifts toward resegregation throughout the nation. First, court injunctions make a significant difference in a school district's effort to desegregate. The release of schools from court injunctions, beginning with the 1991 *Oklahoma City* case, paved the way for schools to transition toward a reflection of its segregated local communities. A nationwide study (Reardon, Grewal, Kalogrides, & Greenberg, 2012) reported that over 200 medium-sized and large districts were released from desegregation court orders between 1991 through 2009. This same study reported that racial segregation rose substantially for those schools released from the court orders. A second reason behind the resegregation of American's public schools is the concentration of racial homogeneity in society. In other words, segregation is on the rise within local communities. The cause for this rise in racial segregation is directly connected with the rise of concentrated poverty in the contemporary United States. Sociologist Patrick Sharkey (2013) found that young African Americans are ten times more likely to live in poor neighborhoods than young Whites. According to Sharkey, mobility out of these poor neighborhoods is much more prominent for Whites than African American residents. This phenomenon, better known as White flight, leaves the public school a very racially homogenous student population to draw from. School and society are linked, and so are race and social class. One cannot be understood without the other. Our next chapter focuses on this linkage behind so many of the daunting challenges before the American public school.

Summary

Racial segregation is a byproduct of the existence of White supremacy as an American social construct. Segregation's historical roots rest in America's long-standing struggle with race, beginning with the introduction of the slave trade in early colonial America. While the American Civil War resulted in the banishment of slavery, it was replaced by a segregationist system (de jure segregation) in the American South that made it illegal for African Americans to experience the same community life as their fellow "White" community members. In the 1896 case *Plessy v. Ferguson*, the U.S. Supreme Court upheld the practice of this segregationist system in states as long as the segregated facilities are equal in nature and practice. This doctrine of "separate but equal" was challenged over 50 years later, in the 1954 Supreme Court case *Brown v. Board of Education*, with the school because of its significance as a socializing agency. The Court's decision under *Brown* to overturn *Plessy* made it illegal to segregate by law anywhere in the United States. It was a struggle for the African American community to ensure that *Brown* was applied in the public school, as many educational and political leaders at the local and state levels refused to comply to the federal ruling. Plus, the legal form of segregation (de jure) helped to foster a cultural form of segregation (de facto) that became webbed in the demographic composition of local communities. By 1968, in *Green v. County School Board New Kent*, the U.S. Supreme Court created an approach that required school districts to achieve unitary status with its schools regarding their racial composition. Unitary status required schools' racial composition to mirror the districts' composition. The 1971 Supreme Court case, *Swann v. Charlotte Mecklenburg School District*, declared that busing students across a school district was an appropriate means to ensure achievement of unitary status. Eventually, a desegregation effort was underway throughout the American South that resulted in a racial balance in schools throughout the region by the 1980s.

The desegregation effort, while statistically successful in forming a racial balance in schools, was unpopular on numerous fronts. The African American community longed for control of their own communities and their neighborhood school whereas school districts found achieving unitary status to be difficult and costly. In 1991, the U.S. Supreme Court ruled in *Oklahoma City v. Dowell* that a district was no longer obligated, by federal injunction, to meet unitary status once it achieved it once. The release of the federal court injunction, along with the White flight phenomenon in urban districts, resulted in a rise in segregation by the 21st century.

Reflection Exercises

1. Compile a list of activities that appear to be segregated by race. Classify those activities as *dejure* or *defacto*. Why do you think those activities are segregated?
2. How could the U.S. Supreme Court allow segregation in 1896 yet disallow it in 1954?
3. Should the community control movement of the 1960s have been allowed to prosper, even though it allowed for segregation (albeit, with African Americans at the helm of the community decision-making rather than the predominant White power structure)?
4. How might the nation properly address its racial resegregation?

References

Board of Education of Oklahoma City v. Dowell (1991). 498 U.S. 237.

Brown v. Board of Education (1954). 347 U.S. 483. Retrieved from Findlaw database: https://caselaw.findlaw.com/us-supreme-court/347/483.html

Fairclough, A. (2004). The costs of Brown: Black teachers and school integration. *The Journal of American History, 91*(1), 43–55.

Goldstein, D. (2014). *The teacher wars: A history of America's most embattled profession.* New York, NY: Anchor.

Green v. County School Board of New Kent County (1968). 391 U.S. 430.

Hlebowitsh, P. (2007). *Foundations of American education.* Dubuque, IA: Kendall-Hunt.

Milliken v. Bradley (1974). 418 U.S. 717.

Orfield, G. (1983). *Public school desegregation in the United States, 1968–1980.* Washington, DC: Joint Center for Political Studies.

Patterson, J. T. (2001). *Brown v. Board of Education: A civil rights milestone and its troubled legacy.* Oxford, England: Oxford University Press.

Plessy v. Ferguson (1896). 163 U.S. 537. Retrieved from the FindLaw database: https://supreme.findlaw.com/supreme_court/landmark/plessy.html

Ravitch, D. (1983). *The troubled crusade: American education, 1945–1980.* New York, NY: Basic Books.

Reardon, S. F., Grewal, E. T., Kalogrides, D., & Greenberg, E. (2012). Brown fades: The end of court-ordered school desegregation and the resegregation of American public schools. *Journal of Policy Analysis and Management, 31*(4), 876–904.

Sharkey, P. (2013). *Stuck in place: Urban neighborhoods and the end of progress toward racial equality.* Chicago, IL: University of Chicago Press.

Swann v. Charlotte-Mecklenburg Board of Education (1971). 402 U.S. 1.

10

Social Class and School

It was the morning of the very first day of school at Bryant Middle School. Mrs. Fowler, the middle school science teacher, greeted each student as they nervously walked into her classroom. "Good morning," she repeatedly announced, "It's good to have you here." The students grimaced back at her and, occasionally, some would greet her back. When the first bell rang, Mrs. Fowler's high heels knocked on the wooden floor as she walked to the front of the room. "This is eighth grade science class and we're going to learn a lot together all year," she confidently told the class, "but first, we need to get to know one another." As was her custom on the first day, Mrs. Fowler had each student stand and share, with the entire class, their name and what they did over the summer break. She asked for volunteers to go first and several students eagerly rose their arms while others, predictably, kept theirs down. "Ok, you may go first," Mrs. Fowler said to Ashli Wright, who proceeded to share herself with the class:

Paradoxes of the Public School, pages 133–147
Copyright © 2019 by Information Age Publishing
All rights of reproduction in any form reserved.

"My name is Ashli. This summer I got to go to Disney World with my family. I also went to ballet class and two volleyball camps."

Ashli was followed by Tony Tompkins:

"My name is Tony. We went to the Grand Canyon and my little league baseball team was runner-up in the regional tournament."

Tony was followed by Sonja Long:

"My name is Sonja. I spent some time with my Grandma and played with my little brother. We had fun together."

The class continued along this path until everyone got a chance to share. Once the class finished with their introductions, Mrs. Fowler began to explain the goals of the class. "Ok, we all have a fresh start with a new school year upon us," Mrs. Fowler announced. "This year we are going to learn about the natural world around us and we will all be successful in this adventure this year."

As we have seen already, the American public school is a byproduct of the local community from which it emerges. School and society are intrinsically linked. This chapter, perhaps more than any other in this book, emphasizes this link. All aspects of the American public school, including disparities between school districts, issues of race, academic achievement, and retention, are rooted in issues of social class. The socioeconomic differences that Mrs. Fowler inherited amongst her students pose possible academic advantages for some students in the class over those who may not have such enriching experiences. In many ways, a chasm exists between the rich and the poor; the haves and have-nots. This chasm exists in our society and permeates amongst classes like Mrs. Fowler's. It is no coincidence that the primary purpose behind most, if not all, federal policy initiatives regarding education are related with uplifting students, and subsequently schools, mired in impoverished conditions.

Unfortunately, social class is seldom explicitly addressed by political and educational leaders. However, in the 1960s, social class was explicitly addressed by federal policy initiatives intended to help schools with a large conglomerate of students mired in poverty. The decade of the 1960s was unique in this effort, primarily due to the explicit efforts of President *Lyndon Johnson* (1908–1973) who used his political power to declare, what he called, "a war on poverty." This explicit emphasis on social class was an unusual endeavor on the part of Johnson since contemporary political leaders often address problems of race or problems with students' academic performance with little attention paid to the significant role social class plays on these fronts. It does great harm to sweep social class under the proverbial rug because of its significance in the problems of our day. Yet, addressing it is no easy matter. Issues of social class, and the problems associated with its effect on the school experience, are complex and challenging. It is much more convenient, though ineffective, to emphasize the symptoms associated with disparities in social class.

Many reform efforts on public education since the latter half of the 20th century have been girded with the notion that issues of academic achievement in schools, therefore, can be quickly fixed by placing punitive measures on school to ensure that it challenges all students to reach specified academic goals. However, a recent analysis (Hanushek, 2016) of national test scores revealed that, while the gap in reading and math scores between "Blacks" and "Whites" have narrowed between 1965 to 2013, the narrowing is occurring at a very slow pace. According to the report, if the current rate of closure of the achievement gap remains steady "it will be roughly two and a half centuries before the Black–White math gap closes and over one and a half centuries until the reading gap closes." Unfortunately, such an emphasis on the Black–White achievement gaps ignores the disparities within racial groups as well as a misnomer that some minority racial groups (i.e., Asian Americans) are experiencing wholesale success in school (Lee, 2015). In a later chapter we will examine these largely unsuccessful reform efforts to narrow the achievement gap. However, the intent with this chapter is to examine the underlying role that social class plays in the American school experience. We will define social class, identify how it is categorized in the contemporary United States, and analyze its effects on the public school. Most importantly, this chapter allows us to understand the nature of gaps among students. The word "gap" is often used by educational critics and policy makers to describe differences in academic achievement among students, usually as a means to demonstrate how the school fails to respond to racial minorities. In this chapter we will challenge this approach of "gap" as something caused within the school environment. Instead, we will approach "gaps" as something the school inherits. Thus, the central paradox of this chapter is the following:

Schools are held responsible for the existence of an achievement gap amongst groups of students, however schools largely inherit this gap.

The 1960s

Social class is a subjective construct in the social science fields aimed at analyzing the *social stratification*, or social differentiation, of groups of individuals in a society. Usually, social class is defined by the socioeconomic level of those groups in relation to one another. The most common categories used to describe social stratification is upper, middle, and lower classes. In a recent report, the Pew Research Center (2015) estimated that middle class can be defined in the following ways using 2014 income levels of individuals living in metropolitan areas of the United States:

- One person household earnings: $24,000–$73,000
- Three person household earnings: $42,000–$125,000
- Five person household earnings: $54,000–$162,000

Therefore, according to this report, the upper class is defined by those with income above the middle class level whereas the lower class is defined with income levels below it. Of course, there is great disparity within these groups (i.e., a $42,000 income earner is in a different financial situation than one who earns $125,000). However, precision is not entirely possible when analyzing social class due to the plethora of differences amongst people and where they live. These defined categories, however, are the means that social sciences use to analyze patterns across groups of people.

As part of the Civil Rights Act of 1964, the United States government commissioned a research survey study aimed at understanding the educational opportunities available for racial and ethnic minority populations at all levels in the United States. The study was led by sociologist *James Coleman* (1926–1995) from Johns Hopkins University and its results were published in 1966 as a report entitled *Equality of Educational Opportunity*, but better known simply as the "Coleman Report" (Coleman et al, 1966). The report is considered one of the most significant sociological studies of public education in the history of the United States. The finding that the report is known primarily for is that students' achievement has less to do with the quality of school but more to do with the students' family background and the social composition of the school (Ravitch, 1983). The Coleman report ran parallel with psychologist *Urie Bronfenbrenner's* (1917–2005) significant breakthrough in understanding human development. Bronfenbrenner devised a theory of human development, popularly known as the *ecological systems theory*, asserting that humans are affected by systematic levels of social influence. These influences range from the microsystem, the network closest to the child that includes family and school, to the macrosystem, the network that involves the larger cultural institutions such as the economy, conventions, and political institutions (Bronfenbrenner, 1994). Bronfenbrenner was instrumental in the federally funded initiatives from the 1960s, such as *Head Start*, aimed at curtailing the effects of poverty on children's performance in school. Bronfenbrenner's work in psychology, alongside the later findings of the Coleman Report, ran parallel in purpose with the passage of the most significant federal legislation ever associated with public education: the *Elementary and Secondary Education Act of 1965* (ESEA). This act was a central component of President Lyndon Johnson's "war on poverty" effort to curtail the negative effects of socio-economic conditions burdening the poor. It allocated federal money, called *Title I funding*, to schools possessing high levels of poverty amidst its student population. This marked the first time the federal government became centrally involved in the functioning of the American public school. As you will see, ESEA is reauthorized annually and morphed in the 21st century as a means for the federal government to hold schools accountable for students' academic achievement.

A Rising Disparity of Social Capital

The Coleman Report and Bronfenbrenner's ecological systems theory point us to an important sociological concept called *social capital*. There are a variety of ways to define social capital depending upon whether one is looking at it from an economic or political perspective. For our purposes, we will consider social capital as something that simply entails the social networking that a person, or groups of people, possess that assists them in achieving success in life. For instance, an individual with educated parents likely will possess a more expansive social capital than one whose parents are not educated. Social capital, in this instance, may be a connection to educational institutions, other educated persons, or a connection to a variety of cultural institutions. One of the most well-known contemporary scholars on social capital, particularly individuals' connection to their communities, is the political scientist *Robert Putnam* (b. 1941). Most recently, Putnam (2015) published research that asserted an escalation in poverty is resulting in an unprecedented level of inequality of opportunity amongst social classes in the United States. Putnam's central conclusion is that this widening disparity amongst social classes brought dramatic changes to family life, communities, and schools that make it even more difficult for those in the lower class to work their way up in society. While poverty has always existed in the United States, Putnam argued that the contemporary nature of poverty in the United States is particularly challenging for those mired in it because of its concentration. In other words, those in poverty seldom associate today with those not in poverty, and visa versa.

The result of this rise in concentrated poverty is that the gap between the lower and upper classes in a multitude of areas, while always in existence in the latter half of the 20th century, dramatically widened as the United States ventured toward the 21st century. The statistical analyses of this development reveals, for instance, a widening gap in education levels between the top and bottom quartiles of family income. In 1970, approximately 40% of the top quartile of family income earners earned a college degree as opposed to roughly 5% of the bottom quartile. By 2011 this gap changed dramatically with nearly 80% of the top quartile earning a college degree with roughly 10% of the bottom quartile doing so (Putnam, 2015). Putnam asserted that this widening gap in areas such as income and education levels also affected the gap in the experiences between children from educated and affluent backgrounds and their peers from less educated and affluent backgrounds. As a case in point, a divergent trend has emerged on a seemingly simple matter as dining together as a family, depending upon the education level of a child's parents. In 1978, according to Putnam (2015), the vast majority of American families ate dinner together regardless of education level (approximately 83% of families whose parents have a BA or more and approximately 79% of families with parents who only have a high school degree or less). By 2005 this gap widened with approximately 75% of the first group dining together as opposed to roughly 63% of the latter group. The significance of this trend in dining together, according to Putnam (2015) is that "better-educated parents were indirectly influenced by the growing recognition of the importance of serve-and-return interactions for child development" while "less educated parents were slower to get the word or were leading such complicated lives that family dinners were not a realistic option" (p. 123).

While effects such as family dining may have an indirect impact on schools, such as students' academic performance, current data reveal that the growing gap between the "haves" and "have-nots" directly affects the school environment as well. As a case in point, Putnam reveals that data findings on student participation in extracurricular activities vary greatly amongst students based on their socioeconomic status (SES). In 2002, nearly 86% of students from the highest SES quartile participated in school-based extracurriculars as opposed to about 65% of students from the lowest quartile. As with other trends, this gap was not as large as decades earlier, in 1972, with roughly 86% of students from the highest socioeconomic quartile participating in extracurriculars as opposed to about 77% of students from the lowest quartile.

Additionally, parents living in a higher SES are likely to spend much more money on their child than parents within a lower SES. Of course, this trend exacerbated over time. In 1972, the top earning households spent just under $3000 (in constant dollars) on each of their children, as opposed to the lowest earning households spending around $550 per child. By 2008, this gap dramatically widened with the top earning families spending approximately $6,500 per child and the lowest earners spending around $700 per child (Putnam, 2015). This entails expenditure on enrichment activities and materials. The demographic trends that Putnam shed light on presents the disturbing reality that children come from vastly different backgrounds depending upon the SES of their families.

Another contemporary researcher whose work mirrors Putnam's findings is the sociologist *Annette Lareau* (b. 1952). In the late 1980s and early 1990s, Lareau (2003) embarked on the difficult endeavor of conducting exhaustive naturalistic observations of a dozen families with children. The families varied in terms of race and SES. Her findings were provocative. In terms of parenting styles, Lareau noticed that the families with a higher SES engaged in a style she called "concerted cultivation." With this approach, according to Lareau (2003), parents make sure to expose their children to a plethora of experiences and a sense of entitlement takes root in the children that "plays an especially important role in institutional settings, where middle-class children learn to question adults and address them as relative equals" (p. 2). The families from a lower SES gravitated toward a parenting style Lareau called "accomplishment of natural growth." According to Lareau, with this style of parenting, "adults do not consider the concerted development of children, particularly through organized leisure activities, an essential aspect of good parenting" but rather "see a clear boundary between adults and children" (p. 3). Parents using this style tend to use directives toward their child rather than persuasion through reason, as those parents do from a higher SES background. This difference in parenting styles results in a difference in experiences among children, based on SES, as well as the child's sense of agency and ability to navigate cultural institutions, such as school.

Table 10.1 displays a summary of Lareau's findings regarding the amount of organized activities (i.e., Brownies, Cub Scouts, music lessons, sports) the children in her study experienced. As you can see, the differences in the number of activities is not dependent on race nor gender, but rather social class. A middle class White and a middle class Black boy or girl experienced a similar amount of organized activities in their life. However, a poor or working class child had much fewer activities organized for them than their middle class peers. Consider these activities as *opportunities to learn* (OTL). The children from a middle class background experience a greater variety of people than their peers from a lower SES. This exposure to more people, often stemming from the middle class, exposes children to individuals from a vast array of professions and educational backgrounds.

Putnam (2015) called these connections to a broad and diverse network of people "weak ties" and stressed their importance in child development:

> The reach and diversity of these social ties are especially valuable for social mobility and educational and economic advancement, because such ties allow educated, affluent parents and their children to tap a wealth of expertise and support that is simply inaccessible to parents and children who are less well off. (p. 208)

While such social ties provide a myriad of opportunities for children as they consider academic or vocational interests, they also relate with another element of social diffusion: the use of words within childhood. Researchers from the University of Kansas, Betty Hart and Todd Risley, entered the homes of 42 families to study vocabulary use in the early to mid 1990s. Their findings revealed that the parent–child interactions differed greatly dependent upon the SES of the family. Primarily focusing on word usage, Hart and Riley concluded that children from higher SES backgrounds are exposed to roughly 30 million more words by the time they are 3 years old than those children from the lowest SES background (Hart & Risley, 2003). Similarly to Putnam's findings, Hart and Risley discovered this word gap incrementally expands with the increase of income level. Studies such as this one, along with the work of Laureau and Putnam, reveal a stunning truth: Money buys more than mere material goods, it buys social capital for children in a multitude of ways.

TABLE 10.1 Average Number of Organized Activities by Social Class, Race, and Child's Gender

	Middle Class	Working Class	Poor
All Children	4.9	2.5	1.5
N	36	26	26
Blacks	5.2	2.8	1.6
N	18	12	14
Whites	4.6	2.3	1.4
N	18	14	12
Girls	4.7	2.6	1.5
N	18	11	15
Boys	5.1	2.5	1.5
N	18	15	11

Source: Lareau (2003, p. 282).

Dropping Out

Inequality among social class affects the school experience on a number of fronts. Among the fronts most studied and analyzed is the graduation rate of students. Graduating from high school is more significant than some might realize. For example, a person who graduates from high school is less likely to land in prison than one who drops out from high school. Nearly 75% of state prison inmates and 59% of federal prison inmates do not have a high school degree (Harlow, 2003). Graduating from high school also results in a higher likelihood of employment. Employers desire hiring individuals who are dependable and earning a high school diploma is one sign that an individual is dependable amidst adversity. In other words, earning a high school diploma is a signal to others that a person can achieve something. Figure 10.1 reveals that only 48% of individuals between 20 to 24 years of age, and without a high school degree, were employed in 2016. This was opposed to 69% of individuals in the same age bracket with a high school degree.

Why does someone drop out of school? There is no singular answer to this question. There are those factors within the school's proximity of influence, called "push factors" that essentially push students out of school. These might be factors such as bullying from students, an ineffective

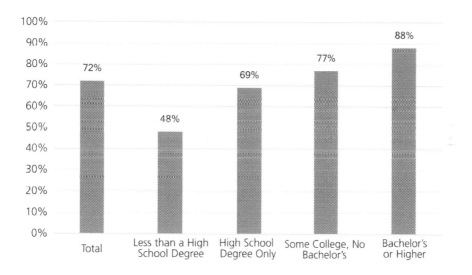

Figure 10.1   Employment rate for 20–24 year olds; by educational attainment: 2016. *Source*: U.S. Department of Commerce, Census Bureau, Current Population Survey (CPS), Annual Social and Economic Supplement, March 2016. See *Digest of Education Statistics 2016*, Table 501.50, 501.60, and 501.70.

curriculum, or an inflexible disciplinary policy. However, the more common reason that may lead a student to drop out of school relate with "pull factors," or factors outside of the school's proximity of influence. Such pull factors may involve situations such as the need to produce additional family income, lack of support from home, or pregnancy. Many pull factors are associated with issues of social class. Recently, researchers (e.g., Wood, Kiperman, Esch, Leroux, & Truscott, 2017) discovered that the SES levels of students and the surrounding community was a primary variable in predicting dropouts. Due to various marginalizing influences in society, there is a strong association between race and SES. However, the research of Wood and others (2017) strongly resonate with the findings of Lareau (2003) that an individual, regardless of race, with a high SES background, possesses many more OTL than an individual from a low SES background. Therefore, Wood and others discovered that an African American from a low SES background is much more likely to drop out from school than an African American from a high SES background.

There are several approaches to measuring dropouts. The two most commonly used for public consumption is the *adjusted cohort graduation rate* (ACGR) and the *status dropout rate*. The ACGR is a relatively recent measurement approach that replaced the aggregate measurement of students who merely began as ninth graders and graduated within a four year span. With the ACGR, however, a state identifies a specific group, or "cohort" of first-time ninth graders in a particular year and also determines how many of those students graduated within 4 years. The distinctive characteristic of the ACGR, however, is that it adjusts the cohort to take into consideration students who transfer into and out of the cohort prior to earning a diploma. In 2014–2015, the total ACGR in the United States was 83%, an increase from previous years. In fact, the high school graduation rate is currently at its highest in the history of the United States. As you can see in Figure 10.2, when the ACGR is measured by race and ethnicity, the findings reveal that African Americans (identified as "Black" in Figure 7), Hispanic Americans (identified as "Hispanic"), and Native American (identified as "American Indian/Alaska Native") represent a lower graduation rate than the average and significantly less than "White" and "Asian/Pacific Islander" populations.

The other measurement popularly used to identify high school dropouts is the status dropout rate. The status dropout rate represents the percentage of 16 to 24 year olds who are neither enrolled in school nor earned a high school credential (either a high school diploma or its equivalency). This rate is arguably the most accurate dropout rate because it includes those students who re-enroll in school after initially leaving. Figure 10.3 displays the status

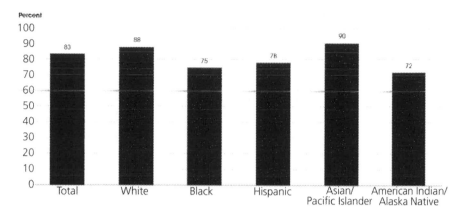

Figure 10.2 Adjusted cohort graduation rate (ACGR) for public high school students by race/ethnicity: 2014–2015. *Source:* U.S. Department of Education, Office of Elementary and Secondary Education, Consolidated State Performance Report, 2014–2015. See *Digest of Education Statistics 2016,* Table 219.46.

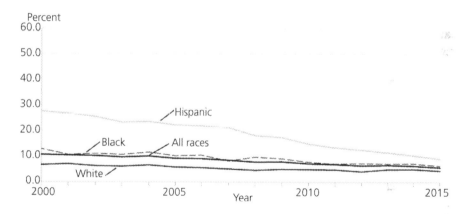

Figure 10.3 Status dropout rates of 16 to 24 year olds by race/ethnicity: 1990–2015. *Source:* U.S. Department of Education, National Center for Education Statistics. (2017).

dropout rates, according to racial composition, from 1990–2015. As you can see, the dropout rate continues to decline across the board, regardless of race. A gap in the dropout, albeit a narrowing one, still remains between races. The dropout rate gap between "White" and "Black" students narrowed from 6.2% in 2000 to 1.9% in 2015. The dropout rate gap between "White" and "Hispanic" students narrowed from 20.9% in 2000 to 4.6% in 2015. These statistics represent a positive trend for the United States as it signals that more students, of all races, are staying in school.

School Funding and Social Reproduction

One way to look upon the decline of the dropout rate is that our society collectively looks upon the public school for assistance in the midst of struggle. However, public schools are funded in a way that directly reflects the nation's growing economic inequality. The sources for funding from public schools include local, state, and federal monies. The allocation of school funding from these sources in 2013–2014 was as follows: local: 45%; state: 46%; and federal: 8.7% (Cornman & Musu-Gillette, 2016). However, it is significant to note that these are averages. Individual states decide the funding formula of schools and often vary with one another with how they fund schools. Some states rely more heavily on local dollars whereas others rely relatively little on local dollars. The primary means for schools to raise local revenue for schools is through property taxes. This matters significantly because some districts possess more valuable commercial and residential property than others, and thus often have the freedom to fund their schools beyond the states' percentage requirement. This is why a school district in one area of a state may be vastly different in how much funds it receives than another merely an hour away (Vevea, 2016).

As a result of the vast inequalities of revenue provided to schools that exist between and within states, some states provide additional funding to assist those districts with lower SES. The Education Law Center, a New Jersey based advocacy group for equal educational opportunity, categorized states according to how they provide equity and opportunity through their school finance systems. According to its most recent report, the states of Delaware, Minnesota, New Jersey, and Massachusetts are the only four states who have both high funding levels and provide a significant amount of additional state funding to districts with highest levels of poverty. States who provide additional funding to local districts with low SES are referred to as having a *progressive funding system*. Other states, such as Nevada, Wyoming, North Dakota, and Illinois, actually rely more heavily on local revenue and have less money allocated to school districts with low SES than those with high SES. States with a funding structure that provides less money to schools mired in poverty are referred to as having a *regressive funding system*. States, such as Oklahoma, Wisconsin, North Carolina, and California, that fund their schools at the relatively same levels regardless of its SES level are referred to as having a *flat funding system* (Baker, Farrie, Johnson, Luhm, & Sciarra, 2017).

Funding schools is a contested political issue. Those who pay a heavier load of taxes likely want to receive direct benefits of their tax dollars. Therefore, they desire schools in their own communities to reflect the money they earned and were required to surrender for taxes (Labaree, 2012). However, advocates for progressive funding systems, such as educational critic Jonathan Kozol (1991), argue that public education is supposed to serve the American democracy rather than the interests of those with a higher SES background. Therefore, public schools should not reflect the socioeconomic disparities in the nation. The unfortunate reality is that these economic disparities do indeed reflect upon the funding of schools.

The funding of schools, alone, does not create a disparity among schools. The characteristics of a school also may likely reflect the characteristics of the local community. Noted educational researcher *Jean Anyon* (1941–2013) conducted a seminal study in the late 1970s on the functioning of schools as it related to the social class they derived from. This study (Anyon, 1980) concluded that schools exhibit a feature in the field of sociology called *social reproduction* where its structure and practices transmit social inequality from one generation to the next. She divided the schools she observed into a four categories based on the school's SES background: working class, middle class, affluent professional, and executive elite. Anyon concluded that the working class school exhibited students' engaging in mechanical procedures, rote behavior, and little decision-making. Students in the middle class school focused on getting "the right answer" with some, but little, decision-making involved. The affluent professional schools provided students with opportunities to be creative and independent. The executive elite school emphasized reasoning through problem solving and conceptual learning with a heavy emphasis upon life application. As Anyon's important work demonstrated, the inequalities produced in a school by the disparity among social classes imbue throughout the school. This is why social class is arguably the most significant factor affecting the American public school.

Summary

In the 1960s, a concern emerged among policymakers, social activists, and educators, regarding the causes for the disparity of measures of academic achievement among races in the United States. The 1966 Coleman Report produced a breakthrough finding that students' academic achievement is primarily affected by his or her SES background. Simultaneously with this important finding, the federal government entered the fray of public education through the Elementary and Secondary Education Act by providing extra money to school districts to help counter the impoverished conditions within their respective communities. In recent times, unfortunately, the disparity has significantly widened between those with a higher SES and those with a lower SES. The research of both Robert Putnam and Annette Lareau demonstrate the growing disparity in the quality of life among children of different social classes. Schools, in fact, inherit gaps among social classes in such areas as students' exposure to words and OTL that affect students' later performance in school.

Even though a disparity is increasing among social classes, the disparity among races regarding students dropping out of school is sharply declining. Perhaps this is a sign that the public looks upon the public school as a means to improve their lives. However, public schools' reliance on property taxes for funding result in a disparity in the funding of schools that actually perpetuates the social class divide rather than narrowing it.

Reflective Exercises

1. How might a teacher effectively narrow the achievement gap in his or her classroom despite the large SES gap amongst the students? Is it reasonable to expect teachers to narrow this achievement gap?
2. How do you see, if at all, poverty being concentrated in your own community?
3. What are some of the consequences that different parenting styles (concerted cultivation, accomplishment of natural growth) have upon students' school experiences?
4. Should schools continue to rely so heavily upon property taxes for revenue? Explain.

References

Anyon, J. (1980). Social class and the hidden curriculum of work. *Journal of Education, 162*(1), 67–92.

Baker, B., Farrie, D., Johnson, M., Luhm, T., & Sciarra, D. (2017). *Is school funding fair? A national report card.* Education Law Center. Retrieved from http://www.edlawcenter.org/assets/files/pdfs/School%20Funding/NRC_VI_Final.pdf

Bronfenbrenner, U. (1994). Ecological models of human development, In *International Encyclopedia of Education*, Vol. 3, 2nd ed. Oxford, England: Elsiver.

Coleman, J., Campbell, E., Hobson, C., McPartland, J., Mood, A., Weinfield, F., & York, R. (1966). *Equality of educational opportunity.* Washington, DC: United States Department of Health, Education and Welfare.

Cornman, S. Q., & Musu-Gillette, L. (2016, October 14). Financing education: National and state funding and spending for public schools in 2014 [NCES Bog]. *National Center for Education Statistics.* Retrieved from

https://nces.ed.gov/blogs/nces/post/financing-education-national
-and-state-funding-and-spending-for-public-schools-in-2014

Hart, B., & Risley, T. (2003). The early catastrophe. *American Educator, 27*(4), 6–9.

Hanushck, E. A. (2016). What matters for student achievement. *EducationNext, 16*(2). Retrieved from https://www.educationnext.org/what-matters-for-student-achievement/

Harlow, C. W. (2003). *Education and correctional populations.* Bureau of Justice Statistics Special Report. Washington, DC: U.S. Department of Justice.

Kozol, J. (1991). *Savage inequalities: Children in America's schools.* New York, NY: Crown.

Labaree, D. F. (2012). *Someone has to fail.* Cambridge, MA: Harvard University Press.

Lareau, A. (2003). *Unequal childhoods: Race, class and family life.* Berkeley: University of California Press.

Lee, S. J. (2015). *Unraveling the "model minority" stereotype: Listening to Asian American youth* (2nd ed.). New York, NY: Teachers College Press.

Pew Research Center. (2015, December 9). *The American middle class is losing ground: No longer the majority and falling behind financially.* Washington, D.C. Retrieved from http://www.pewsocialtrends.org/2015/12/09/the-american-middle-class-is-losing-ground/

Putnam, R. D. (2015). *Our kids: The American dream in crisis.* New York, NY: Simon and Schuster.

Ravitch, D. (1983). *The troubled crusade: American education, 1945–1980.* New York, NY: Basic Books.

U.S. Department of Education, National Center for Education Statistics. (2017). *The Condition of Education 2017* (NCES 2017-144). Retrieved from ERIC database. (ED574257)

U.S. Department of Education, Office of Elementary and Secondary Education. (2016). *Consolidated state performance report, 2014–15.* Retrieved from https://nces.ed.gov/programs/coe/indicator_coi.asp

Vevea, B. (2016, April 17). How Illinois pays for public schools, $9,794 vs. $28,639. *WBEZ News.* Retrieved from https://www.wbez.org/shows/wbez-news/How-Illinois-Pays-For-Public-Schools-$9,794-Vs-$28,639/644c7a51-8232-409f-acc1-bba6188e7d93

Wood, L., Kiperman, S., Esch, R. C., Leroux, A. J., & Truscott, S. D. (2017). Predicting dropout using student- and school-level factors: An ecological perspective. *School Psychology Quarterly, 32*(1), 35–49. Retrieved from http://dx.doi.org/10.1037/spq0000152

11

Exceptionality and School

Cecilia and Christopher were proud parents of a new little girl named Noreen. Noreen was their third child and was different from her siblings in that she had Down Syndrome. While their other children crawled and even began to talk by the age of one year, Noreen mostly sat still and enunciated indecipherable sounds. Frankly, Cecilia and Christopher were not prepared for this unexpected challenge since the development of their other children more or less spawned naturally.

Fortunately, Cecilia and Christopher had help. The local public school district provided an intervention specialist, named Rhonda, to assist them with Noreen's development. Rhonda appeared at their house twice a week with a barrage of new challenges for the parents. Sometimes these challenges involved strapping Noreen in a harness and positioning her to walk while holding her upright. Sometimes it involved positioning Noreen in a high chair and allowing her to feed herself, despite the mess that inevitably followed. Sometimes it involved playing a montage of games that involved

Paradoxes of the Public School, pages 149–160
Copyright © 2019 by Information Age Publishing
All rights of reproduction in any form reserved.

throwing and catching a ball. Rhonda often tag-teamed with a physical therapist, occupational therapist, and speech therapist who regularly challenged Cecilia and Christopher. At times the challenges seemed too daunting for the parents as they regularly asked Rhonda: "Where are we going to find the time to do these things with Noreen when we are already so busy with everything else in our life?" Rhonda's response was always the same: "Noreen is going to go as far as you're willing to challenge her." It was a statement that Cecilia and Christopher despised at the time, but they trusted Rhonda because they knew she cared for them and Noreen.

Days became weeks, weeks became months, and months became years. By the middle of Noreen's third year, she was walking to preschool, eating on her own, and enunciating some words with the assistance of sign language. While outsiders viewed Noreen's progress as a miracle, her parents knew otherwise. Rather than a miracle, Noreen's progressive development was the result of the tenacious guidance from Rhonda and her colleagues mixed in with the hard work of Noreen and her parents.

While the American public school grappled with desegregation and alleviating economic disparity throughout the 1970s, seismic changes emerged in American society. One of these changes, namely the further inclusion of females, will be featured prominently in the next chapter. This chapter, however, focuses upon American society's initial inclusion of individuals identified with disabilities. The legislative changes that required schools to meet the needs of students identified with disabilities paved the way for students like Noreen to reap the benefits of public schooling and contribute in society. Generally speaking, individuals identified with disabilities "have lived lives reflecting a remarkable ambivalence toward their place in American society" (Osgood, 2008, p. xiii). Labels on such individuals reflect this ambivalence. The ever-changing jargon used to describe individuals affected by this significant change is deeply rooted in the school's sturdy connection with the social efficiency movement from the turn of the 20th century (refer to Chapter 7). For example, the term currently employed to describe such individuals is "students with disabilities" but yet that label signifies a deficiency in a student's ability. What, then, is meant by ability? It is not going out on a limb to conjecture that all individuals have their own share of shortcomings, whether it be physical, mental, emotional, moral, or social. Is it accurate, therefore, to state all students fall in the category of possessing a disability? The answer, of course, depends upon one's definition of ability. In real life, people are people with their own set of strengths and shortcomings. In the synthetic life of school, however, ability involves a normative measurement of mental or physical ability that allows teachers to target an intellectually homogenous group of students during the enactment of the curriculum. It is important to note that school labels are used in real life and cast a harmful stigma on students. This is why I prefer to use "exceptionality" rather than "disability" to describe students identified as having mental or physical differences from the mainstream. These students present an exception to the general education program provided by schools since the school may need to adjust the curriculum, services, and sometimes building infrastructure to meet these students' needs. The 1970s was a pivotal moment for these students, whom we will broadly label as "exceptional learners" since it marked the first time the American public school was required to address these students' learning needs. Therefore, the central paradox for this chapter is as follows:

The American public school's central purpose at its inception was to provide an education for all children, but only relatively recently did it even begin to address the needs of all children.

Exceptional Children: A Brief History

During the colonial era, the primary care of exceptional children fell in the hands of families and local communities, with some help from religious organizations. Without any systemization, as was provided to most children in the era, the care was generally uneven from one colony to the next (Altenbaugh, 2003). The first systematic reform efforts for exceptional children emerged in the early to mid-19th century and emphasized those identified as deaf and blind. These efforts were spearheaded and later broadened by a Massachusetts-based social reformer named *Samuel Gridley Howe* (1801–1876) who, in 1832, opened the New England Asylum for the Blind (later to be named the Perkins Institution after a donor). According to historian Richard Altenbaugh (2003), Howe "believed every child had a right to schooling, and he relied on an enlightened, naturalistic approach to education" (p. 99). While the Perkins Institution garnered a national reputation, Howe advocated for further efforts to be taken toward the care of exceptional children. These efforts led the Massachusetts state legislature to support, in 1848, the first public institution for children identified with mental disabilities entitled the Fernald School. The Fernald School emerged at a time, the mid-19th century, when institutionalization of exceptional children was a common practice. *Dorthea Dix* (1802–1887) emerged as a significant activist focused on the improvement of such institutions while further opening others throughout the northern East Coast of the United States.

By the tail end of the 19th century, the care for exceptional children was primarily custodial in nature as institutional administrators "reserved 'school work' for only the most capable of the children" (Osgood, 2008, p. 31). By the turn of the 20th century, a movement emerged, *eugenics*, that curiously looked upon the existence of exceptional children as a genetic deficiency among the human race. The eugenics movement, pioneered by the English scientist, Francis Galton (1822–1911), sought to perfect the genetic quality of the human race. The movement relied heavily on *sterilization*, a medical technique intended to leave an individual unable to reproduce, that eventually became a compulsory practice in many states throughout the United States in the early to mid-20th century. In 1927, the U.S. Supreme Court heard a case, *Buck v. Bell* (1927), that challenged the compulsory sterilization law in the state of Virginia. The case centered around Carrie Buck, an 18 year old patient in a Virginia-based mental institution, who was ordered to undergo a sterilization procedure. In addition to Buck, her mother and child were both identified as possessing a mental disability (Lombardo, 2008). Buck's guardian contested that the order was in violation of her rights of due process spelled out in the 14th Amendment of the U.S. Constitution. The Court ruled in favor of the state, with Justice Oliver Wendell Holmes Jr. composing the majority opinion, stating that

> we have seen more than once that the public welfare may call upon the best citizens for their lives. It would be strange if it could not call upon those who already sap the strength of the State for these lesser sacrifices, often not felt to be such by those concerned, to prevent our being swamped with incompetence. It is better for all the world, if instead of waiting to execute degenerate offspring for crime, or to let them starve for their imbecility, society can prevent those who are manifestly unfit from continuing their kind...Three generations of imbeciles are enough. (Buck v. Bell, 1927, para. 4)

The *Buck* case affirmed states' practices of compulsory sterilization as a means to eradicate humanity from genetic "deficiencies" and legitimized the eugenics movement in the United States. While many states eliminated their compulsory sterilization laws in the latter half of the 20th century, the ruling in *Buck* was never overturned.

While exceptional children were often institutionalized, and subjected to a larger societal movement that viewed them as detriments to society, many schools also sought to create curricular spaces for some of them. More than 100 large city school systems formed special schools and classes for exceptional children by 1911 (Winzer, 1993). The advent of intelligence testing (which we will take a closer look at in a later chapter) and the rise of curricular tracking paved the way for schools to form special classes for exceptional children. Historian Robert Osgood (2008) noted that "Cleveland and Boston both established special class clusters and centers that gathered special class students under one roof and permitted easier movement among settings depending on ability" (p. 48). Altenbaugh (2003) noted that "in Baltimore, enrollment in special schools and classes grew slowly but steadily during the 1920s, from 1,421 in 1926 to 2,722 in 1929" and "enrollment jumped to 10,956 in 1936 because of the Great Depression which reflected the general overall increase in school attendance because of a lack of jobs" (p. 212). Although exceptional children were gradually becoming more integrated in the American public school writ large, they were still generally segregated from other children. However, socio-economic forces in the nation during the mid-20th century began to integrate individuals identified with disabilities into mainstream society. After World War II, "demands for labor, technology, and other innovations began to erode impediment to many" (Altenbaugh, 2003, p. 332). Labor shortage in military production at this time gave opportunities for individuals identified with mental disabilities to succeed in the workforce. At the same time, the dramatic rise of school enrollment in the post-war era included the entry of more exceptional children in the school experience. "School administrators," according to Altenbaugh (2003), began to revise the traditional special education curriculum, which had "relied on repetition, low expectations, and crafts" (p. 332). These forces fed a growing advocacy movement among the American citizenry that sought greater acceptance and improved educational settings for exceptional children.

Numerous activist movements, consisting primarily of parents of exceptional children, sprouted up from local communities in states such as Massachusetts, Minnesota, New Jersey, New York, and Rhode Island (Altenbaugh, 2003). This advocacy turned away from the paradigm of the early 20th century that stipulated exceptional children possessed genetic deficiencies that posed a threat to the human race. Instead, this advocacy focused on the potential possessed by exceptional children who, with educational and medical intervention, could be positive contributors to general society. Eventually, notable personalities in American culture emerged in support of acceptance and improved educational conditions for exceptional children. For instance, Pearl Buck, noted author, wrote a series of essays entitled "The Child Who Never Grew" in the *Ladies' Home Journal* that honestly and empathetically portrayed her life as a mother of an exceptional child. She detailed how she dealt with "ignorance, skepticism, and patronization on the part of family, friends, and professionals" (Osgood, 2008, p. 94).

Perhaps the most influential, and persistent, person to emerge as an advocate for exceptional children was *Eunice Kennedy Shriver* (1921–2009), sister of President John F. Kennedy. Shriver's concern for exceptional children emerged from her relationship with her sister, Rosemary, who was identified with a mental disability (Larson, 2015). Shriver's relentless advocacy for children identified with mental disabilities ranged from being a founder of the National Institute of Child Health and Human Development to the establishment of numerous university programs and health care facilities throughout the country. However, Shriver's most significant advocacy effort was her founding of the Special Olympics in the 1960s that emerged as the largest global sports organization for children and adults identified with disabilities. Shriver raised national and global consciousness toward the plight of individuals identified with disabilities. She advocated for mainstreaming, rather than isolation and institutionalization, of exceptional children into American daily life. The inception of Shriver's advocacy efforts ran parallel with President Kennedy's approval to create the Division of Handicapped Children and Youth in 1963 (Altenbaugh, 2003). The rise of national attention toward the needs of exceptional children eventually led the U.S. Congress to take significant legislative action on their behalf in the mid-1970s.

Federal Intervention

In 1975, the United States created a law that transformed the lives of exceptional children. The law, entitled the *Education for All Handicapped Children Act*, included this important requirement of all schools:

> ...to the maximum extent appropriate, handicapped children, including children in public or private institutions or other care facilities, are educated with children who are not handicapped, and that special classes, separate schooling, or other removal of handicapped children from the regular educational occurs only when the nature of severity of the handicap is such that education in regular classes with the use of supplementary aids and services cannot be achieved satisfactorily. (Education for All Handicapped Children Act, 1975)

The law promised to pave the way for the mainstreaming of exceptional children into general society, a far contrast from past practices. The law was reauthorized, first in 1997 and later in 2004, with a less stigmatic title, the *Individuals With Disabilities Education Act* (IDEA), that identified the individual first as opposed to the disability. The law's emphasis on *inclusion*, or the integration of exceptional children into the general education setting, required schools to assure that it was properly equipped and staffed to fulfill this law.

There are three key components to IDEA that make it transformative for the lives of exceptional children. First, it requires that all students identified with a disability, or who are otherwise eligible for special services, such as speech assistance, must be provided by the school with an *Individualized Education Program* (IEP). Simply put, an IEP is an educational plan aimed toward fulfilling the specific needs of an individual. Some individuals' needs might fall in the *high-incidence category*. These needs may consist of, but are not limited to, various learning disabilities, communication disorders, or emotional disturbance that are more commonly experienced. Other individuals' needs might fall in the *low-incidence category*. These needs may consist of, but are not limited to, various levels of blindness or deafness, and severe intellectual disabilities (Hallahan, Kauffman, & Pullen, 2013) that are less commonly experienced. An IEP is developed in collaboration with a team consisting of the child, parent, school administration, and various teachers and service providers employed by the school district. Together, this team creates educational goals and a plan for services to assist the child in achieving those goals. These goals and services are routinely revisited by the team to ensure that they are appropriate for fulfilling the child's educational needs. Another key component of IDEA is that it ensures that all children are provided a *Free and Appropriate Public Education* (FAPE). This component ensures that all educational services provided to the child through the IEP are publicly funded, without additional charge to the child's family. It also assures that the goals in the IEP are challenging and meets approximate grade-level status for the child. The third component of IDEA that is important for us to note is the concept of providing a child with a *Least Restrictive Environment* (LRE) as they seek to meet their educational goals. The concept of LRE emphasizes the inclusion of exceptional children in the general education setting, unless the nature of the child's disability makes such inclusion impossible. Table 11.1 displays the statistics of students' educational environments according to their identified disability. According to Table 11.1, in 2013, nearly 62% of all students identified with disabilities were included in 80% or more of the regular, general class. The identified disabilities of students most commonly referred to a separate school included deaf-blindness (18.5%), emotional disturbance (12.9%), and the category listed as multiple disabilities (18.7%). These three disabilities likely fall in the category of low-incidence and inclusion in the regular, general classroom may not be as likely for some of these students. However, even with these particular identified disabilities, much of these students school day involved inclusion in the regular, general school setting.

TABLE 11.1 Percentage Distribution of Students 6 to 21 Years Old Served Under Individuals With Disabilities Education Act, by Educational Environment and Type of Disability: Fall 2013

Type of Disability	All Environments	Regular School, Time Inside General Class			Separate School For Students With Disabilities	Separate Residential Facility	Parentally Placed in Regular Private Schools	Homebound/Hospital Placement	Correctional Facility
		Less Than 40%	40–79%	80% or More					
All Students with Disabilities	100.0	13.8	19.4	61.8	2.9	0.3	1.1	0.4	0.3
Autism	100.0	33.3	18.2	39.7	7.4	0.4	0.7	0.3	#
Deaf-blindness	100.0	35.6	11.9	23.1	18.5	7.9	0.1	2.8	0.1
Developmental delay	100.0	16.1	19.4	63.0	0.8	#	0.5	0.2	#
Emotional disturbance	100.0	19.8	17.8	45.1	12.9	1.6	0.3	1.1	1.6
Hearing impairment	100.0	12.2	16.0	59.3	7.7	3.1	1.3	0.2	0.1
Intellectual disbility	100.0	49.4	26.9	16.3	6.1	0.3	0.3	0.5	0.2
Multiple disability	100.0	46.4	16.4	13.3	18.7	1.6	0.3	3.2	0.1
Orthopedic impairment	100.0	21.5	16.1	55.1	4.4	0.1	0.8	1.9	0.1
Other health impairment	100.0	9.6	21.9	64.5	1.7	0.2	0.1	0.8	0.3
Specific learning disability	100.0	6.1	24.4	67.8	0.5	0.1	0.8	0.1	0.3
Speech or language impairment	100.0	4.3	5.4	87.3	0.3	#	2.6	#	#
Traumatic brain injury	100.0	20.1	22.2	49.6	5.1	0.5	0.7	1.7	0.1
Visual impairment	100.0	10.8	13.0	64.8	6.1	3.5	1.2	0.6	#

Source: U.S. Department of Education (2015).

TABLE 11.2 Accomplishments of IDEA, as Stated by U.S. Department of Education in 2010	
Accomplishment	**Data Support**
More young children receive high quality early interventions that prevent or reduce the future need of services.	Approximately, 16% of 3,000 preschoolers receiving special education services in the 2003–2004 school year stopped receiving these services in a two-year span.
More children with disabilities are not only attending neighborhood schools but also are receiving access to the general education curriculum.	In 2008, 5,660,491 students with identified disabilities were enrolled in the general education setting of school. 95% were enrolled in their neighborhood school.
More youths with disabilities graduate from high school.	In 2007–2008, 217,905 students identified with disabilities graduated high school with a regular diploma. Since 1995–1997, there was a 21 point decrease in students identified with disabilities dropping out of school.
More youths with disabilities are enrolled in post-secondary programs.	1987: 14.6% enrolled. 2005: 35% enrolled.

Source: U.S. Department of Education (2010).

A 2010 report on IDEA issued by the U.S. Department of Education revealed a series of accomplishments toward the improvements of the educational experiences of exceptional children since the passage of the law (see Table 11.2). The nature of these accomplishments revolve around increased access to educational opportunities for exceptional children. Undoubtedly, federal intervention was helpful in this regard. One only needs to examine the history of how the American public addressed the needs of exceptional children prior to 1975 to fully appreciate the positive steps forward.

Contemporary Challenges

The achievements of IDEA may lead some to believe a narrative of the education for exceptional children concludes on a positive note. The truth, however, is that the narrative is still being composed despite some success. There is evidence that some schools merely seek to attain minimum standards set forth by IDEA, rather than emphasize the challenge faced with creating an "appropriate" educational plan that meets students' specific needs. A 2017 Supreme Court case, *Endrew F. v. Douglas County School District* (2017), addressed the question: Must schools provide an educational experience where students demonstrate significant progress or can they provide an educational experience for the student so that they demonstrate some improvement? The case involved a boy, named Endrew, who was on an IEP for a diagnosis of autism in a Colorado-based public school. Endrew's parents, out of frustration of a lack of progress in their son's academic and social goals by the time he reached fourth grade, transferred him to a private school where he achieved significant progress in those areas. Since the costly tuition of the private school ran counter to IDEA's emphasis on FAPE, the family took the public school district to court, eventually making its way to the U.S. Supreme Court. In a unanimous decision, the U.S. Supreme Court sided with Endrew's family stating:

> When all is said and done, a student offered an educational program providing "merely more than *de minimis*" progress from year to year can hardly be said to have been offered an education at all. For children with disabilities, receiving instruction that aims so low would be tantamount to "sitting idly...awaiting the time when they were old enough to 'drop out.'...The IDEA demands more. It requires an educational program reasonably calculated to enable a child to make progress appropriate in light of the child's circumstances. (Endrew F. Douglas County School, 2017, para. 44)

Advocates for exceptional children propose that this case has landmark status in that it significantly raises educational expectations for schools to reach all students' learning needs (McKenna, 2017).

While expectations for schools to meet exceptional children's needs may be on the rise, there are reasons to believe that schools are currently ill-prepared to meet those needs. The primary reason for this concern is that general education teachers are poorly prepared in the area of special education (Mader, 2017). A 2007 study of teacher preparation (Cameron & Cook, 2007) reported that, on average, general education teacher candidates take only 1.5 courses in special education as opposed to 11 courses taken by special education teachers. There has been little curricular change in teacher education preparation since this nearly decade old study (Mader, 2017). With an increased emphasis on inclusion, the burden to meet the needs of exceptional children is continually increasing for general education teachers. However, most general teachers are scantly prepared to work with exceptional children.

Summary

The historical narrative of how American society addresses the plot of exceptional children is primarily one of insulation, with significant traces of attempts toward their eradication. Since school is often a mirror image of society, exceptional children have only recently been in the front and center of educational reform. The 1970s proved to be a landmark decade for exceptional children in that the United States took legislative action to secure exceptional children's place in the American public school. Significant achievements for exceptional children have been met since the passage of this legislation. However, children who are identified with disabilities pose a challenge to the American public school since it is generally designed to meet the needs of a homogenous target of students. While legislation and court rulings continually side on behalf of inclusion of exceptional children in the general school setting, schools are ill-prepared to meet these needs with general education teachers woefully prepared to address exceptional students' needs.

Reflective Exercises

1. What effect do you think labels have upon children identified with disabilities?
2. What does the history of the education of exceptional children say about the values of American society, both past and present?
3. Do you think that all children identified with disabilities receive an "appropriate" education? What should an "appropriate" education look like for them?
4. How should teachers be better prepared to meet the needs of exceptional children? What should the nature of their coursework look like?

References

Altenbaugh, R. J. (2003). *The American people and their education: A social history.* Upper Saddle River, NJ: Merrill/Prentice Hall.

Buck v. Bell. 274 U.S. 200 (1927). Retrieved from FindLaw database. https://caselaw.findlaw.com/us-supreme-court/274/200.html

Cameron, D. L., & Cook, B. G. (2007). Attitudes of preservice teachers enrolled in an infusion preparation program regarding planning and accommodations for included students with mental retardation. *Education and Training in Developmental Disabilities, 42*(3), 353–363.

Education for All Handicapped Children Act. (1975). Public Law 94-142. Retrieved from https://www.govtrack.us/congress/bills/94/s6/text

Endrew F. Douglas County School, 580 U.S. (2017) Retrieved from FindLaw database. https://caselaw.findlaw.com/us-supreme-court/15-827.html

Hallahan, D. P., Kauffman, J. M., & Pullen, P. C. (2013). *Exceptional learners: Pearson new international edition: An introduction to special education.* New York, NY: Pearson Higher Ed.

Larson, K. C. (2015). *Rosemary: The hidden Kennedy daughter.* Boston, MA: Houghton Mifflin Harcourt.

Lombardo, P. A. (2008). *Three generations, no imbeciles: Eugenics, the Supreme Court, and Buck v. Bell.* Baltimore, MD: JHU Press.

Mader, J. (2017, March 1). How teacher training hinders special needs students. *The Atlantic.* Retrieved from https://www.theatlantic.com/education/archive/2017/03/how-teacher-training-hinders-special-needs-students/518286/

McKenna, L. (2017, March 23). How a new Supreme Court ruling could affect special education. *The Atlantic.* Retrieved from https://www.theatlantic.com/education/archive/2017/03/how-a-new-supreme-court-ruling-could-affect-special-education/520662/

Osgood, R. L. (2008). *The history of special education: A struggle for equality in American public schools.* Westport, CT: Praeger.

U.S. Department of Education. (2010). *Thirty-five years of progress in educating children with disabilities through IDEA.* Available at https://www2.ed.gov/about/offices/list/osers/idea35/history/idea-35-history.pdf

U.S. Department of Education. (2015). *Office of special education programs, Individuals with disabilities education act (IDEA) database.* Retrieved from https://nces.ed.gov/programs/digest/d15/tables/dt15_204.60.asp

Winzer, M. A. (1993). *The history of special education: From isolation to integration.* Washington, DC: Gallaudet University Press.

12

Gender and School

The cheers of the crowd grew louder as Benton High School's varsity boys' basketball team took the court. Nearly the entire Benton community, adults and students alike, came to watch the big game. It was the big Friday night community event. The public address announcer declared to the filled gymnasium: "Here come your Benton Bulldogs." The cheerleaders, pom-poms in hand, displayed their athleticism and performed their cheers that became a beloved routine for those in attendance. The school band boomed the school's "fight" song. The players formed their layup lines to the adulation of the enthusiastic crowd. They were the pride of Benton.

A day earlier, Benton's girls' varsity basketball team won their biggest game of the year against their local rival. The game was well attended by students and parents alike. Although the band was absent, recorded music played over the public address system. The songs were chosen by members of the girls' team as a way to mentally prepare them for the big game. The first song, Cindi Lauper's (1983) classic hit *Girls Just Wanna Have Fun*,

Paradoxes of the Public School, pages 161–176
Copyright © 2019 by Information Age Publishing
All rights of reproduction in any form reserved.

played as the girls formed their layup lines to the delight of the loyal and loving crowd. The crowd took pride in their girls team—as they worked hard and were known for their teamwork and precision. At the conclusion of the warm-ups, the starting lineups were read by high school junior Andy McDonald, who often filled in wherever the athletic department needed help: "And now, your Lady Bulldogs!"

We like to think that gender equity exists in our society, but the story from Benton high school is familiar to many of us. The truth of the matter is that unless compelled by state or federal law, schools merely follow the path that society lays before them. The 1970s proved to be a pivotal period for gender equity because of a significant piece of legislation that shook the foundation of the public school. While the 1970s proved to be a breakthrough decade for exceptional children's place in the American public school, the same can also be said for females. In 1972, the U.S. Congress passed significant civil rights legislation, called Title IX, that forbade sex-based discrimination in educational institutions. It may seem peculiar that nearly half of the school population, prior to Title IX, experienced discrimination due to their sex. Yet, it was true. Females, for instance, were often forbade from participating in extra-curricular sports. Vintage school yearbooks from the early to mid-20th century reveal that sports were aimed toward males, and females were expected to merely support their male classmates' athletic adventures. However, this changed in the 1970s as a result of Title IX.

Individuals, and groups of individuals, experience marginalization from a power-structure set firmly in place in society. In Chapter 4, we saw the effects of marginalization due to race. Likewise, gender-based marginalization is historically rooted in American society. This chapter examines the changes brought forth from Title IX, but we will venture to look at gender more broadly in the American school experience. The word *gender* commonly refers to the social characteristics of being female or male, whereas *sex* refers to the physical characteristics of males and females. However, many cultures view these two terms interchangeably. For the purposes of simplicity, we will use the word gender to broadly encapsulate both terms. What role does gender and sexuality play in the American school? How do boys fare in school as opposed to girls, and visa-versa? Is school a masculine or feminine institution, and how does one define such categorization? What is the collective experience of the LGBTQ (lesbian, gay, bisexual, transgender, and queer) population in the American public school? These questions emanate from the following paradox:

While sex-based discrimination is illegal in the American public school, gender inequality still exists in the American school experience.

Feminism: Cause and Effect

Many well-educated women were concerned about the status of their gender in the earliest stages of the American republic. As a case in point, on March of 1776, in the midst of the American Revolution, Abigail Adams (1776) implored her then congressman-husband, John Adams, to "remember the ladies" as the Continental Congress sought to build a new political regime. Abigail Adams, an intellectual of high regard, was well aware at how colonial America presumed women should not play a role in public life nor should they have the same individual rights as men. These disparaging views of women emerged from an ancient concept, *misogyny*, borrowed from Ancient Greek culture. Misogyny literally means a hatred of women. The concept is still practiced, but in most instances it has evolved into *sexism*. Sexism is not necessarily a hatred of women, but rather it entails a belief that women should be subjugated to an inferior role than men.

Sexism is an emergent force throughout American history. Throughout the 19th century, women were not allowed to run for political office nor even engage in the practice of voting. Many prominent women throughout the 19th century, most notably *Elizabeth Cady Stanton* (1815–1902), *Lucretia Mott* (1793–1880), and *Susan B. Anthony* (1820–1906) dedicated their lives for the cause of women's suffrage (the right for women to vote). Both Stanton and Mott were leaders of the 1848 Seneca Falls Convention in New York where the *Declaration of Sentiments* emerged as a pioneering document that forcefully accused men of tyranny toward women in America. Anthony was a tireless women's activist who was jailed for voting in the 1872 presidential election. Nearly 2 decades after the death of these three prominent suffragettes, the U.S. Congress passed the 19th Amendment in 1920 that assured women's right to vote in the United States.

In the mid-20th century, a new feminist movement emerged that sought to bring women social and cultural equality. This movement was spearheaded by the 1963 publication of *Bette Friedan's* (1921–2006) provocative book *The Feminine Mystique* (1963). In the book, Friedan details a woman's struggle with subjugation to men and isolation away from the public. Friedan's book was followed by the rise of feminist cultural icon and activist, *Gloria Steinem* (b. 1934) who founded, in 1971, the popular magazine *Ms.* that shed light on women's social issues such as workplace equality and women's reproductive health. As public awareness of women's issues grew, the U.S. Congress passed the legislation pivotal for the women's equal rights movement: Title IX.

Title IX

Title IX was passed by the U.S. Congress in 1972 as a by-product of the Civil Rights Act of 1964 and an amendment to key pieces of education legislation from the 1960s, most notably the Elementary and Secondary Education Act of 1965. The central premise of Title IX is that it forbade discrimination in any educational institution within the United States. The language of the act was as follows: "No person in the United States shall, on the basis of sex, be excluded from participation in, be denied the benefits of, or be subjected to discrimination under any education program or activity receiving Federal financial assistance..." (Title IX, 1972). *Bernice Sandler* (b. 1928), one of the key individuals who lobbied for the passage of Title IX, saw the legislation as central to women receiving equal treatment in American society. Sandler was frustrated that less scholarship money for women than men was provided at universities and that schools were not held responsible for ensuring that women were protected from sexual assault (Morrison, 2017). Interestingly, what Title IX is known most for, namely athletics, was not mentioned in the legislation but rather emerged as a primary by-product from it. Prior to Title IX, female's athletic opportunities paled in comparison to those of males. At the collegiate level, male athletics have a longstanding tradition throughout the 20th century of intercollegiate contests. However, females had to rely heavily on intramural contests within their colleges for athletic competition (Hult, 1994). Title IX shook this enormous male-female disparity to its core. The U.S. Congress granted secondary and post-secondary educational institutions a 6-year period to achieve compliance, meaning that females must have the same number of educational opportunities (i.e., athletic teams) as males (Carpenter, 1993).

The passage of Title IX did not lead to a smooth path to progress for females. While athletic opportunities opened up for females, the quality of these opportunities did not necessarily match those provided for males. *Pat Summitt* (1952–2016), head women's basketball coach at the University of Tennessee, lived through the adversity women faced in the initial wake of the passage of Title IX. Summitt, who led the Tennessee basketball program toward national recognition and acclaim, shared what it was like for her in the 1970s:

> I had to drive the van when I first started coaching. One time, for a road game, we actually slept in the other team's gym the night before. We had

mats, we had our little sleeping bags. When I was a player at the University of Tennessee-Martin, we played at Tennessee Tech for three straight games, and we didn't wash our uniforms. We only had one set. We played because we loved the game. We didn't think anything about it. (Gregory, 2009, para. 5)

Summitt's career rise from obscurity mirrored the effect that Title IX had on females throughout the nation. In 1974, fewer than 300,000 girls participated in high school sports. By 2012, that number remarkably stood at nearly 3.1 million (Simpson, 2012).

Teachers and Administrators by Gender

While females gained the right toward equal opportunity through Title IX, there are numerous other issues unique to each gender. As we saw in Chapter 3, the majority of teachers in the United States are female and has been so for quite some time. Why? This question remains baffling and the lack of empirical research on the topic leaves us to rely on speculation. We know that teaching was advertised in the Common School era as a profession well suited for females. Historian Kathleen Weiler (1989) asserted that many educational leaders in this era, such as Horace Mann and Catherine Beecher, viewed the school as a continuation of the family where "the child was viewed as developing first within the context of maternal care in the family, and then moved naturally to the care of the woman teacher" (p. 17). Perhaps this paradigm has perpetuated, leading later generations to be psychologized that teaching is mostly for women. The lack of professional opportunities, outside of teaching and nursing, may also play a key role in the perpetuation of female domination of teaching. A myriad of factors may play into this issue, such as low pay relative to what is typically available to males in the workforce, or even that females generally remain as the primary caregiver of their children and seek a profession where their work schedules mirror their children's school schedules (Rich, 2014). The truth may likely dwell with a combination of all these factors.

While females dominate the teaching profession (76% of the total teacher workforce), the trend reverses among school administrators. In a recent survey (see Figure 12.1), females account for nearly half (52%) of the nation's school principals but roughly a quarter (27%) of school superintendents. While males have historically dominated administrative positions in school, why has this gender gap remained among superintendents whereas it no longer exists among principals? Once again, we lack a simple and clear answer on this phenomenon. Since women make up the

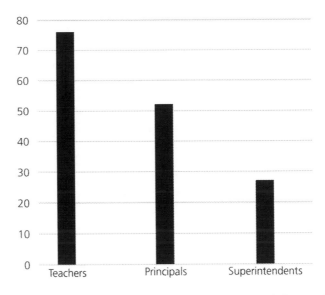

Figure 12.1   Percentage of school position filled by women in 2016. *Sources:* National Council for Education Statistics (2015); The School Superintendents Association. (2015).

vast majority of elementary teachers, women tend to dominate the ranks of elementary school principals. This may play a factor since many school superintendents are drawn from the teaching force in secondary school and it is more common to find males among secondary teachers. Prolonged male domination among superintendents may also leave females less networked than their male colleagues to be encouraged and supported as a potential superintendent. Another possible factor, and one still faced by many females in contemporary America, is the predominance of sexism against females who aspire to positions of power. "When they do get the job," reporter Denisa Superville (2016) said of women in the superintendency, "women often face scrutiny men don't... that includes being told to smile more, having their appearances critiqued, and facing harsh treatment when they assert their authority" (para. 18).

Academic Performance by Gender

Gender-based disparity is not exclusive to school professionals. Data on students' academic performance also illustrate interesting gender differences in school. Academic achievement is often cited as an area where long-standing gender gaps exist. Data analysis of test score results from the National Assessment of Educational Progress (NAEP) reveal a clear pattern: Females generally perform better at reading whereas males generally perform better at mathematics. Figure 12.2 displays reading test score results by gender for 9, 13, and 17 year olds over nearly a forty-year time span. While some variance may exist within the age groups and across the years, a clear pattern exists of females performing better. Why? Some scholars (e.g., Tyre,

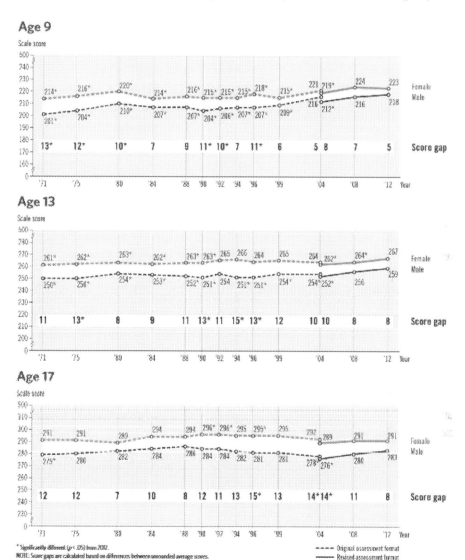

Figure 12.2 Trend in NAEP reading average scores and score gaps for 9-, 13-, and 17-year-old students, by gender. *Source:* U.S. Department of Education (2012). Trends in Academic Progress: Reading 1971–2012.

2008) argue that males' reading interests are often ignored or suppressed by their teachers:

> Unfortunately for our boys, many young men tend to gravitate toward material that many teachers find unacceptable—comic books, books that are goofy and irreverent, and magazines. And rather than encourage their attempts to tackle a new work of literature, their teachers often advise them to leave their copy of *Captain Underpants*, their latest installment of *Spider-Man*, or their new edition of *PC Gamer* at home. (Tyre, 2008, p. 150)

Whether or not teachers are ignoring males' reading interests, there is theoretical support that building upon students' interests is a key approach for improving their academic performance. For instance, John Dewey (1938/2015) emphasized that student growth in certain areas was dependent upon their initial engagement with those areas:

> Any experience is mis-educative that has the effect of arresting or distorting the growth of further experience. An experience may be such as to engender callousness; it may produce lack of sensitivity and of responsiveness. Then the possibilities of having richer experience in the future are restricted. (pp. 25–26)

Dewey's emphasis that future learning experience must be propelled by an intrinsic desire by the student may also speak to the discrepancies in mathematics scores between males and females. Figure 12.3 displays the mathematics test score results by the same age group over the same duration of time. These test scores reveal a pattern nearly reverse to the reading score results, as males consistently perform better than females. However, the score gaps in mathematics are not as large as, nor always as predominant, as the reading scores. Nonetheless, a difference in performance does exist between males and females, albeit a rather minimal difference. This data set leaves us with a central question to answer: Why have boys consistently outperformed girls in mathematics? Recent speculation (i.e., King, 2014) suggests that girls have a waning interest in mathematics due to so few females working in science, technology, engineering, or mathematic (STEM) professions. Table 12.1 supports the fact that females are the clear minority in all such fields. This argument centers on the notion that females may require more role modeling in certain professions in order to be motivated to achieve better in academic disciplines associated with those fields. Therefore, if females knew of more civil engineers who were also female, these students may envision these fields

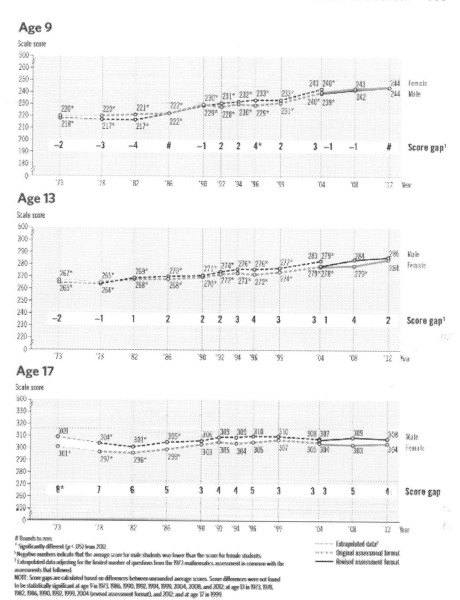

Figure 12.3 Trend in NAEP mathematics average scores and score gaps for 9-, 13-, and 17-year-old students, by gender. *Source:* U.S. Department of Education (2012). Trends in Academic Progress: Mathematics 1973–2012.

TABLE 12.1 Percentage of Employed Persons by Gender, 2016	
STEM Profession	**Percentage of Women in Total Labor Force**
Computer Programmers	21.2%
Software Developers	19.3%
Web Developers	32.5%
Chemical Engineers	16.3%
Civil Engineers	14.8%
Industrial Engineers	23.0%
Electrical Engineers	10.8%
Mechanical Engineers	9.4%
Biological Scientists	47.5%
Chemists	37.7%
Environmental Scientists	33.1%

Source: Bureau of Labor Statistics (2018).

as a possibility to work toward. This may be a simple answer to a complex problem, however it is worth our consideration.

Sexuality, Gender Identity, and Bullying

While there are issues unique to males and females in school, individuals who identify as something other than heterosexual, or who behave in a gender nonconformist manner, face unique issues of their own in school. These individuals stand out in school for a myriad of reasons: same-sex attraction, gender-identity, or gender non-conformist behavior. Individuals who stand out for these reasons are broadly classified as members of the LGBTQ community (GLAAD, 2016). First, let's briefly examine these groups of individuals who are classified as LGBTQ.

Regarding same-sex attraction, several studies demonstrate that approximately six percent of students in middle and high school report attraction to the same sex (Cianciotto & Cahill, 2012). While sexual attraction is a characteristic that may distinguish members of the LGBTQ community from their school peers, *gender identity* and *gender expression* are also necessary constructs to understand the challenges members of the LGBTQ community face within the school experience since many members of the community may identify with or express their gender in a fashion that distinguishes them from the majority of peers. Gender identity "refers to how people understand themselves: as boys or girls, men or women, or something else altogether" whereas gender expression "refers to all the ways that people express their gender identity to the outside world, including through dress, appearance, and behavior" (Cianciotto & Cahill, 2012, p. 15). The label "queer" once was a derogatory term used toward individuals and is currently embraced by some of the LGBTQ community as a word that describes, among other things, gender-nonconforming attitudes and behaviors (GLAAD, 2016). "Gender conforming children are those who prefer sex-typical activities and same-sex playmates; gender-nonconforming children are those who prefer sex-atypical activities and opposite-sex playmates" (Cianciotto & Cahill, 2012, p. 20). While the term receives scrutiny for its vagueness and its past use as a derogatory term, it does acknowledge that a segment within the LGBTQ population cannot be categorized simply for their sexuality.

Individuals within the LGBTQ community have been targets of bullying and discrimination by fellow students as well as school officials. As a case in point, a case heard before the Superior Court of Massachusetts in 2000 entitled *Doe v. Yunits* focused on a middle school aged student who, while biologically male, identified as female. This student was openly transgender and wore makeup to school as well as clothing typically identified for women (i.e., dresses, high heels). The school district forbade the student from dressing female. This, along with harassment from some classmates, led the student to drop out of school altogether. The family of the student sued the school district for sexual discrimination and inhibiting her free speech and expression rights. The Massachusetts court ruled in favor of the student's family, arguing that the school had no right to forbid any student from wearing clothing otherwise acceptable under the general school dress code applicable for all students.

Bullying is a form of intentional aggressive behavior against a person or persons and used repeatedly to demean and cause discomfort toward them. This aggressive behavior may be physical or emotional and may occur face to face or through social media outlets. Figure 12.4 displays the most recent reported statistics on the frequency and type of bullying in school. According to these statistics, nearly 20% of students reported being bullied in school. The reported bullying consisted of such acts as insults, defamation, physical abuse, exclusion, threats, coercion, and vandalism. While bullying does garner some attention that propels schools to be proactive, many students still are uneasy about attending school. A recent school climate survey conducted in 2015 by the LGBTQ advocacy group, GLESN (2015), found that 55% of LGBTQ youth felt "unsafe" in school and that 75% of transgender students said they felt anxiety or fear about going to class. Some support groups for LGBTQ students have emerged in the past few decades to help create a safer,

Type of bullying

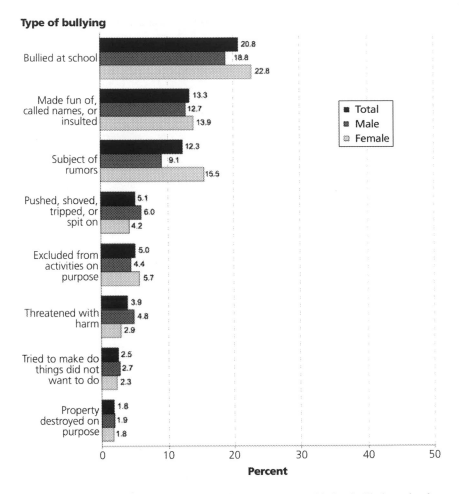

Figure 12.4 Percentage of students ages 12–18 who reported being bullied at school during the school year, by type of bullying and sex: 2015. *Source:* U.S. Department of Education, National Center for Education Statistics (2018). Retrieved from: https://nces. ed.gov/fastfacts/display.asp?id=719
Note: "At school" includes in the school building, on school property, on a school bus, and going to and from school. Students who reported experiencing more than one type of bullying at school were counted only once in the total for students bullied at school.

more welcoming school environment. Perhaps the most notable of these support groups is the Gay–Straight Alliance (GSA). The Gay–Straight Alliance is a student-centered club where LGBTQ students meet along with some heterosexual peers to engage in conversation, share activities, and otherwise engage in mutual support (Mayo, 2013).

Another contemporary issue involving the LGBTQ community, that particularly affects transgender students, is the school's conventional use of sex-segregated restrooms and locker rooms. There is a growing concern among families that, among other things, female students may be sexually assaulted or a victim of voyeurism if a male was permitted to enter a restroom assigned for females. The question becomes: Where may transgender students use a restroom or locker room when they are segregated by gender? This question is currently under litigation in some states. In the Spring of 2017, in what may be a pivotal case to help resolve the question of transgender use of bathrooms, the Wisconsin appellate court considered a civil case entitled *Whitaker v. Kenosha Unified School District* (2017) that focused on a school district that required a transgender student to use a restroom befitting of their anatomical sex rather than their gender identity. The court ruled that the district was in violation of the student's civil rights and discriminated the student based on sex. The court ordered a preliminary injunction on the district that temporarily forbids them from enforcing their restroom policy (Brown, 2017). Eventually the district agreed to a settlement with the plaintiff. However, this issue persists as yet another challenge for the public school to accommodate all students' needs and for the public to be cognizant of what constitutes sex discrimination.

Summary

In the 1970s, gender-based discrimination was forbidden with the passage of Title IX. This federal statute paved the way for females to garner more opportunities, particularly in the arena of athletics. However, gender and sexuality still play a pivotal role in understanding the contemporary school experience. In other words, while school law evokes a sentiment that gender-equality now prevails in the American school experience, gender-equality actually does not exist in full form.

A gender disparity exists among teachers and administrators. While teachers are predominantly female, superintendents are primarily male. Superintendents possess great administrative and political power in the school experience, and females have yet to gain such power on a scale equal to males. However, principals are nearly equal in their gender makeup, signifying some power gains by females.

Gender makes a difference with academic achievement. Generally, females perform better at reading whereas males perform better at mathematics. While the gender gap in mathematics is closing, the gender gap in reading is not. Perhaps there are some gender-specific characteristics about the American school experience that may affect males' achievement in reading. Perhaps, also, the poverty of females in STEM fields may have some effect on females' performance in mathematics.

Students within the LGBTQ community face challenges of their own in school. Bullying is a prevailing concern for this community of students. Another growing concern for transgender students is convention and policies that schools set in place that enforce gender-specific restrooms and locker rooms. Such practices and rules leave a growing challenge for the American public school to resolve, as some parents and students share concern about males and females sharing restrooms and locker rooms, yet transgender students merely desire respect and accommodation rather than coercion away from their gender identity.

Reflective Exercises

1. Is the American public school free from gender-based discrimination, as required under Title IX? Explain your answer.
2. Do you think that a school climate (i.e., classroom practices, routinized schedule, demand for silence) have a more significant effect on males, females, or neither? Explain.
3. Why do you think females currently dominate the teaching profession and males dominate the superintendency? Explain.
4. In addition to bullying and gender-specific policies with restrooms and locker rooms, what are some other challenges faced by the LGBTQ community in school? How might these challenges be accommodated in a reasonable manner?

References

Adams, A. (1776, March 31). Letter to John Adams. Retrieved from https://www.masshist.org/digitaladams/archive/doc?id=L17760331aa

Brown, E. (2017, May 30). Appeals court sides with transgender student in Wisconsin school bathroom case. *Washington Post*. Retrieved from https://www.washingtonpost.com/local/education/appeals-court-sides-with-transgender-student-in-wis-school-bathroom-case/2017/05/30/3f5f6e98-4572-11e7-bcde-624ad94170ab_story.html?noredirect=on&utm_term=.f7d6998b91e7

Bureau of Labor Statistics. (2018). *Labor force statistics from the current population survey*. Retrieved from: https://www.bls.gov/cps/cpsaat11.htm

Carpenter, L. J. (1993). Letters home: My life with Title IX. In G. L. Cohen (Ed), *Women in Sport: Issues and Controversies* (pp. 133–155), Newberry Park, CA: SAGE.

Cianciotto, J., & Cahill, S. (2012). *LGBT youth in America's schools*. Ann Arbor: University of Michigan Press.

Dewey, J. (2015). *Experience and education*. New York, NY: Free Press. (Originally published in 1938)

Doe v. Yunits (2000). No. 001060A. Mass. Cmmw.

Friedan, B. (1963). *The feminine mystique*. New York, NY: W. W. Norton.

GLAAD (2016). *GLAAD media reference guide* (2nd ed.). Retrieved from https://www.glaad.org/reference

GLSEN. (2016). *The 2015 national school climate survey: The experiences of lesbian, gay, bisexual, transgender, and queer youth in our nation's schools. Executive Summary*. Retrieved from https://www.glsen.org/sites/default/files/2015%20National%20GLSEN%202015%20National%20School%20Climate%20Survey%20%28NSCS%29%20-%20Full%20Report_0.pdf

Gregory, S. (2009, February 2). Q & A. Tennessee coach Pat Summitt. *Time*. Retrieved from http://content.time.com/time/arts/article/0,8599,1876213,00.html

Hult, J. S. (1994). The story of women's athletics: Manipulating a dream 1890–1985. In D. M. Costa & S. R. Guthrie (Eds.), *Women and sport: Interdisciplinary perspectives* (pp. 83–107), Champaign, IL: Human Kinetics.

King, D. (2014, July 25). Tech camps, other programs hope to keep girls interested in STEM fields. *Baltimore Sun*. Retrieved from https://www.baltimoresun.com/news/maryland/bs-md-women-in-stem-20140725-story.html

Lauper, C. (1983). Girls just want to have fun. On *She's so unusual* [Vinyl Recording]. USA: Portrait Records.

Mayo, Jr., J. B. (2013). Critical pedagogy enacted in the gay straight alliance: New possibilities for a third space in teacher development. *Educational Researcher, 42*(5), 266–275.

Morrison, P. (2017, August 16). Before Title IX came along, many people didn't believe discrimination against women was a problem. *Los Angeles Times*. Retrieved from https://www.latimes.com/opinion/op-ed/la-ol-patt-morrison-asks-bernice-sandler-title-ix-sex-discrimination-20170816-htmlstory.html

National Council for Education Statistics. (2015). [Data]. Retrieved from https://nces.ed.gov/

Rich, M. (2014, September 6). Why don't more men go into teaching? *The New York Times*. Retrieved from https://www.nytimes.com/2014/09/07/sunday-review/why-dont-more-men-go-into-teaching.html

Simpson, J. (2012, June 21). How Title IX sneakily revolutionized women's sports. *The Atlantic*. Retrieved from https://www.theatlantic.com/entertainment/archive/2012/06/how-title-ix-sneakily-revolutionized-womens-sports/258708/

Superville, D. (2016, November 15). Few women run the nation's schools. Why? *Education Week*. Retrieved from https://www.edweek.org/ew/articles/2016/11/16/few-women-run-the-nations-school-districts.html

The School Superintendents Association. (2015). The study of the American superintendent 2015 mid-decade update. Data retrieved from www.aasa .org

Title IX. (1972). 20 U.S.C. Sections 1681–1688. Retrieved from http://www .dol.gov

Tyre, P. (2008). *The trouble with boys: A surprising report card on our sons, their problems and what parents and educators must do.* New York, NY: Crown.

U.S. Department of Education. (2012). *Trends in scademic progress: Reading 1971–2012, Mathematics 1973–2012.* Retrieved from https://nces.ed.gov/ nationsreportcard/subject/publications/main2012/pdf/2013456.pdf

U.S. Department of Education, National Center for Education Statistics. (2018). *Indicators of school crime and safety: 2017 (NCES 2018-036), Indicator 11.* Washington, DC: Author.

Weiler, K. (1989). Women's history and the history of women teachers. *The Journal of Education, 171*(3), 9–30.

Whitaker v. Kenosha Unified School District (2017). No. 16-3522 (7th Cir.)

13

Technology and School

The Language Arts department at Willow High School consisted of four faculty members: Niles, Maxine, Robert, and Sonja. The department convened every third Thursday of the month for their department meeting. The most recent meeting was contentious because of a disagreement surrounding their collective use of web-based blogging software for student use. Earlier in the year, the department agreed to use the blogging software in each classroom so they could be easily shared with others, particularly so they could foster a curricular partnership with the social studies department's efforts to better engage students in current issues. The problem revolved around Robert's refusal to use the software. The contentious conversation went like this:

Maxine: "We all agreed to use the blogging software earlier in the year, and some students are telling me that they're not using it in their class. What's going on?"

Paradoxes of the Public School, pages 177–185
Copyright © 2019 by Information Age Publishing
All rights of reproduction in any form reserved.

Niles: "Yes, I'm hearing the same thing. The social studies department is depending upon us."

Robert: "Listen, I know you're pointing the finger at me. But, frankly, I've had a lot of success with the bound paper journals we used in the past—and I think it's a disservice to our students to take away something that's been working."

Sonja: "But, you agreed to do the blogs this year."

Robert: "I tried to use the software, and some of the students seemed to have trouble with logging in. I thought this was a ridiculous waste of time. I tried to do it—but I can share the journals with the social studies department, if they want to see it. All they need to do is come by my classroom, and I can hand them out."

Sonja: "But, Robert—the blogs allow for crossway conversation between students in each department. Plus, it's easier to access than carrying those heavy journals around."

That last meeting ended with Maxine, Niles, and Sonja biting their lip. They were irate with Robert. How were they able to integrate new technologies in their department if their colleague resisted? They felt that Robert was dragging the entire department down.

Today marked the day for their new monthly meeting. The four faculty members gathered in Maxine's classroom, each with a smile on their face. But, beneath the surface, tension could be found. How can they help Robert? How can they get Robert to comply? Is there any hope?

While social movements on behalf of individuals identified with disabilities, women, and racial minorities arose in the 1960s and 1970s, the landscape of American culture became jilted with a technological revolution that would greatly affect teaching and learning in the school experience. In the 1980s, home personal computers (PCs) and eventually home video game consoles arose and altered how individuals performed work tasks and found amusement. A technological age arose that jettisoned entrepreneurs such as Microsoft's® Bill Gates and Apple's® Steve Jobs as significant iconic cultural figures who represented a new era in society. In the 1990s, this technological revolution exploded with the advent of the Internet. By the dawn of the 21st century, the Internet became a central means for individuals to communicate, conduct commerce, consume and share information, and be entertained. While technological revolutions have permeated throughout world history, the one in our contemporary era was unique. For instance, this particular technological revolution necessitated school districts to create technology coordinator positions specifically charged with the purpose of ensuring schools were adequately prepared with necessary hardware and software tools. However, while much of American society was transformed by technological advancements during this revolution, its impact in the American school experience has been uneven. Despite the emergence of digital technologies that enable individuals to create, share, and discuss ideas emanating from their experiences, many classrooms, such as Robert's from our story, remain relatively static in how they go about the business of educating. While some teachers permeate their classrooms with digital technologies, many others are reluctant to use them or are otherwise more comfortable with engaging students with instructional practices from an earlier era devoid of digital technologies. This chapter intends to briefly examine the potentialities and problems associated with the integration of digital technologies in the American school experience. Therefore, the central paradox for this chapter is as follows:

Digital technology transforms some teachers' pedagogy while it has a smaller effect on other teachers.

The Nature of Digital Technology

The introduction of technology in the classroom is not a new phenomenon. In the 20th century alone, teachers and students alike experienced new technologies, such as radio, film, and instructional television, that promised to transform teaching and learning (Cuban, 1986). However, the advent of digital technology brought features to the classroom that are drastically different than previous technologies. Digital technologies, such as personal computers, handheld devices, and various software applications, have unique characteristics: They can be used in different ways and they are rapidly changing (Koehler & Mishra, 2009). These technologies bring forth new challenges to teachers. For example, software applications have unique affordances and constraints. Therefore, in order to effectively use these applications in the classroom, teachers must be aware of these affordances and constraints prior to understanding how they might effectively employ them in the classroom. This takes more time than merely turning on an audio or video recorder because of the numerosity and wide variety of applications to pick from and the ever-changing nature of these applications. Audio or video players and recorders, on the other hand, remained much more constant in how they operated.

However, as the historian Larry Cuban (1986) pointed out, the teachers who first jumped at the chance to use the new technologies from the 20th century, such as audio and video players, in their respective classrooms were a minority compared to those less willing. Teacher practices over time, Cuban argued, reflect more continuity than change. There are numerous reasons why this may be the case. Cuban argues that the nature of teacher work, with minimal contact time among and between teachers (especially at the secondary level) likely plays a factor in some teachers' recalcitrance to use new technologies. There may be is some validity to this argument, but in this chapter we will re-examine why technology adoption is so uneven across the teaching profession. First, however, let's examine an important framework that explains how technology fits into a teacher's pedagogical repertoire.

TPACK

In 1986, *Lee Shulman* (b. 1938), an educational psychologist, conceived a workable framework to understand teachers' unique professional knowledge. This framework, called *Pedagogical Content Knowledge* (PCK), joined together a teacher's knowledge of pedagogy with their knowledge of content to create a knowledge form that emphasizes how a teacher transforms subject matter for student comprehension and understanding. A teacher's PCK, according to Shulman (1986), "includes an understanding of what makes the learning of specific topics easy or difficult" and "knowledge of the strategies most likely to be fruitful in reorganizing the understanding of learners" (p. 9). Thirty years later, two educational researchers named *Punya Mishra* and *Matthew Koehler* (2006) shared their idea of adding technological knowledge to Shulman's PCK framework that created a dynamic framework for understanding the role of technology in a teachers' professional knowledge. This framework is appropriately entitled *Technological Pedagogical and Content Knowledge* (TPACK).

As you can see in Figure 13.1, the TPACK framework allows for examination of a teacher's content knowledge (C), pedagogical knowledge (P), and technological knowledge (T). In other words, the TPACK model enables analysis of a teacher's understanding of an area of subject matter (C), their ability to transform that content knowledge for student understanding (P), and how they use digital technologies during this process of teaching and learning (T). The TPACK model also possesses a dynamic feature in that along with looking at each component (technology, pedagogy, and content) in isolation, each feature can also be looked at in pairs: PCK, Technological Content Knowledge (TCK), Technological Pedagogical Knowledge (TPK), and the summation of the three as Technological Pedagogical Content

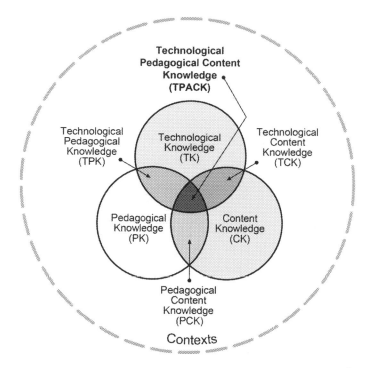

Figure 13.1 TPACK model. *Source:* http://tpack.org (Reproduced by permission of the publisher, ©2012 by tpack.org).

Knowledge (TPACK; Mishra & Koehler, 2006). While PCK has already been addressed, it may be helpful to explain TCK and TPK. Technological Content Knowledge (TCK) consists of the knowledge of how certain technologies may be more adept at teaching particular areas of subject matter, and how the subject matter may dictate how the technology should be used. Technological Pedagogical Knowledge (TPK) consists of the knowledge how a technology may be used beyond its conventional use (i.e., data entry, entertainment) and instead used to enhance teaching and learning.

The emergence of all these knowledge forms is the essential makeup of TPACK (which can be found at the very center of the model in Figure 13.1). In sum, the TPACK model is a visual heuristic that enables analysis or reflection of a teacher's ability to teach content using digital technologies.

Numerous kinds of digital technologies pose tremendous possibilities to enhance teaching and learning in a subject-specific manner. For instance, history education has been evolving toward the need to better position students to create historical narratives of their own using primary sources (a primary source stems from a particular time period whereas a secondary source is a narrative written about a time period, but not from the time period). A growing interest in the use of filmmaking software such as Microsoft's *Moviemaker*® or *Photostory 3*® and Apple's *iMovie*® software has emerged in many history classrooms as a means to position students to craft meaningful and sophisticated historical narratives that creatively weave together images with audio.[1] Recent research (e.g., Schul, 2012, 2014) demonstrates that desktop documentary making may provide students with a rich history learning experience.

Yet another technology that can be used in a subject-specific manner, is the vast reservoir of statistical databases that exist on the Internet. For instance, throughout this book I retrieved information from the Bureau of Labor Statistics, the National Center for Education Statistics, and the National Assessment of Educational Progress. These databases, as well as a multitude of others, are a tremendous source of statistics that could be effectively used in a mathematics, sociology, or government course.

An example of a technology that can be used in a subject-specific manner is software, such as Google Docs®, that allow individuals to collaboratively edit a document or share information with one another. This software may prove to be helpful in a language arts classroom where students are required to collaborate on a writing project together. It could also be employed generically in a discussion-centered classroom experience where students are posed questions and may answer anonymously.

These examples are a mere snapshot of the reservoir of digital technologies available to teachers as a tool to improve teaching and learning in their particular curricular setting. It is paramount that the teacher understand their particular academic discipline and how that technology enhances the learning within the realm of that discipline. Teachers who can effectively integrate digital technology to improve learning within an academic discipline have a robust TPACK. However, some teachers are more capable at doing this than others.

Teacher Integration With Technology

It has been my experience throughout my teaching career that some teachers are more willing to integrate technology than are others. Like any pedagogical strategy, those that involve digital technology require a commitment by the teacher toward being a creative-generative teacher. As we saw in Chapter 6, creative-generative teachers desire to place their students in positions where they are required to solve problems. This approach to teaching often requires risk-taking and an openness to employing new strategies that may effectively engage students in problem-solving. In a small research study I conducted with a workshop of middle and secondary social studies teachers, as well as teacher candidates, I discovered that some teachers viewed desktop documentary making as something they would employ in their classroom for the mere purpose of providing students with a technological experience (Schul, 2017a). However, some of the teachers envisioned documentary making in a subject-specific manner for their own classroom. In other words, some of the teachers isolated the technology as a separate entity apart from their subject matter whereas others saw it as closely tied to how they would approach teaching their subject matter. As my own experience with colleagues and teacher candidates runs parallel with my research finding, the following essential question emerges: Why do some teachers integrate technologies better than others?

This question likely resonates with any question that begs for understanding why some teachers are generally better than others. While talent undoubtedly plays a role, I have known very intelligent teachers who struggle with being an effective teacher. Therefore, talent alone should not be the lone answer to our question. A more helpful answer may involve exploring a teacher's decision-making process. Many factors play a role in teachers' decisions. It may be safe to say that teachers' decisions toward technology integration depend upon two primary factors: training and openness to change (Vanatta & Fordham, 2004).

Training involves a teachers' professional preparatory program as well as ongoing professional development. Teachers with a high TPACK likely were prepared in coursework that modeled effective technology integration and, in the case with instructional methods coursework, they were explicitly taught how some technologies enhance their particular disciplines. It is also crucial for a teacher candidate to be placed in field settings where they may collaborate with practicing teachers who show a willingness and interest toward integrating digital technologies (Schul, 2017b). Working alongside other teachers, particular experienced teachers, who are open to the changes that integration of digital technologies brings to the teaching and learning experience, provides teachers with opportunities to enhance their TPACK. Yet, what causes some teachers to be more open to changes than others? Technology educator Marc Prensky (2001) posed a popular argument that individuals who grew up alongside the rise of digital technologies (digital natives) are more adept at using the technologies than those who grew up beforehand (digital migrants). While Prensky's argument may have some substance, it does not explain those older teachers who are quite adept at integrating technology. Some research (e.g., Barton & Levstik, 2003) sheds light on the notion that teachers who lack a commitment student inquiry are more likely to allow their pedagogical decisions to be centered around covering content and controlling the class rather than taking risks like technology integration requires. Therefore, teachers' openness to change, with technology or anything else that relates with self-improvement, may depend on a myriad of factors such as training, work environment, and an individual's own personal attributes rather than merely the age of the teacher.

Summary

Teachers have been challenged to integrate new technologies throughout the history of the school experience. However, the advent of digital technologies at the turn of the 21st century introduced a transformation of the American culture. As digital technologies became capable of new tasks and the public grew accustomed to these technologies, it became pertinent that schools successfully integrate digital technologies into the lives of teachers and students. A new framework, TPACK, was conceptualized that took into consideration the knowledge necessary for teachers to successfully integrate digital technologies to enhance teaching and learning in a subject-specific manner. However, teachers' TPACK is unevenly dispersed throughout the profession enabling some teachers to be more willing to integrate digital technologies than others.

Reflective Exercises

1. Consider the past three generations in our nation. How has technology influenced each generation differently and similarly? Did these changes affect their schooling experience? Explain.
2. Look at the TPACK framework in Figure 13.1. Of all the different types of knowledge displayed in the TPACK framework, which one might be the most challenging to improve upon for teachers? Which one might be the easiest?
3. Describe how some teachers you know successfully integrated technology in their own classroom.
4. Why do you think some teachers are more adept than others at integrating digital technology into their classroom?

Note

1. For more about desktop documentary making, refer to the following article I wrote: Schul, J. (2014). Film Pedagogy in the History Classroom: Desktop

Documentary Making Skills for History Teachers and Students. *The Social Studies, 105*(1), 15–22.

References

Barton, K. C., & Levstik, L. S. (2003). Why don't history teachers engage students in interpretation? *Social Education, 67*, 358–361.

Cuban, L. (1986). *Teachers and machines: The classroom use of technology since 1920.* New York, NY: Teachers College Press.

Koehler, M., & Mishra, P. (2009). What is technological pedagogical content knowledge (TPACK)? *Contemporary issues in technology and teacher education, 9*(1), 60–70.

Mishra, P., & Koehler, M. J. (2006). Technological pedagogical content knowledge: A framework for teacher knowledge. *Teachers college record, 108*(6), 1017.

Prensky, M. (2001). Digital natives, digital immigrants. *On the Horizon, 9*(5), 1–2.

Schul, J. E. (2012). Compositional encounters: Evolvement of secondary students' narratives while making historical documentaries. *The Journal of Social Studies Research, 36*(3), 219–244.

Schul, J. E. (2014). Emotional evocation and desktop documentary making: Secondary students' motivations while composing historical documentaries. In W. Russell (Ed.), *Digital Social Studies* (pp. 439–466). Charlotte, NC: Information Age.

Schul, J. E. (2017a). Technology for its own sake: Teachers' purpose and practice with desktop documentary making. *Social Studies Education Review, 6*(1), 43–62.

Schul, J. E. (2017b). Clinical entrepreneurship: A student teacher's integration of desktop documentary making. *Research in Social Sciences and Technology, 2*(2), 1–35.

Shulman, L. S. (1986). Those who understand: Knowledge growth in teaching. *Educational researcher, 15*(2), 4–14.

Vannatta, R. A., & Fordham, N. (2004). Teacher dispositions as predictors of classroom technology use. *Journal of Research on Technology in Education, 36*(3), 253–271.

14

Accountability and School

"Remember to show them what you know," Ms. Lutz announced on the loudspeaker. Tomorrow is a big day at Herman Middle School, for the entire student body will take the end-of-year state standardized test. Ms. Lutz, the school's principal, was nervous despite her tough exterior. She knew that her job depended upon the students' test results, as the students did not do so well last year. This year has been particularly challenging for the school, as several students who performed well academically had transferred to the local private school or to the adjacent public school district. "Do you think your students are prepared?" Ms. Lutz asked Mrs. Crescent as she walked in the office to check on her mailbox. "I think so. All I know is that we've done our best. I've never reviewed lessons so often for students as I have this year," Mrs. Crescent replied. Mrs. Crescent knew what tomorrow meant for her. She was in her 20th year at Herman and was, by all means, a sterling teacher. However, the last 3 years have been tough on her. Her annual evaluation now includes students' performance

Paradoxes of the Public School, pages 187–203
Copyright © 2019 by Information Age Publishing
All rights of reproduction in any form reserved.

on the standardized tests, and the students' performance has been less than spectacular. The two didn't talk any further and Mrs. Crescent walked back to her classroom. She, too, wondered in her thoughts if this would be her last year at Herman. Yes, tomorrow is a big day for the school.

The American public school, as we saw in Chapter 5, has experienced numerous reform efforts. These reform efforts pushed the school to do such things as be more relevant to society, more efficient in how it conducts affairs, and more just in how it treats marginalized populations. Some argue (e.g., Labaree, 2012) that reform efforts in the school experience have reaped little success since the common school movement of the mid-19th century. With that said, we are currently mired in the midst of an aggressive, widespread, and largely controversial movement that has been transformative in the school experience: the high stakes-accountability movement. Its effects are strongly felt on the teachers and students at Herman Middle School and yet the stress Mrs. Lutz and Mrs. Crescent experience is an unnecessary and dangerous consequence to an unsuccessful and dangerous reform movement.

The high-stakes accountability movement is historically rooted in the public's effort to hold its institutions accountable to the taxpayer. However, ideological opposition to public schooling also plays a significant role in pushing forward this reform effort. In many ways, the entire project of public education is more vulnerable than ever before and may be at risk of being lost. In this chapter we will examine this accountability effort, including its origins, means of operation, and an analysis of its effect on the public school experience. As you will see, this reform effort pushes classroom policies that run contrary to research in the learning sciences and boldly touts changes that are dispelled by empirical research. Yet, the high-stakes accountability movement is perpetually robust and strong in its effects on the project of public education. The central paradox of this chapter, therefore, is:

Policies and practices are pushed upon the public school experience in the name of improving it, however educational theory and research asserts that these policies and practices are, as a whole, harmful to the school experience.

A National Crisis

In 1983, the U.S. Department of Education released a report filled with fear and peppered with calls for action. The report, entitled *A Nation at Risk*, spelled out, among other things, that the United States was falling behind other industrialized nations in academic achievement and this was a key reason behind the lackluster performance of American industry. The report blasted American public education as having "lost sight of the basic purposes of schooling" and resolved to "renew the Nation's commitment to schools and colleges of high quality throughout the length and breadth of our land" (U.S. Department of Education, 1983). The report failed to take into consideration the characteristics that make the United States more distinct than other nations, most notably Japan, and how those distinctions may affect international test score comparisons. Among these distinct characteristics, the typical U.S. high school serves "a full range of students" whereas many other nations "operate educational systems in which only selected students are allowed to enter high-status high schools and comparative data from these countries may be collected only from those high-status schools" (Berliner & Biddle, 1995, p. 54). The report's rhetoric had an impact on future education policymaking that reshaped the entirety of the American school experience. At the center of these new policies was high-stakes standardized testing.

The origins of standardized tests rest in the social efficiency movement of the early 20th century. Initially called "objective tests" for their supposed objective portrayal of a feature of life, devoid of the need for human expertise and limiting the scope of human error, these tests first arose as a means to survey school performance such as time spent on a particular subject (Lagemann, 2002). Eventually, E. L. Thorndike (recall him from Chapter 7) employed these tests to measure "anything and everything relevant to education—mental capacities, changes in behavior, and even the aims of education" (Lagemman, 2002, p. 59). As Thorndike's use of tests popularized them, they soon became a tool to measure an individual's intelligence and then school achievement. By the 1930s and 1940s, a multitude of objective tests were available that aimed to assess anything from intelligence, personality, or vocational aims (Reese, 2005). A division arose in the mid-20th century among those who created and employed tests in the school experience. Historian Nicholas Lemann (2000) asserted that this division saw the emergence of four separate advocacy groups of standardized testing: (a) those who viewed the test as a measure of individual growth, (b) those who sought to impose tough uniform standards via strict test protocols, (c) those who sought to measure aptitude and reward pure inherited brain power, and finally (d) those who sought to inform teachers of their students' learning needs. The fourth group, whom Lemann called the "educational expanders," were led by two prominent figures in the testing landscape: *Ralph Tyler* (1902–1994) from the University of Chicago and *E. F. Lindquist* (1901–1978) from the University of Iowa. The expanders believed that "schools should be used to transform unlettered Americans, as many as possible, into people who read and thought and had training and skills and therefore who could get on in the world more successfully" (Lemann, 2000, p. 25). The expanders sought to use tests to expand educational opportunities for as many people as possible by allowing teachers to focus on those students who required special attention. Lindquist's creation of the American College Test (ACT) in the mid-20th century is a prime example of educational expansionism since it was originally geared to inform universities of the educational needs of its incoming students so they could fashion a curriculum well suited for them. While remnants of testing as a means of educational expansionism exist in the American school experience, policy makers tend to gravitate toward the second group Lehmann referred to: those who sought to impose tough uniform standards via strict testing protocols. This is exactly what happened in the aftermath of the publication of *A Nation at Risk.*

By the late 1980s, the federal government's cry for educational reform led several states to take action. This call for action came in the package of state academic standards and mandated testing to assure student proficiency of the standards. As a case in point, the Ohio state legislature passed a law in 1987 that required all public school students to pass a proficiency test in order to graduate from high school. These initial Ohio tests consisted of reading, writing, mathematics, and citizenship. The cohort of students to take the exams was the 1994 incoming high school class. Eventually, by 1999, all nonpublic school students in Ohio would also be required to pass the proficiency tests (Ohio Department of Education, 1998). While states such as Ohio took the lead in the wave of standards and testing, the federal government followed up on the growing concern brought forth from *A Nation at Risk* with the 1994 passage of Goals 2000: Educate America Act. Initially created by a coalition of state governors in 1989, Goals 2000 was interestingly passed by a Democratic Congress and signed by Democratic President Bill Clinton. The political party that created Goals 2000 is noteworthy because *A Nation at Risk* was created by a Republican Presidential administration a decade earlier. Goals 2000 put forth eight educational goals for the United States to achieve by the year 2000. These goals, as written by the U.S. Congress (1994) were as follows:

- School Readiness: All children in America will start school ready to learn.
- School Completion: The high school graduation rate will increase to at least 90%.
- Student Achievement and Citizenship: All students will leave Grades 4, 8, and 12 having demonstrated competency over challenging subject matter including English, mathematics, science, foreign languages, civics and government, economics, arts, history, and geography, and every school in America will ensure that all students learn to use their minds well, so they may be prepared for responsible citizenship, further learning, and productive employment in our Nation's modern economy.
- Teacher Education and Professional Development: The Nation's teaching force will have access to programs for the continued improvement of their professional skills and the opportunity to acquire the knowledge and skills needed to instruct and prepare all American students for the next century.
- Mathematics and Science: The United States will be first in the world in mathematics and science achievement.
- Adult Literacy and Lifelong Learning: Every adult will be literate and will possess the knowledge and skills necessary to compete in a global economy and exercise the rights and responsibilities of citizenship.
- Safe, Disciplined, and Alcohol and Drug Free Schools: Every school in the United States will be free of drugs, violence, and the unauthorized presence of firearms and alcohol and will offer a disciplined environment to learning.
- Parental Participation: Every school will promote partnerships that will increase parental involvement and participation in promoting the social, emotional, and academic growth of children.

Federal grant money was provided to states that cooperated with the Goals 2000 initiative. These ambitious goals were not met for the obvious reason that many of them, if not all of them, required significant socio-cultural changes in the American landscape. As we saw in Chapter 10, there are many socioeconomic factors that contribute to student performance in school. However, Goals 2000 signaled the widespread acceptance of the use of an *outcome-based* approach to hold schools accountable. In other words, by the dawn of the 21st century, the success of the U.S. public school experience was assessed by immediate outcomes it produced, much like a manager assesses the success of a factory operation: Inputs should equate specified outputs. By this time, alternatives to the traditional public school were entrenched in American society and would eventually be used by the federal government as a means to foster competition amidst public education.

The Charter School Movement

In the midst of a national call for change in public education arose an idea that promised to spark progress: charter schools. Charter schools were first conceived by *Ray Budde* (1923–2005), an education professor at the University of Massachusetts in Amherst. Budde laid out his conception of charter schools in his publication of the book entitled *Education by Charter*. In the book, Budde listed 12 goals for what he called the "reorganized school," including giving teachers responsibility for and control over instruction, establishing a budgeting/accounting system where educational programs may be planned and implemented over a span of 3 to 5 years, and enable principals to revitalize their roles as school leaders (Budde, 1988). Budde proposed that a creative approach where schools could attain such goals was if any teacher, or group of teachers, within a district could submit an application to their superintendent for charter funds to embark on an educational endeavor, for a short period of time, as a means to try out new ideas. Budde coined the term "charter school" because he believed the idea was akin to the charters given by European monarchs to navigators in the 15th century's era of exploration. Budde's idea remained stagnant for nearly a decade until *Albert Shanker* (1928–1997), well-known president of the American Federation of Teachers, picked up the idea in the late 1980s and proposed it nationwide. Shanker saw Budde's conception of charter schools as empowering teachers and improving the teaching profession. In 1988, Shanker spoke at an event hosted by the Minneapolis Foundation, a Minnesota-based community organization and proposed his idea to the gathering of community leaders. Later, a group of individuals at that gathering met together to discuss the possibilities of infusing the charter school concept in Minnesota. One of these individuals, *Ted Kolderie*, director of a Minneapolis-based public policy group called the Citizens League, proposed opening up the charter school concept to individuals or agencies outside of the school experience, essentially allowing a private business to start its own school using public money. Kolderie's ideas gained popularity among the group, including members of the Minnesota state legislature, leading Minnesota to pass, in 1991, the first charter school law in the history of the United States. As you can see in Table 14.1, the idea spread widely across the country in the 1990s with well over half the nation's states adopting charter school laws. Charter schools' rise in popularity was a bipartisan undertaking. Political leaders from both major U.S. parties (Presidents Clinton, a Democrat, and George W. Bush, a Republican, were

TABLE 14.1 Charter Law Passage in the United States

1991	1992	1993	1994	1995	1996
Minnesota	California	Colorado	Arizona	Alaska	Connecticut
		Georgia	Hawaii	Arkansas	DC
		Massachusetts	Kansas	Delaware	Florida
		Michigan		New Hampsire	Illinois
		New Mexico		Louisiana	New Jersey
		Wisconsin		Rhode Island	North Carolina
				Wyoming	South Carolina
					Texas

Source: Vergari (2002); Schul & Reineke (2015)

TABLE 14.2 Expansion of Charter Schools vs. Traditional Public Schools (1999–2012)

Selected Characteristic	1999–2000		2011–2012	
	Traditional Public Schools (Non-Charter)	Charter Schools	Traditional Public Schools (Non-Charter)	Charter Schools
Number of Schools	90,458	1,524	92,632	5,696
Student Enrollment	46,350,000	340,000	47,199,000	2,058,000
Number of Teachers	2,622,678	13,599	2,920,353	107,929

Source: U.S. Department of Education, National Center for Education Statistics, Common Core of Data (n.d.); Schul & Reineke (2015). (This table was prepared in March 2014.)

both strong supporters of charter schools). Philanthropists, such as Bill and Melinda Gates, and celebrities, such as Oprah Winfrey, also lent significant support to the charter school movement. As you can see in Table 14.2, the outpouring of public support led to increased student enrollment in charter schools. The number of students enrolled in charters grew from 340,000 in the 1999–2000 school year to 2,058,000 in the 2011–2012 school year.

Although both Ray Budde and Albert Shanker perceived charter schools as a method to rejuvenate traditional public schools, education policy makers throughout the nation embarked on an effort to make charter schools into a competitor to the traditional public school system. Kolderie's decision to allow outsiders, particularly businesses, to embark on a venture to create schools made public education into a source of private gain. A widespread belief in the possibilities of a free market influence upon American education helped to pave the way for some of the most significant legislative reforms of education in the history of the nation.

The No Child Left Behind Act

In the beginning of the 20th century, the United States embarked on an effort to reshape American public education in ways not seen since the mid-1960s (Sunderman, Kim, & Orfield, 2005). Led by then Republican President *George W. Bush* (b. 1946), but widely applauded by Democratic Senators such as Massachusetts' Ted Kennedy, this bipartisan effort was branded the No Child Left Behind Act (NCLB). It was hailed by political leaders as an innovative way to improve education while holding public schools accountable for educating all of its children, particularly racial minorities and the underprivileged.

Prior to NCLB, the Elementary and Secondary Education Act of 1965 (ESEA) was cornerstone education legislation aimed at improving the plight of public schools that serve a high percentage of low income families (called Title I schools). Among other things, ESEA provided federal funding to those targeted schools. Each year ESEA has been reauthorized, and in 2001 it was reauthorized as NCLB with a new and significant twist: Receipt of federal funding was to be contingent on compliance with the new accountability measures put in place.

Accountability measures seeped throughout NCLB's provisions on schools. The first, and foremost, measure put in place by NCLB was that each state needed to follow the path of states such as Ohio and create a proficiency test. Students' test results must meet a proficiency level constructed by each individual state. This proficiency level became part of an annual yearly progress (AYP) formula constructed by the state. This AYP formula set by the state was designed to incrementally lead all students toward proficiency. For instance, a state may assert that 50% of all students must meet a proficiency cut score by 2005 and must gradually improve upon that on a schedule the state created. The end goal of NCLB was that all students throughout the United States were to reach full proficiency by 2012. What happened if a school failed to meet the states' AYP level? First, if a school failed to meet AYP for 2 consecutive years, it was placed on a "needs improvement" list and would receive assistance from the federal government toward its targeted areas of improvement. For instance, a school might use the money to create intervention programs in math or reading, depending upon its test score results. In addition to the intervention, students in schools on the "needs improvement" list were permitted to transfer to a school not on the list (Hlebowitsh, 2007a).

A series of harsh punitive measures were placed upon schools who failed to meet AYP for 4 or more consecutive years. The measures after 4 consecutive years of noncompliance include an allowance for schools to replace staff perceived as most responsible for failure to reach AYP. A fifth consecutive year of non-compliance meant that the school could be dissolved and, among other things, recreated as a charter school. It should be noted that while NCLB targeted Title I schools, any public school could be labeled as failing and vulnerable to transfer policies put in place by NLCB and subsequently threaten attendance-based state funding. As a result, NCLB affected all public schools, regardless of the amount of federal monies received.

The No Child Left Behind Act was an abysmal failure. States did not meet full proficiency by 2012 and the high-stakes placed on standardized tests had a negative effect on the school curriculum. Rather than attempting to create a dynamic school curriculum, NCLB had the effect of pushing school leaders to focus on fulfilling the policy's requirements in lieu of emphasizing improvement on the whole school experience not tied to NCLB, particularly curricular areas such as arts, music, and physical education. As evidence of the detrimental effect of NCLB, many schools engaged in gaming strategies where, for instance, they either pushed for failing students to transfer schools, pushed for their enrollment in special education (which eventually became immune to NCLB requirements) or, even worse, to drop out of school. There were also several reported instances of school administrators and teachers engaging in cheating with test results in order to escape punitive measures (Strauss, 2015).

Current Policy Trends

President *Barack Obama* (b. 1961) sought to end NCLB, arguing that it enforced "cookie-cutter" reforms upon schools (Resmovitz, 2015). While Obama argued, throughout his administration, that standardized testing was too dominant in the American school experience, he continued the pattern of using it as an accountability measure. Prior to putting an end to NCLB, the Obama administration spearheaded a federal reform effort entitled *Race to the Top* in 2009 that sought to empower states and local districts to create their own reform that aimed at improving school quality, especially teacher quality. Funded by the American Recovery and Reinvestment Act of 2009, *Race to the Top* provided competitive grants as a means to spur educational innovation within states. States applied for the monies by articulating a reform initiative that sought to improve teachers and narrow achievement gaps amongst students. A key component of this reform effort was that test scores were used to assess teacher performance, rather than the school writ large. A new approach to teacher evaluation, *value-added assessment*, was encouraged throughout the era of *Race to the Top*. Value-added assessment compares a teachers' current test scores of their students to the scores of those same students in previous school years, as well as to other students in the same grade. The purpose of doing this is to isolate the role of the teacher, or value-added, that the teacher plays in students' academic performance. While value-added assessments were often hailed as a fairer assessment, it assumes that students are fixed variables with very little influence from outside the teacher's classroom. The reality is that value added assessment is an unstable measurement of teacher performance because, among other reasons, student performance depends on a wide conglomerate of factors, in addition to the classroom teacher, that may include home life, parent educational level, and even other classroom teachers (Darling-Hammond, 2013).

Race to the Top eventually subsided when, in 2015, the federal government repealed NCLB and reauthorized the ESEA with a new reform initiative entitled *Every Student Succeeds Act* (ESSA). This new reform effort took a page from *Race to the Top* and required states to create reform plans of their own unlike the strong role of the federal government under NCLB. However, like NCLB, ESSA relies heavily on standardized testing as a means of accountability. There are, of course, differences between NCLB and ESSA such as ESSA's funding for professional development of teachers. These differences, though, are relatively minimal in light of the primary framework of ESSA: standardized testing as a key accountability measure.

Another current reform movement is the Common Core State Standards Initiative that provides nationwide standards in two areas: reading and language arts as well as mathematics. This initiative was spearheaded by the National Governors Association as a means to provide consistent academic standards across states and to ensure that graduating students are adequately prepared for college or the workforce. While this reform echoes the nearly three-decade-old concerns from Goals 2000 to raise academic performance, its effort to streamline and, essentially, nationalize standards is new. States were incentivized to accept the Common Core Standards as part of *Race to the Top*. While most states adopted the Common Core, some such as Indiana have not. Others, like Minnesota, adopted only the reading and language arts standards and not the math standards. Among the criticisms of the Common Core is that it usurps power from states to create their own standards and it paves the way for nationalized standardized tests. Advocates of the Common Core claim that national standards and assessment tied to those standards is necessary to ensure all students in the nation are provided a high quality educational experience and are prepared for the challenges of the 21st century.

Effects of Reforms

While the rhetoric surrounding efforts to reform school in the past 3 decades evoke a crisis, the reality is that these reforms have not improved the school experience. While we earlier addressed the problems associated with the international comparisons used to judge the rigor of the American school experience, longitudinal data within the school experience call to question if a crisis ever really existed. For instance, results from the National Assessment of Educational Progress (NAEP), the lone national assessment we have on student achievement in the American public school experience, paint a picture of a steady rise in student achievement since the early 1970s. According to Figure 14.1, reading scores from the NAEP exam actually were on the rise in 1983, at the time of the publication of *A Nation at Risk*. Scores on mathematics also signaled a rise in 1983, with the small exception of a slight decrease for 17 year olds when compared to how that age group fared in 1971 (see Figure 14.2). However, these scores in no way signal a crisis. Interestingly, the data from Figures 14.1 and 14.2 actually signal a steady rise over time without a significant change in scores taking place with the advent of high-stakes accountability reform efforts in the 21st century. Accountability reform efforts also failed to dramatically affect SAT scores, as you can see in Table 14.3. The SAT exam, taken by high school juniors and seniors who are considering college, is an aptitude test aimed at gauging how well students may succeed in college. SAT mathematics scores

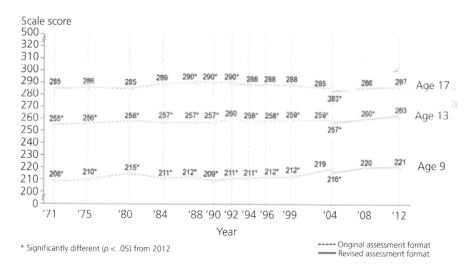

Figure 14.1 Trend in NAEP reading scores (1971–2012). *Source:* National Center for Education Statistics (2013).

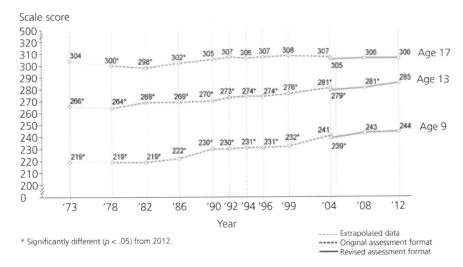

Scale score

* Significantly different (*p* < .05) from 2012.

········· Extrapolated data
••••• Original assessment format
——— Revised assessment format

Figure 14.2 Trend in NAEP mathematics average scores for 9-, 13-, and 17-year-old students. *Source:* National Center for Education Statistics (2013).

TABLE 14.3 SAT Scores: 1990–1991, 2000–2001, 2010–2011, 2014–2015; by Race				
Group of Students	**1990–1991**	**2000–2001**	**2010–2011**	**2014–2015**
Critical Reading				
All	499	506	497	495
White	518	529	528	529
Black	427	434	428	431
Mathematics				
All	500	514	514	511
White	513	530	535	534
Black	419	426	427	428

Source: U.S. Department of Education, National Center for Education Statistics (2018).

have increased over the past quarter of a century, whereas the reading scores actually regressed overall. These patterns remained true regardless of race, testifying to the point that so called "achievement gaps" perpetuate throughout the school experience. Again, this is another data source that minimizes any forgoing crisis in American public education and debunks the notion that high-stakes accountability measures are effective at improving academic achievement.

The high-stakes accountability movement focused exclusively on the ills of the traditional public school, as private schools have been exempt from the scope of the policies. Throughout the duration of this accountability movement, charter schools have been hailed by policy makers and politicians as a viable remedy for fixing schools it deemed in need of improvement. However, charter schools have a poor track record when compared to traditional public schools' performance on standardized tests. In 2009 and 2013, for instance, an independent research group entitled Center for Research in Education Outcomes (CREDO) housed at Stanford University conducted a national charter school study where it compared test score results of traditional public schools (see Table 14.4). The 2009 report, which examined test results from 16 states, revealed that 17% of charter schools were better with producing results in academic achievement than traditional public schools, leaving 46% of charters the same and 37% worse. The 2013 study, which expanded upon the 2009 study to include test results from 26 states, had slightly more favorable results for charter schools than the 2009 report. However, the 2013 results still revealed that three-fourths of American charter schools were either the same or worse than traditional public schools. Despite this evidence, charter schools remain popular among many politicians who tout them as a viable alternative to the traditional public school system they deem as failing. The reality is that there very well may be a dichotomy between politicians' and parents' general perceptions of charter schools. It may be that many parents may approve charter schools because they may, for instance, divert from influence of social-efficiency placed upon the traditional public school, something that the high-stakes accountability movement actually reinforces (Schul & Reineke, 2015).

The net result of the nearly three-decade-old accountability school reform movement is that high-stakes standardized testing has infiltrated the American school experience. The American Federation of Teachers

TABLE 14.4 Charter Schools Performance Compared With Traditional Public Schools

Year of Study	Charter School Better Than Traditional Public Schools	Charter Schools Same as Traditional Public Schools	Charter Schools Worse Than Traditional Public Schools
2009	17%	46%	37%
		Total: 83%	
2013	25%	56%	19%
		Total: 75%	

Source: Center for Research on Education Outcomes (2013); Schul & Reineke (2015).

issued a recent report that revealed the outrageous cost of standardized testing. The report revealed that nearly \$200–\$400 per student were spent for Grades K–2 and \$600-\$800 per student for Grades 3–8, with one high school in the Eastern Coast of the United States spending above \$1,100 per student in Grades 6–11 (Nelson, 2013). This emphasis on standardized testing, while yielding little positive results in the school experience, has affected it for the worse. One critic of standardized testing, curricularist Peter Hlebowitsh (2007b), noted on the damaging effects of high-stakes testing:

> We have known for years that school experiences in high-stakes-testing environments generally reduce themselves to what is being tested. The effect is that art, music, and such skills sets as critical thinking, creativity, cooperative behavior, and many others get short shrift in the classroom, primarily because such matters typically have little or no place on the exams. (p. 28)

In fact, the rise of high-stakes testing runs contrary to the growing amount of research in the learning sciences that has surged in recent years. As a case in point, Allison Gopnik's (2009, 2012) research on infants and young children reveals the necessity of play and exploration in an individual's learning process. Learning environments where individuals are exposed to set-standards and then assessed on them with singular standardized tests, often at the end of a school year, harbors stress for students and teachers alike. There is even some evidence of students vomiting on tests due to experiencing fear and anxiety associated with the tests (Chasmar, 2013).

If contemporary use of tests in the school experience bring forth such negative consequences, what role should tests play in the classroom? Perhaps Ralph Tyler, the primary architect of the NAEP, is the most helpful source of advice on the role of tests in school. Tyler placed parameters around NAEP upon its creation in the late 1960s. First, Tyler removed all incentives to convert the NAEP into a curriculum by making it a no-stakes exam with only a randomly chosen testing population As a result, no teacher is compelled to teach to the NAEP, cheat on the NAEP, or otherwise catapult the NAEP as the basis of the school experience (Schul, 2013, 2015). Second, Tyler believed that evaluation needs to be inherently tied to instructional purposes and learning experiences. Tyler was an educational expansionist who saw tests' role being primarily to inform teachers and administrators on students' learning needs and their progress in learning. Taken out of the school context, tests are provided more power than they were intended. It is misleading, and dangerous, to gauge school performance by a singular assessment. There are too many factors that play a role in student performance in school for a school to be judged by a singular test. If high-stakes standardized testing is so deeply flawed as an accountability measure upon schools, why is it still prominent in the school experience? This remains a mystery.

Summary

In the early 1980s, the American public school was blamed by political leaders and critics for a perceived decline of the United States on the world stage. This paved the way for a reform movement that promised to hold the American public school accountable to fulfilling its mission of educating the American public. This reform movement involved the implementation of curriculum standards throughout the states, with a singular standardized test used to assess student proficiency with those standards. By the turn of the 21st century, the federal government initiated wide-sweeping educational reform that aimed to ensure that the public school delivered on a promise to assure all students were adequately educated. While this reform employed standards and high-stakes accountability measures, it also jettisoned charter schools as a viable competitor to the American public school. Nearly two decades later, evidence points to high-stakes accountability efforts as being wholly ineffective in improving the American public school experience. In fact, high-stakes accountability efforts run counter to most curriculum theory on the role of assessments as well as findings from growing research in the learning sciences.

Reflective Exercises

1. It is natural to desire public institutions to perform at their maximum. However, the *A Nation at Risk* report signaled an alarm that schools were in dire straits. Yet, NAEP data reveals a steady increase in student achievement in reading and mathematics at the time the report was published. Should the report have referenced the NAEP scores? If it did, how might this have changed the current landscape of American public education?
2. What makes an assessment "high stakes"? What are the problems associated with high-stakes assessments?
3. Charter schools originated as an idea to rejuvenate American public education. However, charter school legislation throughout the nation altered this original vision of charter schools by allowing businesses to start up charter schools. What were the implications of this decision? Should it have happened?
4. How might schools be held accountable to the public without the use of high-stakes standardized testing?

References

Berliner, D. C., & Biddle, B. J. (1995). *The manufactured crisis: Myth, fraud, and the attack on America's public schools.* New York, NY: Longman.

Budde, R. (1988). *Education by charter: Restructuring school districts : Key to long-term continuing improvement in American education.* Andover, MA: Regional Laboratory for Educational Improvement of the Northeast & Islands.

Chasmar, J. (2013, November 25). Common Core testing makes children vomit, wet their pants: NY principals. *The Washington Times.* Retrieved from https://www.washingtontimes.com/news/2013/nov/25/common -core-testing-makes-children-vomit/

Center for Research on Education Outcomes. (2013). *National charter school study, 2013.* Retrieved from https://credo.stanford.edu/documents/NCSS% 202013%20Final%20Draft.pdf

Darling-Hammond, L. (2013). *Getting teacher evaluation right: What really matters for effectiveness and improvement.* New York, NY: Teachers College Press.

Gopnik, A. (2009). *The philosophical baby: What children's minds tell us about truth, love, and the meaning of life.* New York, NY: Farrar, Straus and Giroux.

Gopnik, A. (2012). Scientific thinking in young children: Theoretical advances, empirical research, and policy implications. *Science, 337*(6102), 1623–1627.

Hlebowitsh, P. S. (2007a). *Foundations of American Education.* Dubuque, IA: Kendall-Hunt.

Hlebowitsh, P. S. (2007b, November 6). First, do no harm. *Education Week.* Retrieved from https://www.edweek.org/ew/articles/2007/11/07/11hleb owitsh.h27.html.

Labaree, D. F. (2012). *Someone has to fail.* Cambridge, MA: Harvard University Press.

Lagemann, E. C. (2002). *An elusive science: The troubling history of education research.* Chicago, IL: University of Chicago Press.

Lemann, N. (2000). *The big test: The secret history of the American meritocracy.* New York, NY: Farrar, Straus and Giroux

National Center for Education Statistics. (2013). *The nation's report card: Trends in academic progress 2012 (NCES 2013-456).* Washington, DC: National Center for Education Statistics, Institute of Education Sciences, U.S. Department of Education. Retrieved from https://nces.ed.gov/programs/ coe/pdf/coe_cnj.pdf

Nelson, H. (2013). Testing more, teaching less: What America's obsession with student tests costs in money and invested time. *American Federation of Teachers.* Retrieved from http://www.aft.org/pdfs/teachers/testingmore 2013.pdf

Ohio Department of Education. (1998). *Proficiency testing in Ohio—A summary.* Retrieved from http://www.chuh.net/school/FAQs/OPTs.background .html

Reese, W. J. (2005). *America's public schools: From the common school to "No Child Left Behind."* Baltimore, MD: JHU Press.

Resmovitz, J. (2015, December 10). Obama signs Every Student Succeeds Act, marking the end of an era. *Los Angeles Times.* Retrieved from https://www.latimes.com/local/education/standardized-testing/la-me-edu-essa-obama-signs-end-no-child-left-behind-20151210-story.html

Schul, J. E. (2013). Ensuing dog fight: The AHA commission on the social studies' testing controversy. *Journal of Educational Administration and History, 45*(1), 1–27.

Schul, J. E. (2015). The sphinx of American education: Ralph Tyler's peculiar relationship with standardized testing. *The Journal of Educational Thought, 48*(3), 217–238.

Schul, J. E., & Reineke, J. (2015). Chartered waters: The twisted navigation of the American charter school movement. *Curriculum History,* 56–72.

Strauss, V. (2015, April 1). How and why convicted Atlanta teachers cheated on standardized tests. *Washington Post.* Retrieved from https://www.washingtonpost.com/news/answer-sheet/wp/2015/04/01/how-and-why-convicted-atlanta-teachers-cheated-on-standardized-tests/?utm_term=.77a6a972d4d0

Sunderman, G. L., Kim, J. S., & Orfield, G. (2005). *NCLB meets school realities: Lessons from the field.* Thousand Oaks, CA: Corwin Press.

U.S. Congress. (1994). *Goals 2000: Educate America act.* 20 USC 5812. Retrieved from https://www2.ed.gov/legislation/GOALS2000/TheAct/index.html

U.S. Department of Education. (1983). *A Nation at Risk.* Retrieved from https://www2.ed.gov/pubs/NatAtRisk/risk.html

U.S. Department of Education, National Center for Education Statistics. (2013). The Nation's Report Card: Trends in Academic Progress 2012 (NCES 2013-456). Washington, DC: Author.

U.S. Department of Education, National Center for Education Statistics. (2018). Digest of Education Statistics, 2016 (NCES 2017–094), Chapter 2. Retrieved from https://nces.ed.gov/fastfacts/display.asp?id=171

U.S. Department of Education, National Center for Education Statistics, Common Core of Data (n.d.). Public Elementary/Secondary School Universe Survey Data, 1999–2000 through 2011–2012. Retrieved from https://nces.ed.gov/ccd/pubschuniv.asp

Vergari, S. 2002. *The charter school landscape.* Pittsburgh, PA: University of Pittsburgh Press.

About the Author

James E. Schul is an associate professor in the Education Studies department at Winona State University. He has published numerous educational research articles ranging from classroom studies to histories. Prior to his time in academia, he was a high school social studies teacher for 10 years. He lives in Winona, MN with his wife and four children.

Index

Paradoxes of the Public School, pages 207–213

Copyright © 2019 by Information Age Publishing

Printed in the United States
By Bookmasters